magimix cookery

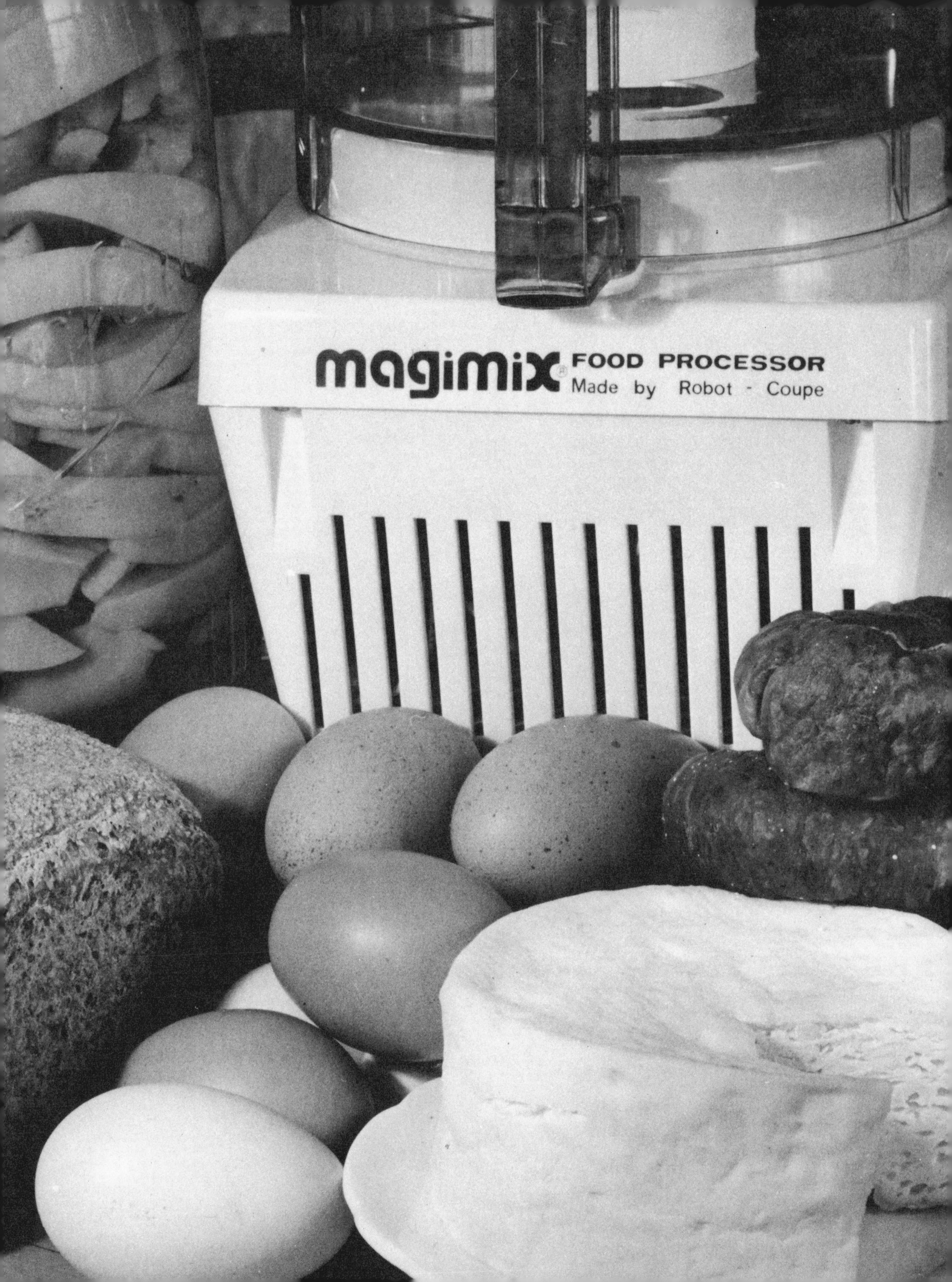
magimix FOOD PROCESSOR
Made by Robot - Coupe

magimix cookery

Marika Hanbury Tenison

ictc

First published 1982 by the Publishing Division of ICTC Ltd.,
632–652 London Road, Isleworth, Middlesex, TW13 4EZ

Reprinted 1982, 1983 (twice), 1984 (twice)

British Library Cataloguing in Publication Data

Hanbury Tenison, Marika
    Magimix cookery
    1. Food processor cookery
    I. Title
    641.5'89   TX840.F6

ISBN 0 907642 04 7

Design and photography by Edward Piper
Edited by Tessa Hayward

Food for photographs by Martin Bates M.C.F.A (C.G)

Printed in Great Britain by Chorley and Pickersgill Ltd, Leeds.

ICTC Stock Number: 54120

Contents

Illustrations

Foreword

There can hardly be a day that goes by when I don't thank the culinary gods for my Magimix and Grande Famille food processors; like plastic bags and tinfoil one wonders what on earth one ever did without them.

Take an average day in the Hanbury Tenison household. First thing in the morning scramble the eggs in the Magimix and chop the bacon with the double-bladed knife because it makes it cook so much more quickly; squeeze fresh orange juice with the citrus fruit juice extractor for the daily dose of vitamin C. Then, whip up some buns for the farm men when they come in for their elevenses; make a pâté for a dinner party in the evening, some home made tagliatelli to follow it and then flip up a flan to finish with. On to lunch; chop vegetables for a hearty soup with the double-bladed knife, grate cheese for macaroni pie, grate and slice ingredients for a salad, whip up the salad dressing with the plastic blade and make a scrumptious strawberry pudding in seconds. In the afternoon make three cakes for the haymakers to keep them happy. Mix a respectable daiqueri cocktail in the evening (using the Grande Famille since the dinner party is for ten), decide to have vichysoisse before the pâté at the last minute and make that in no time at all in the Magimix, produce an excellent sauce for the tagliatelli in minutes and even have time to put my feet up for half an hour before anyone arrives. On a rough count I have used my Magimix at least thirty times during the day. What would I do without it?

Often one gets bored with kitchen gadgets. I have a cupboard of them I flirted with but now never use, but the Magimix is different, it becomes like an extension of yourself, it makes life easier, cookery quicker and more efficient and, even more important, it makes the job of producing daily food more fun.

When Magimix first came on the market it only had one or two accessories. Now there is a wide range of discs to perform every chore from fine grating to thick slicing; watch out for new discs, they can be invaluable. It is also worth, I believe, buying yourself, at no great cost, one or two extra bowls to fit your Magimix. However carefully you plan your menus there are times when you need a clean dry bowl for processing ingredients and it saves time if you don't just have one bowl which may need to be washed up in a hurry. I also find it useful to have two or three double-bladed knives, the attachment I find I use most, so that you don't need to wash the knife between processing savoury and sweet ingredients.

The problem I find most with people who are using a Magimix for the first time is that they tend to under estimate the strength of their machine and so over-process ingredients. If in doubt switch the machine on and off when chopping or grinding ingredients so that they will have no chance of being over-processed. I have made a clear definition in the recipes between "coarsely" and "finely" chopped to help prevent you letting the machine run away with you.

In this book I have tried to produce a good balance of new recipes to suit almost every situation and pocket; at the same time I have repeated a few of the 'basic' recipes. Many of the recipes are classics adapted to be made in half their normal time with the help of a Magimix, as many again are original recipes worked on in my own kitchen and designed especially for you; all have been tested and I would like to think they suit all moods and all circumstances.

Enjoy your Magimix, enjoy the recipes, and, above all, have a good appetite. .

Marika Hanbury Tenison,
Maidenwell.

This one, above all, is for Rosa who flatters my food, corrects my grammar and picks me up when I slip on onion skins.

Weights and Measures

All the recipes in this book are given in both Imperial and Metric measurements. Use either of them, but be consistent and do not mix them or the recipe may not work. When dry measurements are given by the spoonful it means, unless otherwise stated, a rounded spoonful.

American Measurements:
In America when dry measurements are given by the spoonful it always means a level spoonful. This means that two American tablespoons are equal to one English tablespoon.

With all liquid measurements:
Cup equals ⅓rd pint: 8 fl oz: 240 ml.

One Cup U.S.A. equals approximately the following:

Flour	5 oz	150 g
Sugar (Granulated, Caster, Demerara)	7 oz	200 g
Sugar (Icing)	4 oz	100 g
Butter	8 oz	225 g
Dried Fruit	5 oz	150 g
Nuts (whole)	5 oz	150 g
Ground Almonds	4 oz	100 g
Golden Syrup	12 oz	350 g
Rice	8 oz	225 g
Grated Cheese	3½ oz	90 g
Chopped Onions	5 oz	150 g

How to get the best out of your ingredients with the Magimix

Almonds   Grind blanched almonds with the double-bladed knife into a paste to use for puddings, cakes, etc.

Anchovy fillets   Process anchovy fillets (with or without oil) to a smooth paste with the double-bladed knife to use as a flavouring ingredient for soups, stews, sauces and savoury butters etc.

Apples   Slice peeled and cored apples through the thick, medium or thin slicing discs to use for puddings and pies (for neat slices halve and core the apple, cut a slice from the bottom and stand them, upright, in the feed tube – exert a medium pressure on the pusher). Put slices of apple into cold water into which a teaspoon of lemon juice has been added, to prevent them discolouring before use. Purée cooked apples with the double-bladed knife for making puddings and sauces. Grate peeled and cored apples through the coleslaw disc for salads.

Apricots   Process cooked fresh or dried apricots into a purée with the double-bladed knife for puddings and sorbets etc. Chop dried apricots with the double-bladed knife to use in pilaffs, savoury pies, etc.

Asparagus   Purée cooked asparagus stalks or whole asparagus to make delicious soups.

Aubergines   Slice aubergines through the medium or thick slicing disc for vegetable and meat dishes.
Process aubergines through the chipper or coarse grating disc to add to meat and poultry dishes (aubergines take on the flavour of other ingredients as they cook and therefore proving a useful meat stretching ingredient).
Purée cooked aubergines to make a purée for dips and first courses.

Avocados   Purée avocados with some lemon juice with the double-bladed knife to use for mousses, soups, dips and also for exotic creamy puddings.

Bacon   Use the double-bladed knife to coarsely chop, finely chop or reduce to a paste bacon (with rind removed) for soups, larding, casseroles, stews, pâté, forcemeat, etc.

Beans   *Broad beans* Purée tender, cooked, broad beans to make soup bases and vegetable purées.
Runner beans Cut top and tailed runner beans to fit the feed tube lengthwise and process into slices through the thin or medium slicing discs to use as a vegetable or for freezing. Sliced or chopped runner beans can also be used in soups and casseroles and cooked runner beans, processed with the double-bladed knife, make an excellent vegetable purée.

French beans Arrange the beans, upright in the feed tube and process through the thick slicing blade to use in soups, stews, casseroles and to cook to use in salads, etc.

Beetroot Slice cooked beetroot for pickling and to serve with cheese or sweet and sour sauce as a vegetable. Process raw beetroot through the julienne disc for salads and soups.

Bread Bread can easily be processed, with your food processor, into breadcrumbs of the size and substance you require. Use day old or stale bread to make 'fresh breadcrumbs'. Process bread with the crusts removed to make coarse or fine breadcrumbs. In the place of white bread you can use granary or brown bread to make crumbs for coating etc.
Make bread sauce in the normal way and process it to make a thick, smooth and rich sauce.
Make dried breadcrumbs by baking stale bread, with or without the crusts removed, until crisp and dry. Process the dried bread in your food processor until it is reduced to crumbs of the desired consistency. For fried breadcrumbs to go with roast poultry or game see page 146.

Brussel sprouts Thinly slice your Brussel sprouts to use for winter salads. Purée cooked Brussel sprouts to use for vegetable purées, soups, etc.

Butter Process with the double-bladed knife or plastic blade to soften butter for incorporation into sauces, cakes, biscuit mixtures etc.
Soften butter with the double-bladed knife to use for savoury butters.

Butter beans Purée cooked or tinned butter beans to use as a thickening for soups or as a vegetable purée.

Cabbage Process cabbage through the coleslaw disc (if using the standard Magimix) or through the thick, medium or thin slicing discs to use for soups, stews, vegetable dishes and coleslaw etc.

Carrots Slice peeled carrots through the thin, medium or thick slicing discs for vegetable dishes, stews and casseroles.
Grate carrots through the fine or thick discs or, if using the standard Magimix, the coleslaw disc to serve raw or cooked in salads, soups, stews, etc.
If using the standard Magimix process peeled carrots through the julienne disc for use in soups, cooked dishes and salads. (Photograph p. 293).
Chop carrots with the double-bladed knife for use in soups, stews and sauces.
Process peeled carrots through the chipper disc to use for vegetable dishes, soups, stews and casseroles, etc.
Cut peeled carrots to fit the feed tube lengthwise and process through the thin slicing disc for Chinese stir-fry dishes.
Note To slice one carrot only – cut off the bottom of a peeled carrot, place it upright in the right hand side of the feed tube and exert a firm pressure on the pusher.

Cauliflower Slice raw cauliflower through the thick or medium discs to use in salads. Purée cooked cauliflower with the double-bladed knife to use as a vegetable or for soups.

Celeriac Grate celeriac through the coarse grating disc or, if using the standard Magimix, through the julienne disc, plunge into cold water to which some lemon juice has been added to prevent the celeriac browning and use for salads. Purée cooked celeriac with the double-bladed knife for vegetable dishes and soups.

Celery Slice celery with the thin, medium or thick slicing disc for use in soups, stews, casseroles and salads.
Chop celery with the double-bladed knife for use in soups and sauces. Chop celery leaves with the double-bladed knife for use as a flavouring ingredient and as a garnish for soups and cold dishes.
Arrange celery stalks sideways in the feed tube and process with the julienne or grating disc to produce a lovely textured vegetable for soups and salads. Purée a little cooked celery with other cooked root vegetables to make an excellent vegetable purée to serve with meat and vegetable dishes.

Cheese Slice Gruyère, Cheddar, Edam and other firm cheeses through the thin or medium slicing discs to use as a sandwich filling or for topping savoury dishes.
Grate cheeses through the fine, medium or thick grating discs to use for sauces, toppings and salads. (Photograph p. 293).
Crumble cheese with the double-bladed knife to use in sauces, savoury pastries and, combined with crumbled bread as a gratinée topping.
Process Parmesan cheese through the Parmesan grating disc (available for some machines) to produce fresh tasting Parmesan which is infinitely nicer than the commercial grated products. (Photograph p. 294).

Chicken Process cooked chicken with the double-bladed knife for pâtés, soups, salads and savoury dishes. (Photograph p. 288).
Process raw chicken with the double-bladed knife for use in pâtés, terrines and forcemeats etc.

Chilli peppers Finely chop red or green chilli peppers with the double-bladed knife for use as a flavouring ingredient in Chinese stir fry dishes, soups and stews, etc.

Chips Make thin French fries through the chipper disc and game chips with the ripple cut or thin slicing disc. (Photograph p. 292).

Citrus fruit Squeeze oranges, lemons, limes and grapefruit with the citrus fruit juice extractor which is available for some machines. Use squeezed three quarter lemons or oranges as an attractive vehicle for serving ice creams, fruit mousses etc. (Photograph p. 294).
Chop citrus fruit to make marmalade and candied peel.
Slice lemons through the medium slicing disc for use in puddings, marinades and sauces (cut a slice off the bottom and top of small lemons, place them in the feed tube and press with an even pressure on the pusher.

Cooked vegetables
Chop crisply cooked vegetables with the double-bladed knife to use in salads and soups.
Process cooked vegetables with the double-bladed knife to make excellent vegetable purées, thickening agents for sauces and soup bases.

Courgettes
Make full use of this versatile vegetable with your Magimix.
Slice courgettes through the fine, medium or thick slicing discs for use as a vegetable, for casseroles and stews or for salads.
Process courgettes through the chipper disc for soups, stews, salads and quiches.
Process courgettes through the coarse grating disc for salads and quiches.
Purée cooked courgettes with the double-bladed knife for delicious soups.

Cranberries
Purée cooked or raw cranberries with the double-bladed knife for use in jams, jellies, sauces, etc.

Cucumber
Slice cucumber through the thin, medium or thick slicing disc for salads or cruditiés. (Photograph p. 293).
Grate it through the fine or coarse grating disc before adding to mousses, etc.

Currants (red, black and white)
Purée cooked or raw currants with the double-bladed knife to use for jams, sweet sauces, fools, ice creams and sorbets, etc.

Dried fruit
Process dried fruit until coarsely or finely chopped with the double-bladed knife for use in cakes, puddings, salads and rice dishes etc.

Eggs
Beat whole eggs for sauces, cakes, mousses, custards, etc. with the double-bladed knife or plastic blade.
Beat egg yolks until smooth, fluffy and pale for use in sauces, puddings, etc.
Chop hard boiled eggs with the double-bladed knife for salads and garnishing.
Incorporate whole eggs or egg yolks into other ingredients through the feed tube with the machine switched on.

Fennel
Slice fennel through the medium or thick slicing discs to add to salads. Purée cooked fennel with the double-bladed knife for soups and vegetable purées.

Fish
Process raw fish with the double-bladed knife for use in pâtés, terrines and forcemeats etc.
Process cooked fish with the plastic mixing blade or double-bladed knife for use in pâtés, mousses, potted fish etc.
Reduce cooked shellfish roe to a paste with the double-bladed knife for adding to sauce and soups.

Game
Process raw game with the double-bladed knife to use for pâtés, terrines and forcemeat. Chop leftover cooked game with the double-bladed knife to use for potted dishes, risottos and soups etc.

Garlic
Finely chop peeled garlic with the double-bladed knife for savoury dishes, soups, sauces, etc.

Garlic sausage Slice firm garlic sausage through the medium or thick slicing disc; cut the garlic sausage to fit the feed tube and exert a medium pressure on the pusher.
Process garlic sausage through the chipper disc, exerting a medium pressure, to use in salads.

Gooseberries Purée cooked gooseberries with the double-bladed knife to use for fools, sorbets, etc.

Ham Process ham with the double-bladed knife until finely or coarsely chopped to use for potted dishes, sauces, salads, etc.

Herbs Process fresh herbs with the double-bladed knife until finely chopped to use for flavouring and garnishing. Make sure the herbs and the bowl are dry before processing. (Photograph p. 290).

Horseradish Grate fresh peeled horseradish root to use for sauces to give a delightfully hot and sharp flavouring.

Leeks Process cleaned leeks through the thin, medium or thick slicing disc for use in vegetable dishes. If one leek only is to be sliced position it in the right hand side of the feed tube. Purée cooked leeks with the double-bladed knife to use as a flavouring ingredient for soups.

Lettuces Shred crisp lettuces with the thick slicing or coleslaw disc to use for salads.

Mangoes Process raw, peeled mangoes with the double-bladed knife to make delicious purées for use in ice creams, sorbets and mousses etc.

Meat Process raw meat with the double-bladed knife to use for minced meat dishes, hamburgers, meat loaves, pies, etc. Cut the meat into cubes before processing and remove any excess fat and gristle.
Process cooked meat with the double-bladed knife until finely or coarsely chopped to use in leftover dishes and for spaghetti sauces, etc. Cut top quality meat to fit the feed tube, chill in the deep freeze until firm and slice through the thin or medium slicer for Chinese stir fry dishes, etc.

Mincemeat Make delicious well flavoured mincemeats by chopping ingredients with the double-bladed knife.

Nettles Process cooked, young, nettle shoots to a purée to make a delicious soup.

Nuts Chop nuts with the double-bladed knife to use for garnishing and in cakes etc. (Photograph p. 291).

Onions   One probably chops more onions in the kitchen than one does any other vegetable. With a Magimix, slicing, chopping and mincing onions is done with the minimum of effort and no tears. Peel and quarter small or medium onions or roughly chop large ones and process them with the double-bladed knife until coarsely, finely or very finely chopped. Peel small onions (or cut large peeled onions to fit the feed tube) and process them through the thin, medium or thick slicing discs. Peel onions and process them through the coarse or coleslaw grating discs for recipes that require grated onions. Purée cooked onions with the double-bladed knife. (Photograph p. 290).

Oranges   (See Citrus Fruit)

Parsnips   Purée cooked parsnips with the double-bladed knife to use as a vegetable. Process raw parsnips through the chipper disc for vegetable dishes.

Peas   Purée cooked peas with the double-bladed knife to make a base for soups and a delicious vegetable.

Peel   (See Citrus Fruit)

Peppers   Slice red and green peppers through the fine, medium or thick slicing disc for salads or for adding to casseroles etc. (Photograph p. 292).

Pork fat   Use the double-bladed knife to finely chop pork fat for pâtés and terrines.

Potatoes   Process raw, peeled potatoes through the chipper disc to make pommes frites. (As soon as the potatoes have been processed rinse them well in cold water to remove excess starch, drain them well and dry on kitchen paper before cooking).
With the standard Magimix process raw, peeled potatoes through the julienne disc to make fine straw fried potatoes (rinse as above).
Process raw, peeled potatoes through the ripple cut, thin or medium slicing discs to make game chips (rinse as above before deep frying).
Grate raw potatoes through grating discs to make potato pancakes, etc.
Process raw, peeled potatoes, through the medium or thick slicing discs to use as a topping for stews and casseroles etc. and for vegetable dishes. (Photographs p. 292).
Note Do not mash cooked potatoes with the double-bladed knife as they become sticky. Cooked potatoes can be riced through the coarse grating blade.

Radishes   Slice radishes through the thin or medium slicing discs for use in salads and as a garnish.

Raspberries   Purée raspberries with the double-bladed knife for puddings, mousses, fools, ice cream, sorbets and sauces, etc.

Root vegetables Use the fine or coarse grating disc, or with the standard Magimix the coleslaw disc or julienne disc to grate raw vegetables for use in salads and soups, etc.
Process root vegetables through the chipper disc for use in salads, vegetable dishes, soups and stews.
Purée cooked root vegetables with the double-bladed knife to use as vegetable dishes and in soups.

Salami Choose a small salami that will fit the feed tube, or cut a larger one in half. Chill in the refrigerator and you can obtain even slices with the thin or medium slicing disc.

Salsify Process raw or cooked salsify through the chipper disc to make a delicious vegetable.

Spinach Roughly chop raw spinach with the double-bladed knife to use in soups and as a vegetable. Purée or chop cooked spinach with the double-bladed knife to use as a vegetable and for soups, etc.

Strawberries Slice firm strawberries through the medium or thick slicing discs for salads and tarts, etc.
Purée strawberries with the double-bladed knife for jam, sauces, mousses, ice creams and other puddings.

Sugar Process granulated sugar with the double-bladed knife to produce caster sugar.

Swede Process raw swede through the coarse grating disc or, with the standard Magimix, the julienne disc for use as a winter salad ingredient. Process raw swede through the chipper disc to use as a vegetable, in soups, stews and casseroles, etc.
Process cooked swede with the double-bladed knife to make a delicious vegetable purée or to use as a soup base.

Tomatoes Purée skinned tomatoes with the double-bladed knife to use for soups, stews etc. (Remove tomato skins by covering the tomatoes with boiling water for three minutes, draining and then sliding off the skins: remove the core and seeds for a smooth purée).
Process small, firm, ripe tomatoes through the medium slicing disc or chipper disc for use in salads.

Turnips Process small, young peeled turnips through the thin or medium slicing discs or the coarse grater to make a good, crisp winter salad ingredient.
Process turnips through the chipper disc for adding to soups, stews, etc.

Watercress Chop watercress with the double-bladed knife for use in sauces and soups.

Yoghurt Stabilize yoghurt by beating it with the double-bladed knife with a little cornflour and a white of egg to prevent it curdling during cooking. Make a sweet sauce by combining yoghurt and sugar and processing with the double-bladed knife.

SOUPS

Iced Vichyssoise

One of the queens of soups; elegant, smooth, satiny and light. There is only one problem – Vichyssoise is essentially a summer soup and it is best served cold but, during the summer, it is nearly impossible to find any leeks about. I freeze leeks especially to make this soup.

For four to six people

6 leeks
1 onion
4 medium sized potatoes
2 oz (50 g) butter
1½ pints (900 ml) chicken stock

Salt and freshly ground black pepper
Pinch ground nutmeg
½ pint (10 fl oz 300 ml) single cream
2 tablespoons finely chopped chives

Trim leeks and remove the green tops (the soup should be creamy white in colour). Peel the potatoes. Peel the onion.

Medium slicing disc
Slice the leeks, and the onion.

Chipper disc
Process the potatoes through the chipper disc. Heat the butter in a heavy saucepan. Add the leeks, onion and potato and cook over a low heat, stirring to prevent sticking, until the butter has been absorbed. Add the stock, season with salt, pepper and nutmeg, bring to the boil and simmer for about 30 minutes until the vegetables are absolutely soft. Drain off the stock.

Double-bladed knife
Process the vegetables until puréed. Return them to a clean pan, add the stock, bring to the boil, adjust the seasoning and simmer for 10 minutes. Cool. Stir in the cream and chives and refrigerate until well chilled before serving.

Clear Gazpacho Soup

Much more sophisticated this than the rather heavy and over flavoured gazpacho one so often gets in restaurants. This is a true Mexican recipe and is often accompanied by a number of different condiments or side dishes which guests help themselves to as they wish. The basic soup is light and very subtle but must have a basis of good jellied stock or consommé (tinned jellied consommé is very useful here).

For eight people

6 medium tomatoes
1 small onion
1 tablespoon white wine vinegar
½ teaspoon dried oregano

1½ tablespoons olive or sunflower oil
Salt and freshly ground black pepper
4 pints (2·4 litres) chicken consommé or
    jellied chicken stock

Cover the tomatoes with boiling water for three minutes and slide off their skins. Cut the tomatoes into quarters and remove the cores and seeds. Peel and roughly chop the onion.

Double-bladed knife

Process the onion until finely chopped. Add the tomatoes and process until roughly chopped. Add the vinegar, oregano, oil and seasoning and continue to process until the tomatoes are finely chopped. Add the processed ingredients to the stock or consommé, mix lightly and chill in the refrigerator for at least two hours before serving.

Serve with bowls of the following:— Finely chopped red and green peppers; Chopped, peeled and seeded tomatoes; Chopped spring onions; Croutons of crisply fried bread.

Iced Cucumber Soup

I add peas to a cold cucumber soup to give a little more green colouring.

For six people

2 medium cucumbers
1 small onion
6 oz (175 g) fresh or frozen peas
½ oz (13 g) butter
1¾ pints (1 litre) chicken stock

3 bay leaves
1 carton (5 fl oz 150 ml) soured cream
Salt and white pepper
Few mint leaves
Grated peel and juice of ½ lemon

Chipper disc

Peel the onion and all but ½ in. of the cucumbers. Process the onion and all the cucumber excepting the unpeeled piece, through the disc. Heat the butter in a saucepan. Add the onion and cucumber and cook, stirring, over a medium low heat until the onion and cucumber are really soft. Add the peas and continue to cook until the peas are soft.

Double-bladed knife   Process the vegetables until smooth and return to a clean pan. Add the stock and bay leaves, season with salt and pepper, bring to the boil and simmer for five minutes. Remove the bay leaves, add the lemon juice and peel and leave to cool. Add a little of the soup to the sour cream and mix until smooth and add to the remainder of the soup and chill until ice cold. Check seasoning before serving.

Thin slicing disc   Process the unpeeled cucumber. Garnish the soup with slices of cucumber and some finely chopped mint.

Consommé

Consommé is clarified good stock and is delicious served hot or cold either plain or flavoured with a variety of ingredients.

For eight people

4 pints (2·4 litres) good beef stock
10 ozs (275 g) shin beef
1 leek

2 egg whites
Pinch mixed herbs
Salt and white pepper

Double-bladed knife   Wash and trim the leek, drain well and roughly chop.
Process the beef and leek until very finely chopped. Add the egg whites, and herbs and process to break up the egg whites and mix the ingredients. Add ½ pint (300 ml) of the stock and process to mix. Heat the remaining stock in a large saucepan. Add the meat mixture stirring all the time over a low heat until the sauce comes to the boil. As soon as the liquid boils, reduce the heat until the soup is just simmering and simmer gently for eight minutes. Season with salt and pepper and strain very slowly through a damp layer of double cheese cloth or muslin.
Note The stock should now be clear – if it is still cloudy add two more beaten egg whites to the stock, bring to the boil stirring all the time, simmer for five minutes and then strain again. Remove any fat from the surface with sheets of kitchen paper skimmed across the surface of the liquid until all the fat has been removed.

Variations Add 1 carrot peeled and process through the julienne disc to the finished consommé and simmer until the carrot is just tender.
Add 2 peeled, seeded and cored tomatoes which have been finely chopped with the double-bladed knife, to the consommé and simmer for five minutes before serving.

Avgolemono (Greek Egg and Lemon Soup)

For four people

1¾ pints (1 litre) clear chicken stock (see how to clarify beef stock on page 18)
2 oz (50 g) rice

2 eggs
Juice 1½ lemons
4 tablespoons single cream

Double-bladed knife

Cook the rice in the stock until it is just tender and drain off the stock. Combine the eggs with the lemon juice and process until smooth. Add about ¼ pint (5 fl oz 150 ml) of the chicken stock and process until smooth. Add the egg mixture to the remaining stock and heat through stirring all the time, without boiling, until the soup is thick and satiny. Add the rice and mix in the cream.
Note The soup can also be served cold in which case the stock and egg mixture should be allowed to get cold before the cream is added.
The cold soup can be garnished with a little finely chopped mint.

French Onion Soup

The real brew as served in Paris as a cure for late night hangovers.

For five to six people

1 lb (450 g) onions
2 oz (50 g) butter
3 cloves garlic
2 tablespoons flour
2½ pints (1·5 litres) good beef stock (or use water and stock cubes, but the stock must be *strong*)

2 oz (50 g) Gruyère or Emmenthal cheese
1 teaspoon made English mustard
Salt and freshly ground black pepper
5 or 6 slices French bread
1 tablespoon grated Parmesan cheese

Thin slicing disc

Peel the onions and garlic cloves.
Slice the onions and two of the garlic cloves. Heat the butter in a saucepan, add the onions and garlic and cook over a moderately low heat, stirring every now and then to prevent sticking, until the onions are a good golden brown (this will take longer than you expect but care must be taken not to allow the onions to burn ..... about 30 – 40 minutes). Add the flour and stir until the flour is also brown. Gradually add the stock, stirring continually until all the stock has been used and the soup has come to the boil. Season with salt and pepper and simmer for 20 minutes.

Double-bladed knife

Process the Gruyère and Emmenthal cheeses together with the remaining clove of garlic until all are finely chopped. Add the mustard and Parmesan and process until the ingredients are well mixed. Spread the cheese mixture over the slices of bread. Place the slices of bread in pottery soup bowls, pour over the soup and when the slices of bread have risen to the top put the bowls under a hot grill until the cheese is golden brown.

Cream of Watercress Soup

A lovely pale green soup for summer evenings. Watercress is full of goodness and not only makes a delicious soup but also an extremely nutritious one.

For six people

2 onions
12 oz (350 g) watercress
1 ½ oz (40 g) butter
2 tablespoons plain flour
2 pints (1·2 litres) chicken stock
Salt and freshly ground black pepper

1 teaspoon dried chervil
2 egg yolks
¼ pint (5 fl oz 150 ml) double cream
Sprigs of watercress and thin slices of
   lemon to garnish

Pick over the watercress. Peel and roughly chop the onions.

Double-bladed knife
Process the onions until fairly finely chopped. Melt the butter in a large, heavy, saucepan. Add the onion and cook over a low heat until the onion is completely soft and transparent. Add the watercress and stir over a low heat for about five minutes or until the watercress has wilted. Stir in the flour and then add the chicken stock, season with salt and pepper, mix in the chervil, bring to the boil and simmer for 5 minutes. Strain the soup.

Double-bladed knife
Process the vegetables with a little of the stock until a coarse purée has been obtained. Return the purée and the stock to a clean pan and mix well. Process the egg yolks with the cream until smooth. Add a few tablespoons of the soup and process to mix well. Add the egg and cream mixture to the soup and heat over a low heat, stirring, without boiling. Check the seasoning and serve with a garnish of watercress and a thin slice of lemon in each bowl.

Cream of Florence Fennel Soup

How I wish more people would grow this delicious vegetable (especially market gardeners). It is not difficult to grow and is one of the best late summer vegetables I know having the muted aniseed flavour of the fennel herb with none of its overpowering qualities. I serve the fennel bulbs braised as vegetables, in a delicious crisp salad or as this sophisticated and delicate pale green soup.

For seven to eight people

3 medium fennel bulbs
1 onion
4 oz (100 g) frozen peas
2 oz (50 g) butter
1 oz (25 g) flour
2 pints (1·2 litres) chicken or ham stock

½ pint (10 fl oz 300 ml) milk
Salt and freshly ground black pepper
Pinch nutmeg
2 egg yolks
¼ pint (5 fl oz 150 ml) single cream

Trim the fennel bulbs, removing a little of the green feathery tops and reserve for garnish.

Peel and halve the onion.

Medium slicing disc   Slice the onion and fennel. Melt the butter in a large saucepan. Add the fennel and onion and cook over a low heat, stirring to prevent sticking, until the onion is soft. Mix in the flour and gradually add the stock and milk, stirring continually over a medium heat until the mixture comes to the boil. Add the peas, season with salt, pepper and a pinch of nutmeg and simmer for about 30 minutes until the fennel is really soft. Strain off most of the stock.

Double-bladed knife   Purée the strained vegetables until smooth. Return the purée and the stock to a clean pan and mix well. Process the egg yolks and cream together until smooth. Add the egg and cream mixture to the soup and reheat, stirring all the time, without boiling. Serve with a little of the finely chopped fennel tops floating on top of the soup.

Potage Lorraine

A versatile soup which has made the journey from France to Scotland and ended up not knowing quite who it belongs to. Not to worry, the soup is so good who cares what its origins are.

For four people

4 oz (100 g) blanched almonds
12 oz (350 g) cooked chicken
2 hardboiled egg yolks
1 thick slice white bread with the crusts removed
¼ pint (5 fl oz 150 ml) milk
2 pints (1·2 litres) chicken stock

Salt and white pepper
Pinch nutmeg
Juice ½ small lemon
2 egg yolks
¼ pint (5 fl oz 150 ml) double cream
Small bunch parsley

Double-bladed knife   Process the almonds until reduced to a paste. Add the chicken, hardboiled egg yolks and bread and continue to process until the ingredients are all finely ground. Add the milk and process the mixture into a smooth paste. Add a little of the chicken stock and process to mix. Transfer the mixture to a saucepan, mix in the remaining stock, season with salt, pepper and nutmeg and the lemon juice, bring to the boil and simmer for 15 minutes.

Double-bladed knife   Process the egg yolks with the cream until smooth. Add a little of the soup and process until well mixed. Add the cream and egg yolk mixture to the rest of the soup and mix well, heating through without boiling.

Double-bladed knife and a clean dry bowl   Remove any tough stalks from the parsley and process until finely chopped. Serve the soup very hot with a garnishing of finely chopped parsley.

Autumn Soup

A beautiful soup made from avocado pears with a flavouring of chicken stock, onion and celery. It comes out a rich pale green colour and tastes both elegant and warming – what more could one ask for the start to an autumn meal.

For four people

1 medium to large, ripe, avocado
3 outside stalks of celery with leaves
1 medium onion
2 cloves garlic

2 pints (1·2 litres) chicken stock (or use water and 2 stock cubes)
4 tablespoons single cream
Salt and freshly ground black pepper
1½ oz (40 g) butter

Roughly chop the celery. Peel and roughly chop the onion and garlic. Peel and halve the avocado, and roughly chop the flesh.

Double-bladed knife

Combine the celery, onion and garlic in the Magimix bowl and process until the ingredients are very finely chopped. Remove the ingredients from the bowl scraping it really clean.

Heat the butter in a saucepan. Add the celery, onion and garlic and cook over a low heat, stirring, until the onion and celery are soft. Add the avocado and stock, season with salt and pepper (be careful with the salt if you are using stock cubes), bring to the boil and simmer for 15 minutes. Strain the soup.

Double-bladed knife

Transfer the avocado and vegetables to the Magimix bowl and process until the ingredients are puréed. Put the purée into a clean saucepan, add the stock, mix well and add the cream. Check seasoning and heat through without boiling.

Note The soup can be garnished with extra finely chopped celery leaves or with separately served croutons of crisply fried bread. The soup can also be served cold but may need a little squeeze of lemon juice to sharpen it and bring out the flavour of the avocado.

Mushroom Soup with Bacon Garnish

Mushroom soup, I feel, is basically rather uninteresting. If you agree with me try my version which is garnished with delicious crumbled bacon and thin slices of uncooked mushrooms.

For five to six people

12 oz (350 g) mushrooms
2 oz (50 g) butter
2 tablespoons flour
1¾ pints (1 litre) good chicken stock

Salt and white pepper
Pinch ground nutmeg and ground mace
¼ pint (5 fl oz 150 ml) single cream
2 rashers streaky bacon.

Double-bladed knife   Process 10 oz (275 g) of the mushrooms until fairly finely chopped.

Melt the butter in a saucepan, add the chopped mushrooms and cook, stirring, over a medium heat for three minutes. Stir in the flour and mix well. Gradually add the stock, stirring continually over a medium high heat until the soup comes to the boil, season with salt and pepper, mace and nutmeg and simmer for ten minutes.

Double-bladed knife   Process the bacon rashers until fairly finely chopped and remove.

Thin slicing disc   Slice the remaining mushrooms and remove.

Fry the bacon without extra fat until crisp and drain well on kitchen paper.

Double-bladed knife   Strain the soup and process the mushrooms with a little stock until smooth. Return to a clean pan adding the remaining stock and the cream and heat through without boiling. Garnish the soup at the last minute with the bacon pieces and sliced mushrooms.

Chicken and Celery Soup

A quickly made and deliciously nourishing winter soup with a creamy, satiny, texture.

For four people

The leaves from one bunch of celery
4 large stalks celery
1 small onion
6 oz (175 g) raw chicken (preferably white meat)
1 oz (25 g) butter

1 tablespoon flour
1½ pints (900 ml) good chicken stock
Salt and freshly ground black pepper
Pinch ground nutmeg
¼ pint (5 fl oz 150 ml) single cream
2 egg yolks

Peel and roughly chop the onion. Roughly chop the celery. Cut the chicken into cubes.

Double-bladed knife   Process the celery leaves until finely chopped and remove.

Process the onion and celery until finely chopped and remove. Process the chicken until fairly finely chopped – do not overprocess.

Melt the butter in a saucepan, add the onion and celery and cook over a medium heat, stirring to prevent sticking, until the onion and celery are soft. Add the chicken and stir until it becomes opaque. Add the flour and mix well. Gradually blend in the stock, stirring continually, over a medium high heat until the soup comes to the boil. Season with salt, pepper and a little nutmeg and simmer for 15 minutes or until the vegetables and chicken are tender.

Double-bladed knife   Combine the egg yolks and cream and process until smooth. Add the cream mixture to the soup and stir over a low heat, without boiling, until the soup is thick, rich and satiny.

Garnish the soup with the chopped celery leaves.

Curried Cauliflower Soup

The light flavouring of curry with this excellent soup makes it into a sophisticated starter.

For four people

1 small cauliflower
1 medium onion
2 teaspoons curry powder
¼ teaspoon ground nutmeg
1 pint (20 fl oz 600 ml) good chicken
  stock

½ pint (10 fl oz 300 ml) milk
1 egg
¼ pint (5 fl oz 150 ml) double cream
Salt and freshly ground black pepper

Cut off the florettes, roughly chop the cauliflower stalks and the tenderer leaves. Peel and roughly chop the onion. Combine the vegetables, curry powder, nutmeg, stock and milk, bring to the boil and simmer for about 20 minutes until the cauliflower is just soft. Strain off the stock from the vegetables.

Double-bladed knife Process the vegetables until reduced to a coarse purée – the soup is better if it has some texture in it. Add the egg and cream and process until the ingredients are well mixed. Return the vegetable purée to a clean pan, add the stock and milk and heat through without boiling, stirring all the time. Season with salt and pepper and serve hot with crisply fried croutons of bread.

Curried Carrot and Apple Soup

A delicious and versatile soup which can be served either as a thin, subtle elegant starter before a substantial main course or as a thickened and creamy aromatic brew to have before a lighter main course.

For four people

1 medium onion
2 cloves garlic
1 piece of fresh root ginger ½ in. (1·25
  cm)
3 tablespoons sunflower oil
1 tablespoon Madras curry powder
4 large carrots

2 firm eating apples
2 bay leaves
2 pints (1·2 litres) chicken stock (or use
  water and stock cubes)
2 tablespoons tomato purée
4 tablespoons single cream (if making
  the thick soup)

Peel and roughly chop the onion, garlic and ginger root. Peel, core and roughly chop the apples. Peel and roughly chop the carrots.

Double-bladed knife Process the onion, garlic and ginger until very finely chopped and remove. Heat the oil in a saucepan, add the onion, garlic and ginger and cook over a low heat, stirring every now and then until the onion is soft. Add the curry powder, mix well and cook for 2 minutes.

Double-bladed knife

Process the carrot and apple together until the carrot is finely chopped. Add the carrot, apple and tomato purée to the curry mixture, mix in the stock, add the bay leaves bring to the boil and simmer for 30 minutes.

For a Thin Soup
Strain the soup through a very fine sieve.

For a Thick Soup

Double-bladed knife and a clean bowl

Strain the soup and process the vegetables in the Magimix until smooth and transfer to a clean saucepan. Add the stock and heat through, stirring well. Add the cream, check for seasoning and serve piping hot with tiny croutons of crisply fried bread.

Swede Soup

Swedes have a subtle taste that is very underrated. They must be one of the cheapest vegetables on the market during the dreary winter months and yet it is strange how seldom you find them mashed, mashed with half a quantity of mashed potato, roasted around the meat or made into a light and delicious soup like the following recipe.

For four to five people

1 small onion
1 oz (25 g) butter
2 tablespoons flour
1½ pint (900 ml) good chicken stock
1¼ lb (575 g) swede

Bouquet garni
Salt and freshly ground black pepper
¼ pint (5 fl oz 150 ml) single cream
Chopped parsley to garnish

Peel and roughly chop the onion. Thinly peel and roughly chop the swede.

Double-bladed knife

Process the onion until finely chopped and remove.
Process the swede until coarsely chopped.
Combine the onion and swede with enough stock to cover, add the bouquet garni, season with salt and pepper; bring to the boil and simmer for about 25 minutes until the swede is soft. Strain off excess stock.

Double-bladed knife

Process the swede and onion until smooth.
Melt the butter in a large saucepan. Add the flour and mix well. Gradually blend in the remainder of the stock, stirring continually over a medium high heat until the mixture is smooth. Add the vegetable purée, check seasoning, mix in the cream and heat through without boiling. Garnish with finely chopped parsley.
Note If the soup is too thick thin it with more stock.

Barley Soup with Vegetables

People seem to have forgotten about the use of pearl barley in soups, but it is delicious and forms the basis of some very nourishing and inexpensive starters.

For six people

2 oz (50 g) pearl barley
2¼ pints (1·4 litres) chicken stock
1 large carrot
1 large onion
1 large leek

2 large potatoes
2 small firm tomatoes
Salt and freshly ground black pepper
4 oz (100 g) frozen peas
1 tablespoon finely chopped parsley

Peel the carrot, peel and roughly chop the onion; clean the leek. Peel the potatoes. Remove the stalks from the tomatoes.

Chipper disc Process the carrot, onion, leek and potatoes through the disc putting very little pressure on the chipper (this will produce short chipped lengths of the vegetables). Process the tomatoes through the chipper disc with the pusher in place but putting no pressure on the pusher. Combine the pearl barley and chicken stock together with the chipped vegetables in a saucepan, season with salt and pepper, bring to the boil and simmer for about 1 hour or until the barley is tender. Add the peas and cook for a further 15 minutes. Check seasoning, mix in the parsley and serve piping hot.

Winter Pea Soup

An excellent soup for a cold, foggy, night which warms the cockles and delights the appetite.

For eight people

1 lb (450 g) dried green peas, soaked
    overnight.
1 stick celery
3 rashers streaky bacon with the rinds
    removed
1 large onion

2 carrots
4 pints (2·4 litres) chicken stock
Salt and freshly ground black pepper
Few drops Tabasco sauce
¼ pint (5 fl oz 150 ml) single cream

Trim the leaves from the celery. Roughly chop the celery stick. Roughly chop the bacon. Peel and roughly chop the onion and carrots.

Double-bladed knife Finely chop the celery leaves and remove. Process the bacon until finely chopped and remove. Combine the onion, carrots, and celery in the Magimix bowl and process until the ingredients are all finely chopped.

Cook the bacon in a heavy saucepan until the fat runs. Add the onion, carrots and celery and cook over a low heat until the vegetables are softened. Drain the peas and add them to the vegetables together with the stock. Season with salt and pepper, add a few drops of Tabasco sauce and bring to the boil. Simmer for about two hours or until the peas are really soft. Drain off and reserve any liquid.

Double-bladed knife Process the soup until smooth and return it to a clean pan with the liquid. Heat through, adjust seasoning, stir in the cream and garnish with the chopped celery leaves.

Cream of Pea and Ham Soup

This is only really worth making when you have a ham or bacon bone handy. Delicatessens or grocery shops will often let you have a ham bone for very little after they have carved off all the ham. Sadly these days very few grocers carve their own ham off the bone so if you know of one stick to him like a leech; the alternative is to use the bone from a bacon joint you cook at home (I usually bone and roll my bacon joints myself in order to have the bone for this rich, inexpensive and nourishing winter soup.

For four to five people
6 oz (175 g) dried split green or yellow peas
Water
1 ham bone
1 small onion
½ oz (13 g) butter

Chicken or white stock
2 oz (50 g) cooked bacon or ham
Bouquet garni
Freshly ground black pepper
Finely chopped parsley
Crisp croutons of fried bread to garnish.

Cover the peas with water and leave to soak overnight.
Drain off excess water.
Peel and roughly chop the onion.

Double-bladed knife Finely chop the onion with the double-bladed knife. Melt the butter, add the onion and cook over a low heat until the onion is soft and transparent. Add the peas and enough stock to cover. Season with pepper, put in the ham bone and bouquet garni, bring to the boil and simmer gently for about 40 minutes or until the peas are tender (this can be done in a pressure cooker).

Remove the bouquet garni and ham bone. Transfer the soup to the Magimix bowl and purée the peas. In the standard Magimix you may need to do this in two batches. Return to a clean pan, add the coarsely chopped bacon or ham and enough stock to make up to 2 pints liquid and heat through. Check seasoning and garnish with finely chopped parsley. Serve a bowl of crisply fried bread croutons separately.

Smoked Haddock Soup

A subtle flavoured soup which can be served cold in the summer. Make sure you get smoked haddock fillets and not the more coarse smoked cod.

For six people

1 lb (450 g) potatoes
2 pints (1·2 litres) milk
1 chicken stock cube crumbled
3 small leeks
2 oz (50 g) butter

12 oz (350 g) smoked haddock
¼ pint (5 fl oz 150 ml) single cream
White pepper
1 tablespoon finely chopped chives or spring onion tops

Peel and roughly chop the potatoes. Clean and trim the leeks. Cut the fish into 1 in. (2·5 cm) cubes.

Double-bladed knife

Process the potatoes until fairly finely chopped.

Thin slicing disc

Process the leeks through the thin slicing disc. Heat the butter in a heavy saucepan. Add the potatoes and leeks and cook over a low heat, stirring every now and then, until the butter has been absorbed. Add the milk and stock cube, mix well, bring to the boil, add the smoked haddock and simmer for about 15 minutes until the vegetables are tender.
Strain off most of the stock.

Double-bladed knife

Process the ingredients until puréed and return to a clean pan. Add the stock and cream, season with white pepper and thin the soup if necessary with a little extra milk (it should be the consistency of velvety cream). Heat through without boiling and garnish with finely chopped chives just before serving.

Crab Soup

Illustrated on page 41

Not as extravagant as it sounds since the strong flavour of crab can be stretched by the addition of potatoes when this soup is made in your Magimix. The result is a rich aromatic soup which can be further enhanced by the addition of a little brandy poured into each bowl just before serving.

For four people

12 oz (350 g) potatoes
1 medium onion
1½ oz (40 g) butter
1 pint (600 ml) fish fumet or chicken stock
½ pint (10 fl oz 300 ml) milk
2 oz (50 g) brown crabmeat, fresh, frozen or tinned

2 oz (50 g) white crabmeat, fresh, frozen or tinned
Salt and freshly ground black pepper
Few drops Tabasco sauce
Few drops anchovy essence
¼ pint (5 fl oz 150 ml) single cream
Chopped parsley

Double-bladed knife Peel and roughly chop the potatoes. Peel and roughly chop the onion.
Melt the butter in a heavy saucepan. Add the potatoes and onion and cook over a low heat, stirring now and then, until the butter is all absorbed into the vegetables. Add the stock, bring to the boil and simmer until the potatoes are soft. Strain off most of the stock and process the potatoes and onion until smooth. Mix the brown crabmeat with a little of the stock until smooth. Return the purée to a clean pan with the stock and crab mixture, add the milk and bring to the boil. Season with salt, pepper and a little Tabasco and anchovy essence.
Mix in the white crabmeat and cream, heat through without boiling and serve in bowls sprinkled with chopped parsley and accompanied with slices of buttered brown bread.

Stilton Soup

This unusual soup has recently become popular on the menus of quite a number of restaurants. It has a pleasant tangy flavour but care has to be taken not to make it too rich. I find cider gives a lighter and less astringent flavour than wine in this soup.

For five to six people

1 onion	1½ pints (900 ml) chicken stock
1 clove garlic	½ pint (10 fl oz 300 ml) milk
2 sticks celery	8 oz (225 g) Stilton
2 oz (50 g) butter	4 tablespoons single cream
3 tablespoons flour	Salt and white pepper
¼ pint (5 fl oz 150 ml) dry cider	Pinch cayenne and ground nutmeg

Peel and roughly chop the onion and garlic. Roughly chop the celery, reserving the leaves for garnish.

Double-bladed knife Combine the onion, garlic and celery in the Magimix bowl and process until the vegetables are fairly finely chopped.
Heat the butter in a saucepan, add the vegetables and cook, stirring, over a low heat for five minutes. Mix in the flour and gradually add the cider, stock and milk stirring continually over a medium high heat until the soup comes to the boil. Season with salt, pepper, cayenne and nutmeg and simmer for 10 minutes. Strain the soup.

Double-bladed knife Purée the strained vegetables with the Stilton and return them to a clean pan with the strained liquid. Add the cream, check seasoning and heat through without boiling. Garnish with chopped celery leaves.

Old Fashioned Chestnut Soup

This is the sort of soup one only wants to have once a year. It is very rich and velvety and once is enough but *that* time it is sensational. Be careful only to serve a light main course after the soup – I often serve it at Christmas time if I have leftovers and salad to bring out for the main course.

For five to six people

1½ lb (675 g) chestnuts	2 pints (1·2 litres) good strong chicken
1 large potato	stock (or use water and stock cubes)
1 small onion	Salt and freshly ground black pepper
1 carrot	Few drops lemon juice
Bouquet garni	½ pint (10 fl oz 300 ml) thin cream
2 bay leaves	Fried bread croutons for garnishing

Cut a cross in the top of the chestnuts with a small sharp knife and bake them for 20 minutes in a moderately hot oven (400°F. 200°C. Reg. 6) until the chestnuts are soft. Leave to cool and then remove the shells and inner skins of the chestnuts. Peel the potato, onion and carrot.

Thin slicing disc Process the potato, onion and carrot through the slicing disc. Combine the chestnuts, potato, onion and carrot in a saucepan, add the bouquet garni, bay leaves, season with salt and pepper and pour over enough stock to cover the chestnuts and vegetables. Bring to the boil and simmer for about 25 minutes until the vegetables are soft. Remove the bouquet garni and bay leaves and drain off excess stock.

Double-bladed knife Process the chestnuts and vegetables in the Magimix bowl until puréed. Return the purée to a clean pan, mix in the remaining stock, bring to the boil, add a few drops of lemon juice to counteract the sweetness of the chestnuts and check the seasoning. Lower the heat, stir in the cream, and heat through without boiling. Garnish the soup with crisp croutons of fried bread.

STARTERS

Fish and Broccoli Pâté with a Rosey Sauce

For six people

12 oz (350 g) broccoli or calabrese
12 oz (350 g) monkfish off the bone
2 eggs
4 egg whites
Salt and freshly ground black pepper

Few drops Tabasco sauce
4 tomatoes
4 oz (100 g) rhubarb
Chicken stock

Cook the broccoli or calabrese in boiling stock until tender and drain well. Cut the fish into cubes.

Double-bladed knife
Process the fish until reduced to a purée. Add the broccoli and continue to process until the ingredients are puréed. Add the eggs and egg whites, season with salt, pepper and a little Tabasco sauce and process to mix well.

Turn the pâté into an oiled loaf tin with the bottom lined with non stick paper. Cover with foil and place in a bain marie with enough hot water to come half way up the sides of the loaf tin.

Cook in a hot oven (400°F. 200°C. Reg. 6) for about 35 minutes or until the pâté is firm. Turn out and leave to cool.

Cover the tomatoes with boiling water for two minutes and then slide off the skins. Remove the cores and seeds from the tomatoes. Cook the rhubarb in a little chicken stock until just tender and drain well.

Double-bladed knife
Process the rhubarb and tomatoes together until smooth and fluffy and leave to cool.

Serve the pâté garnished with watercress, cut into slices, with the sauce separately.

Prawn Pâté

A light tasting and refreshing pâté made of prawns and cream cheese with a good seasoning and some chopped chives for flavouring. Serve with hot brown toast and lemon quarters. Defrost frozen prawns in the refrigerator overnight – the more slowly they are defrosted the better will be their flavour and texture.

For four to five people

½ lb (225 g) peeled prawns
4 oz (100 g) butter
2 tablespoons mayonnaise
3 tablespoons cream cheese

Salt and freshly ground black pepper
Pinch cayenne pepper
1 teaspoon chopped chives

Double-bladed knife

Cut up the butter and process until soft and fluffy scraping the sides down if necessary. With the machine switched on add the mayonnaise a teaspoon at a time through the feed tube. As soon as the mayonnaise has been amalgamated with the butter add the cream cheese and seasonings and process until smooth and light. Add the prawns and chives and switch on and off to roughly cut up the prawns. Pack into small ramekins and chill in a refrigerator for at least one hour before serving. Garnish with sprigs of parsley.

Smoked Fish Pâté

Illustrated on page 42

The smoked fish you use depends on your purse strings but the basic recipe remains the same. Try this with smoked mackerel, smoked salmon trimmings if you can get them, kipper, cooked smoked haddock, smoked eel or even smoked snoek.

For six people

8 oz (225 g) smoked fish with skin and
    bones removed.
5 oz (125 g) butter
½ a small onion
½ clove garlic

Juice ½ a small lemon
Freshly ground black pepper and a
    pinch mace and cayenne
¼ pint (5 fl oz 150 ml) double cream

Peel and roughly chop the onion and garlic.
Heat half the butter in a saucepan, add the onion and garlic and cook over a low heat until the onion is soft and transparent.

Plastic blade

Combine the onion, garlic, fish and remaining butter in the Magimix bowl and process until smooth. Add the lemon juice and cream, season with pepper, mace and cayenne and process until well mixed. Pack into small pots and chill until firm. Serve with hot toast.

Brandade of Smoked Haddock

A brandade is a smooth, delectable, pounded paste served as a first course with hot French bread. The classic brandade is made from salt cod and served with bread, crisply fried in hot oil. Smoked haddock is a lot easier to find and milder in flavour.

For five to six people

1 lb (450 g) smoked haddock fillet
1 large cooked potato
1 clove garlic
½ pint (10 fl oz 300 ml) olive or
   sunflower oil

Freshly ground black pepper
Chopped parsley
Wedges of lemon

Roughly chop the potato.
Poach the haddock fillet in water until just tender. Peel the clove of garlic.

Double-bladed knife
Process the garlic until finely chopped.

Plastic blade
Add the haddock and the potato to the garlic and process until a smooth paste is formed. With the machine switched on add the oil in a slow steady stream through the feed tube as though you were making a mayonnaise. Season with pepper, and some salt if necessary.
Turn into a serving dish, dust with chopped parsley and garnish with wedges of lemon.
Serve warm or cold.

Potted Prawn Pâté

A mixture of pâté and those lovely potted shrimps one used to have but never seem to see nowadays (I believe it is something to do with shrimps being too much trouble to peel – one of the sad symptoms of today's gastronomic delights).

For four people

8 oz (225 g) peeled prawns (if they are
   frozen defrost them as slowly as
   possible in a refrigerator to preserve
   as much as possible of their flavour)
6 oz (175 g) butter

Salt and freshly ground black pepper
Good pinch cayenne pepper and ground
   mace
½ teaspoon lemon juice
½ teaspoon brandy

If the prawns are at all damp, dry them on kitchen paper. Melt the butter over a medium heat until foaming and strain it through a fine sieve or a piece of muslin.

Double-bladed knife
Process the prawns until coarsely chopped.
Add the butter, seasoning, lemon juice and brandy and process for just long enough to mix the ingredients and finely chop the prawns. Pack the prawn mixture into a small mixing bowl and chill in a refrigerator for at least three hours. Dip the bowl into very hot water, turn out and cut into wedges, like a cake. Serve with hot toast and wedges of lemon. Cayenne pepper should also be on the table.

Smoked Salmon Rosettes

Delicate mounds of smoked salmon encasing a delicious pâté of cream cheese and avocado pears.

For eight people

24 thin slices smoked salmon
2 ripe avocado pears
1 teaspoon lemon juice
½ small onion
Salt and white pepper
4 oz (100 g) cream cheese

½ pint (10 fl oz 300 ml) double cream
Few drops Worcestershire sauce
Pinch cayenne pepper
Small bunch watercress
8 radishes

Use the smoked salmon to line 8 small bowls.
Peel the avocados and remove the stones. Peel and roughly chop the onion.

Double-bladed knife

Process the onion until finely chopped.
Add the cream cheese to the onion and process until the cheese is smooth and creamy. Add the avocado and lemon juice and continue to process until the mixture is smooth. Add the cream, season with salt, pepper, Worcestershire sauce and cayenne, and process until the pâté is thick and light – do *not* over process.
Fill the smoked salmon lined bowls with the pâté, smooth out the pâté and fold over the edges of the smoked salmon. Chill in the refrigerator for at least one hour and turn out by inverting and gently tapping the bottom of the bowls. Garnish the top of the smoked salmon mounds with a radish cut into a rose and a few leaves of watercress. Accompany with halves of lemon neatly wrapped in a layer of muslin so that the juice, but not pips, can be squeezed out as required. Accompany with thin slices of buttered brown bread.

Potted Crab

A delicious simple starter for any meal. Serve it with plenty of hot brown toast preferably made from granary bread.

For six people

8 oz (225 g) mixed brown and white
    crabmeat
Salt and freshly ground black pepper
½ teaspoon lemon juice

Ground mace
6 oz (175 g) butter
Few drops Worcestershire sauce
8 fl oz (240 ml) whipping cream

Melt the butter.

Double-bladed knife

Combine the crab with the lemon juice in the bowl. Add salt and pepper to season, a little ground mace, a few drops of Worcestershire sauce, and the melted butter. Process to mix well. Remove and leave to cool but not set.

Plastic blade

Process the cream until thick and fold it into the crab mixture. Turn into six ramekin dishes and chill in a refrigerator for at least an hour.

Mussels Provençal

Mussels cooked in the style of snails and just as delicious.

For four people

5 pints (3 litres) mussels (about 10 – 12 per person)
¼ pint (5 fl oz 150 ml) dry white wine
2 teaspoons green peppercorns
2 cloves garlic

4 oz (100 g) butter
1 small bunch parsley
2 oz (50 g) sliced bread with the crusts removed
Salt

Scrub the mussels with a wire brush and pull out the "beards" which protrude from the opening side of the mussels. Place them in a large, heavy, saucepan, pour over the wine and bring to the boil over a high heat, shake the pan as the mussels open and as soon as they have all opened remove the pan from the heat discarding any mussels that have not opened after about six minutes.

Remove the mussels one at a time onto flat open serving dishes pulling off the top, empty, shells. Remove the coarse stems from the parsley. Peel and roughly chop the garlic.

Double-bladed knife Process the parsley until finely chopped. Add the garlic and process until finely chopped (scrape down the sides if necessary). Add the butter, bread and peppercorns and process until the mixture is reduced to a smooth paste. Season with salt and process for just long enough to mix in the salt.

Spread a teaspoon of the stuffing over each mussel and put under a hot grill until golden brown. Serve at once.

Crab and Cucumber Salad

A light first course salad with Japanese overtones.

For four people

1 cucumber
6 oz (175 g) white crab meat
1 in. (2·5 cm) fresh root ginger
1 tablespoon vinegar

1 tablespoon soy sauce
Salt and freshly ground black pepper
Pinch sugar
Crisp lettuce leaves

Leave the cucumber whole without peeling.

Chipper disc Process the cucumber through the chipper disc, remove, sprinkle with salt and leave to stand in a sieve or colander to remove excess liquid for 30 minutes. Pat dry with kitchen paper and mix with the crab meat.

Peel the ginger root.

Double-bladed knife Process the ginger until finely chopped.

Add the vinegar and soy sauce and process until well mixed, season with salt, pepper and a pinch of sugar and process for just long enough to mix in the seasonings. Pour the sauce over the cucumber and crab and toss lightly to mix. Turn into bowls lined with crisp lettuce leaves and serve chilled garnished with thin slices of lemon.

Ratatouille Mousse with Prawns

This really is the most delicious starter, but it is fairly substantial so serve it before a light main course.

For six people

1 onion
2 cloves garlic
1 medium courgette
1 small aubergine
1 green pepper
2 tablespoons olive or sunflower oil
1 tin tomatoes
2 tablespoons dry white wine
Pinch of mixed herbs and oregano

Salt and freshly ground black pepper
1 packet gelatine powder
Warm water
¼ pint (5 fl oz 150 ml) double or whipping cream
8 oz (225 g) prawns
Crisp lettuce leaves
Mayonnaise (optional) (see page 250)

Peel and roughly chop the onion and garlic.
Remove the core and seeds from the pepper.

Double-bladed knife
Process the onion and the garlic and green pepper until finely chopped and remove.

Coarse grating disc
Process the courgette and aubergine through the coarse grating disc. Heat the oil. Add the onion, garlic and pepper and cook until the onion and garlic are soft and transparent. Add the aubergine and courgette, mix well, add the wine and cook until the wine has evaporated. Add the tomatoes, season with salt and pepper and mix in the herbs. Bring to the boil and simmer, uncovered until the vegetables are absolutely tender and the ratatouille is thick. Leave to cool. Soften the gelatine in three tablespoons warm water.

Double-bladed knife
Process the vegetables until smooth, and remove. Add the gelatine mixture to the puréed vegetables and leave until beginning to set.

Double-bladed knife and a clean bowl
Process the cream until thick. Fold the cream into the setting vegetable purée. Turn half the mixture into dampened patty or ramekin moulds. Spread the prawns (reserving about one third of the prawns for decoration) over the puréed vegetables, cover with the remaining vegetables and chill for about two hours in a refrigerator until set firm. Run a knife around the edge of the moulds, dip them quickly into boiling water to loosen the bottoms and turn out the moulds on to crisp lettuce leaves. Garnish with the reserved prawns and serve with a little mayonnaise on the side if you like.

Chicken Mousses with Spring Onion Sauce

Individual chicken mousses on top of which you float a delicate and deliciously light sauce. The advantage with these dishes which can be served as a first or light lunch or supper dish is that they utilize leftover cooked chicken.

For four people	Butter	2 tablespoons cream
	4 oz (100 g) cooked chicken, with the skin removed	Salt and freshly ground black pepper
	2 oz (50 g) mushrooms	Pinch nutmeg and mace
	2 eggs, separated	Spring onion and wine sauce (see page 257)

Double-bladed knife Process the chicken until fairly finely chopped. Add the mushrooms and process until finely chopped. Add the egg yolks and cream and season with salt, pepper, nutmeg and mace. Process until the ingredients are well mixed. Butter four ramekin dishes. Whip the egg whites until stiff and fold them lightly into the chicken mixture. Turn into 4 ramekin dishes and bake in a moderate oven (350°F. 175°C. Reg. 4) for 15 minutes.

Serve with a spring onion and wine sauce (see page 257) on the side.

Mousseline of Chicken

Deliciously light moulds which are served warm as a first course with a variety of accompaniments and sauces.

For four people	8 oz (225 g) raw chicken breast with the skin removed	½ pint (10 fl oz 300 ml) double cream
	1 large egg	Salt, white pepper, pinch cayenne and mace

Butter six dariole moulds (muffin tins) making sure that both sides and bottom of the moulds are really well coated with butter (I find the easiest way to do this is to dip a piece of kitchen paper in a little melted butter).

Roughly chop the chicken breast.

Double-bladed knife Process the chicken breast until finely chopped. Add the egg and process until the mixture is just smooth (do not over process). Add the cream, season with salt, pepper and a small pinch of cayenne and mace and process for just long enough to mix the cream into the other ingredients. Half fill the moulds with the mixture, cover each one with well buttered foil, place them in a bain marie or a roasting tin half filled with nearly boiling water and bake them in a moderately hot oven (375°F. 190°C. Reg. 5) for 20 minutes. Remove the moulds from the hot water and leave them to stand for 3 – 4 minutes before running a sharp knife around the edge of the mousselines, turning them upside down and tapping the bottom sharply to remove the moulds.

Serve the Chicken Mousselines on individual plates in the following way:

On a small bed of savoury rice with a tomato or spring onion and wine sauce (see page 257).

With a surround of spinach purée and a tomato sauce (see page 259).

On a bed of rice with a curry sauce (see page 266).

Artichoke Bottoms with Chicken Liver Mousse

For four people

8 tinned artichoke bottoms
1 small onion
8 oz (225 g) chicken livers
4 oz (100 g) butter
Salt and freshly ground black pepper

Pinch mixed herbs
1 tablespoon brandy
¼ pint (5 fl oz 150 ml) whipping or
   double cream
Watercress for garnishing

Peel and roughly chop the onion.
Trim the chicken livers of any fibres or yellowish pieces.

Double-bladed knife
Process the onion until very finely chopped. Heat 1 oz (25 g) of the butter in a saucepan. Add the onion and cook over a low heat until the onion is soft and transparent. Add the livers, season with salt and pepper and mix in the herbs. Cook, shaking the pan for three minutes until the livers are browned on the outside but still pink inside. Add the brandy, bring to the boil and set light to the brandy with a match; shake the pan until the flames die down.

Double-bladed knife
Process the liver mixture with the remaining butter until smooth and remove.

Plastic blade
Process the cream until thickening (do not over process, the cream should be mousse-like not thick) add the chicken liver mixture and process for just long enough to incorporate the ingredients. Chill in the refrigerator until firm.
Using a forcing bag, pipe the chicken liver mousse on top of the artichoke bottoms and garnish with watercress.

Artichoke Bottoms with Smoked Salmon and Prawn Cream

An elegant and quickly made starter. Try to get the large tinned artichoke bottoms if you can and if as happened to me once, you can't get any tinned artichoke bottoms at all, serve the cream surrounded by crudités of carrot, celery, green pepper and cucumber sticks and accompany it with delicious granary bread.

For six people

6 large or 12 small artichoke bottoms
2 tablespoons oil
1 tablespoon white wine vinegar
Salt and freshly ground black pepper
4 oz (100 g) smoked salmon (I use the
   cheaper trimmings of Canadian
   salmon for this dish)

2 tablespoons horseradish sauce
2 oz (50 g) cottage cheese
4 oz (100 g) defrosted prawns
¼ pint (5 fl oz 150 ml) double cream
Cayenne pepper
Spring onion tops or chopped chives to
   garnish

Drain the artichoke bottoms. Combine the oil and vinegar, season with salt and pepper, pour the dressing over the artichokes and refrigerate for two hours (this takes away any 'tinned' flavouring in the artichoke bottoms)
Roughly chop the smoked salmon.

Double-bladed knife Combine the cottage cheese and horseradish and process until smooth. Add the smoked salmon, half the prawns and a seasoning of salt, pepper and cayenne and process until the salmon and prawns are finely chopped. Add the cream and process until thick. Drain the artichoke bottoms and pat them dry on kitchen paper. Place the bottoms on six serving dishes, mound up the smoked salmon cream in the centre and garnish with the remainder of the prawns and a sprinkling of spring onion tops or chives. Serve chilled with buttered brown bread.

Tomato Mousse with Artichoke Bottoms

An attractive and sophisticated, cool, first course. See ideas for alternative ways of using the mousse below. Tinned artichoke bottoms are available from good delicatessens.

For six people

1 onion
1 clove garlic
2 tablespoons olive or sunflower oil
1 tin (15 oz 425 g) tomatoes
2 tablespoons tomato purée
¼ pint (150 ml) dry white wine
1 teaspoon dried tarragon

1 tin (15 oz 425 g) consommé
1 packet gelatine
Salt and freshly ground black pepper
½ pint (10 fl oz 300 ml) whipping or
   double cream
4 tinned artichoke bottoms
Watercress and lemon slices for garnish

Peel and roughly chop the onion and garlic

Double-bladed knife Process the onion and garlic until finely chopped. Heat the oil, add the onion and garlic and cook over a medium heat until the onion is soft and transparent. Add the tomatoes, tomato purée, white wine and tarragon, season with salt and pepper, bring to the boil and cook over a moderately high heat, uncovered, for 30 minutes until most of the liquid has been absorbed. While the tomato mixture is cooking put the consommé into a saucepan and cook over a high heat until it is reduced by about a half to ½ pint. Remove from the stove, sprinkle the gelatine over the surface and leave until the gelatine has dissolved. Stir well.

Double-bladed knife Process the tomato mixture until reduced to a purée and rub through a coarse sieve to remove the tomato seeds. Add the consommé to the tomato mixture and mix well. Leave to cool and then chill until first beginning to set.

Medium slicing disc Slice the artichoke bottoms and mix them into the setting tomato jelly.

Plastic blade Process the cream until thick and mousse like but not too stiff. Add the tomato mixture and switch on and off to mix. Turn into six dampened moulds and chill in a refrigerator until firm. Turn out the moulds and garnish with watercress and slices of lemon.

Variations on the tomato mousse theme Turn the mousse into a dampened ring mould and chill until firm. Turn out onto a serving dish and fill the centre with whipped cream flavoured with chopped, smoked, oysters and a little horseradish; grated seasoned cucumber with yogurt and finely chopped mint or shredded tongue with a sauce verte. (see page 258).

Guacamole (Avocado Dip)

For eight people

2 large ripe avocados
1 large ripe tomato
2 cloves garlic
1 red pepper

2 tablespoons lemon or fresh lime juice
½ teaspoon ground coriander
Salt and freshly ground black pepper
Few drops Tabasco sauce

Cover the tomato with boiling water for three minutes, drain, slide off the skin and remove the seeds and core from the tomato flesh. Peel the garlic. Remove the core and seeds from the red pepper. Peel the avocados, remove the stones and roughly chop the flesh.

Double-bladed knife

Process the garlic until finely chopped. Add the pepper and tomato and process until the pepper is fairly finely chopped. Add the avocado, lemon or lime juice and coriander, season with salt, pepper and Tabasco and process until the mixture is thick and creamy and the avocados are smooth. Serve chilled with crudités or with Tortillas (see page 235).

Avocados with Grated Carrot and Raisins

An extremely simple but very successful combination to serve as a first course or to have for lunch when you are trying to lose a few pounds.

For four people

2 ripe avocados
Lemon juice
¼ pint (5 fl oz 150 ml) vinaigrette
    dressing (see page 246)

2 tablespoons seedless raisins
2 medium sized carrots

Make the vinaigrette, add the raisins and leave in a warm place for the raisins to plump out for 30 minutes.
Peel the carrots.
Halve the avocados, remove the stones and brush the cut surfaces with lemon juice.

Coarse grater or julienne disc

Process the carrots.
Add the grated or julienne carrots to the vinaigrette and raisins and toss lightly until all the carrot is coated with dressing. Pile the carrot mixture in the centre of the avocados and chill before serving.

Crab Soup (Page 28)

Avocado with Crab and Mayonnaise

A rich starter so serve a light main course to follow it.

For four people

2 ripe avocados
¼ pint (5 fl oz 150 ml) mayonnaise (see page 250)
Lemon juice
1 teaspoon curry paste

Few drops Worcestershire and Tabasco sauce
3 oz (75 g) brown crab meat
3 oz (75 g) white crab meat

Double-bladed knife

Halve the avocados, remove the stones and brush the cut surfaces with lemon juice. Combine the mayonnaise, curry paste and brown crab meat, flavour with a little Worcestershire and Tabasco sauce and process to mix. Add the white crab meat and switch the machine on and off a couple of times to incorporate the ingredients. Pile the filling into the centre of the avocado halves and serve chilled.

Avocados with Chicken Salad

This makes a good winter starter or a useful light main course for a summer lunch.

For four people

2 ripe avocados
Juice ½ lemon
6 oz (175 g) cooked chicken
2 sticks celery
1 small green pepper

3 fl oz (90 ml 6 tablespoons) mayonnaise (see page 250)
Salt and freshly ground black pepper
Few drops Tabasco and Worcestershire sauce

Double-bladed knife

Halve the avocados, remove the stones and rub the exposed avocado with lemon juice. Remove the core and seeds from the green pepper.
Process the celery and pepper until coarsely chopped. Add the chicken and mayonnaise, season with salt and pepper, add a little Tabasco and Worcestershire sauce and process for just long enough to mix the ingredients and fairly coarsely chop the chicken (do not over-process).
Pile the salad in the avocado halves and serve chilled.

Smoked Fish Pâté (Page 32)

Cucumber, Melon and Tomato Cocktail

This is a deliciously cool and refreshing starter which I have pinched unashamedly from that excellent of all restaurants "The Horn of Plenty" at Gunnislake, Nr. Tavistock, Devon. My version is not quite the same as that of Sonia Stevenson but the principle is there. Serve this before a robust main course.

For six people

4 firm ripe tomatoes
1 firm but ripe melon
1 cucumber
1 teaspoon French Dijon mustard
1 teaspoon curry powder

5 tablespoons olive or sunflower oil
2 tablespoons vinegar
Pinch sugar
Salt and freshly ground black pepper
Pinch dried or finely chopped fresh dill

Cover the tomatoes with boiling water for three minutes and slide off the skins. Quarter the tomatoes and remove the cores and seeds. Peel the cucumber, cut it in half lengthwise and remove the seeds. Peel and halve the melon and remove the seeds.

Double-bladed knife
Process the tomatoes until fairly finely chopped and remove.

Chipper disc
Process the cucumber and melon using a light pressure on the pusher. Remove the cucumber and melon.

Double-bladed knife
Combine the mustard, curry powder, oil and vinegar and season with salt, freshly ground black pepper and a pinch of sugar, add the dill and process for just long enough to mix the ingredients. Pour the dressing over the cucumber, tomato and melon, toss lightly and chill in the refrigerator for at least 45 minutes. Turn into six glass goblets and garnish with a sprig of mint if this is available.

Pâté Stuffed Deep Fried Mushrooms

An elegant, savoury starter with a succulent filling. Choose fairly large button mushrooms that are absolutely fresh and firm. Allow about five mushrooms per serving depending on their sizes.

For four people

20 medium sized firm button
    mushrooms
4 oz (100 g) country style pâté
Small bunch parsley
2 slices white bread
1 small onion or shallot

2 cloves garlic
1 tablespoon oil
Salt and freshly ground black pepper
Pinch mixed herbs
1 egg
Oil to deep fry

Remove any coarse stems from the parsley. Peel and roughly chop the onion and garlic.

Double-bladed knife	Cut off the crusts and process the bread until reduced to fine crumbs and remove. Process the parsley until finely chopped and remove. Process the onion and the garlic until finely chopped. Heat the oil in a small frying pan. Add the onion and garlic and cook over a low heat, stirring to prevent sticking until the onion is soft and transparent.
Double-bladed knife	Process the pâté with the parsley and onion and garlic, season with salt and pepper, add the herbs and process until well mixed, scraping down the sides of the bowl if necessary. Remove the stalks from the mushrooms and, using a teaspoon, fill the mushroom caps with the pâté mixture pressing it down firmly. Chill the filled caps in the refrigerator for 1 hour.
Double-bladed knife	Process the egg until smooth. Dip the mushrooms into the beaten egg, roll in the breadcrumbs and deep fry, a few at a time, until they are crisp and golden. Drain on kitchen paper and serve with a garlic mayonnaise (see page 251).

Halved Grapefruit with Sea Food Salad

For six people

3 grapefruit
Half crisp (iceburg) lettuce
3 oz (75 g) peeled prawns
2 oz (50 g) white crabmeat
24 mussels, cooked (or use tinned
  mussels in brine)
1 spring onion
7 fl oz (210 ml) mayonnaise
  (see page 250)

2 tablespoons tomato ketchup
1 tablespoon sherry
2 tablespoons dry white wine
Juice ½ orange
1 teaspoon lemon juice
Pinch dried dill
Salt and freshly ground black pepper
Few drops of Tabasco sauce

Halve the grapefruits (you can make an attractive pattern by cutting around the centre with a sharp pointed knife in a zig-zag pattern.) Cut out all the membrane and flesh, separate the flesh from the membrane and discard the pips and membrane.

Thin or medium slicing disc
Slice the lettuce, and remove.

Double-bladed knife
Combine the spring onion, mayonnaise, tomato ketchup, sherry, white wine and orange and lemon juices, add the dill and season with salt, pepper and Tabasco and process until the onion is chopped and the sauce smooth and well mixed.
Divide the lettuce between the grapefruit halves. Top with the prawns, crab, mussels and grapefruit flesh and spoon over the mayonnaise sauce.
Serve well chilled.

Stuffed Mushrooms

For four people

12 large flat mushrooms
3 tablespoons olive or sunflower oil
3 oz (75 g) cooked ham
1 small onion
2 cloves garlic
Small bunch parsley

2 slices white bread
1 egg
2 tablespoons single cream
1 tablespoon sherry
Salt and freshly ground black pepper

Remove and reserve the stems from the mushrooms. Brush the mushrooms with 1 tablespoon oil and bake them in a hot oven (425°F. 225°C. Reg. 7) for five minutes. Roughly chop the ham. Peel and roughly chop the onion and garlic. Remove the tough stems from the parsley. Remove the crusts from the bread.

Double-bladed knife

Process the bread until it is reduced to fine crumbs and remove. Process the parsley until finely chopped and remove. Process the onion and garlic until finely chopped. Heat the remaining oil in the saucepan. Add the onion and garlic and cook over a low heat, stirring to prevent sticking, until the onion is really soft and tender. Process the mushroom stalks and ham until finely chopped. Add the ham and mushroom stalks and cook gently for 2 minutes.

Double-bladed knife

Process the egg with the cream and sherry until smooth. Add the cream mixture to the ham with the parsley. Season and stir over a low heat for 1 minute. Fill the mushroom caps with the ham mixture, sprinkle over the breadcrumbs and brown under a hot grill until the breadcrumbs are crisp and golden and the mushrooms are sizzling hot.

Stilton Pears

An elegant starter that cannot fail to get a meal off to a good start.

For four people

3 tablespoons olive or sunflower oil
1 tablespoon lemon juice
½ teaspoon dry mustard
Salt and freshly ground black pepper
4 oz (100 g) Stilton cheese
4 oz (100 g) cottage cheese

1 tablespoon sour cream
Pinch cayenne pepper
4 large pears
2 bunches watercress
2 slices Parma ham (optional)

Double-bladed knife

Combine the oil, lemon juice and mustard, season with salt and pepper, process to mix well, and remove.
Combine the Stilton, cottage cheese and sour cream in the Magimix bowl, season with salt, pepper and a little cayenne and process to mix well.
Use an apple corer to remove the centre of the pears and fill them with the cheese mixture, using a small teaspoon and pressing the cheese down firmly.

Brush the top of the pears with the dressing to prevent browning and chill them in the refrigerator.

Cut the pears into thin slices and arrange them on the watercress. Spoon over the dressing making sure all the cut surfaces of the pear are covered with the dressing. Cut the ham into very thin strips. Garnish the pear slices with the ham strips and serve chilled.

Timbale of Rice and Ham

An elegant mound of ham filled rice which can be served as a first or light main course.

For four people

1 small onion
2 slices bread with crusts removed
6 oz (175 g) long grain rice
3 oz (75 g) butter
1 tablespoon oil
¾ pint (450 ml) chicken stock
1 egg yolk
2 oz (50 g) grated Parmesan cheese

6 oz (175 g) ham
4 oz (100 g) cooked spinach
2 tablespoons quick tomato sauce (see page 259)
1 tablespoon of dry white wine
Salt and freshly ground black pepper
Pinch dried oregano

Peel and roughly chop the onion. Roughly chop the ham.

Double-bladed knife Process the bread until reduced to very fine crumbs and remove. Process the onion until finely chopped.

Heat 1 oz (25 g) butter with the oil in a heavy saucepan. Add the onion and cook over a low heat until the onion is soft and transparent. Add the rice and stir until the grains become transparent. Add the stock stirring continually until the mixture comes to the boil. Season with salt and pepper, cover and cook over a low heat, stirring every now and then, until the rice is just tender and the liquid has been absorbed.

Double-bladed knife Process the egg yolk until well mixed. Add the rice and 1 oz (25 g) butter and the Parmesan and process for just long enough to mix the ingredients. Remove and leave to cool.

Double-bladed knife Process the ham and spinach until finely chopped. Heat ½ oz (13 g) butter in a saucepan. Add the ham and spinach and the wine and cook over a high heat stirring, until the wine has evaporated. Add the tomato sauce and oregano, season with salt and pepper and cook over a low heat, stirring until the sauce is thick. Use rest of butter to well grease a large mould and coat with breadcrumbs reserving some for the tops of the mould. Pack the rice risotto around the bottom and sides of the mould reserving some for the top. Fill the centre with the ham mixture, top with the remaining risotto and sprinkle the top with the remaining breadcrumbs. Bake the mould in a moderately hot oven (350°F. 175°C. Reg. 4) for about 30 minutes until the top is golden brown and crusty. Turn out the mould and serve at once with extra tomato sauce on the side.

Tartlets en Chemise

Elegant little tartlets with a casing of young spinach leaves rather than a high calorie quiche pastry.

For two people

18 young spinach leaves
4 oz (100 g) lean ham
Small bunch parsley
1 oz (25 g) Cheddar cheese
1 teaspoon finely chopped chives

Pinch dried tarragon
1 whole egg
1 egg white
Salt and freshly ground black pepper
Pinch cayenne and ground nutmeg

Blanch the spinach leaves in boiling salted water for three minutes, drain well, separate and pat dry on kitchen paper. Roughly chop the ham. Remove the stalks from the parsley.

Double-bladed knife

Process the parsley until finely chopped and remove. Process the cheese until very finely chopped, add the ham and process until the ham is very finely chopped. Add the egg and egg white and process to mix well. Add the parsley, chives, tarragon and season with salt, pepper, a pinch of cayenne and ground nutmeg and process to mix well.

Line 2 × 6 in. (15cm) diameter oiled patty tins with the spinach stalks with the top of the leaves in the centre of the tins and leaving an overlap over the sides of the tins. Fill the tins with the ham mixture and lightly fold over the stalk ends of the leaves. Cover tightly with foil and place in a bain marie with enough hot water to come halfway up the sides of the tins. Bake in a hot oven (400°F. 200°C. Reg. 6) for 20 minutes or until firm.

Hot Stuffed Tomatoes

Vegetables like tomatoes make an excellent vehicle for stuffing. They need to be highly herbed and seasoned and can be prepared in advance although they should be served as soon as they are cooked.

For six people

6 large tomatoes
2 slices white bread
4 oz (100 g) cooked beef or lamb
2 oz (50 g) streaky bacon rashers
1 clove garlic
1 small onion

2 oz (50 g) mushrooms
6 tablespoons olive or sunflower oil
Salt and freshly ground black pepper
1 egg
Pinch mixed herbs
1 tablespoon tomato purée

Cut off a slice from the top third of the tomatoes and using a teaspoon scoop out the seeds, core and half the flesh leaving a firm tomato shell. Scoop out the flesh from the tomato tops. Discard the seeds and any coarse core. Turn the tomatoes upside down and leave them to drain. Remove the crusts from the bread. Roughly chop the meat. Remove the rinds from the bacon rashers and roughly chop the bacon. Peel and roughly chop the garlic and onion.

Double-bladed knife Process the bread until reduced to fine crumbs and remove.

Process the meat until finely chopped and remove. Process the bacon until finely chopped and remove. Process the onion and garlic until finely chopped and remove.

Process the mushrooms until coarsely chopped. Add the tomato flesh and process until the tomato flesh is fairly finely chopped. Heat four tablespoons of oil. Add the bacon, onion and garlic and cook over a medium low heat, stirring to prevent sticking, until the onion is soft and transparent. Raise the heat, add the meat and cook over a high heat until the meat is browned. Add the mushrooms and tomato flesh, season with salt, and pepper, add the herbs and stir in the tomato purée. Cook over a medium heat for five minutes.

Double-bladed knife Process the egg until smooth and stir it into the meat mixture. Fill the tomatoes with the meat mixture, place them in a baking tin, sprinkle with the breadcrumbs and dribble over the remaining oil. Bake in a hot oven (400°F. 200°C. Reg. 6) for 30 minutes.

Tomatoes Stuffed with Tuna, Black Olives and Red Peppers

These produce an appetising cold first course or light lunch or summer supper dish.

For four people

4 large ripe tomatoes
2 oz (50 g) long grain rice (I like to use wild rice for this dish)
½ red pepper
12 stoned black olives

1 tin (8 oz 225 g) tuna fish
¼ pint (5 fl oz 150 ml) mayonnaise (see page 250)
1 teaspoon curry paste

Cover the tomatoes with boiling water, leave them to stand for three minutes and then slide off the skins. Cut a slice off the top third of the tomatoes, cut out the centre flesh and seeds and scoop out the flesh leaving a firm tomato cup. Discard the seeds and hard core of the tomatoes. Leave the tomatoes to drain upside down in a sieve. Discard the core and seeds of the pepper. Drain the tuna fish. Cover the rice with cold salted water, bring to the boil and simmer until the rice is tender. Rinse in cold water.

Double-bladed knife Combine the pepper, tomato flesh and black olives and process until the olives are fairly finely chopped. Add the mayonnaise, curry paste, tuna and rice process for just long enough to mix the ingredients.

Spoon the filling into the tomato cups, piling it up in a mound, put on the tops and chill the tomatoes in the refrigerator before serving.

Note The tomatoes can be garnished with sprigs of small bay leaves, fresh parsley, lemon balm, mint or coriander.

Stuffed Tomatoes with Crab

Aromatic stuffed tomatoes make a fairly substantial first course and are ideal to serve before a light fish or poultry main course. They can be served, in their own right, as a light main course with other vegetables. Choose the richly flavoured Mediterranean tomatoes or our own hot house ones.

For four people

4 large tomatoes
1 green pepper
1 cucumber
2 stalks celery

8 oz (225 g) white crabmeat
¼ pint (5 fl oz 150 ml) mayonnaise
  (see page 250)
Tabasco and Worcestershire sauce

Cover the tomatoes with boiling water and leave them to stand for three minutes. Drain well and slide off the skins. Cut a slice from the top third of the tomatoes and, using a teaspoon scoop out the flesh core and seeds, leaving a firm casing. Discard the seeds and tough core. Leave the tomatoes upside down to drain. Remove the core and seeds from the pepper. Peel the cucumber, cut it in half lengthwise and remove the seeds. Trim the celery.

Double-bladed knife
Process the pepper until finely chopped and remove. Process the celery until finely chopped and remove. Process the tomato flesh until fairly finely chopped and remove.

Chipper disc
Process the cucumber through the chipper disc place it in a sieve, sprinkle it with salt and leave it to stand for twenty minutes. Press out the excess liquid.

Plastic blade
Combine the crabmeat, mayonnaise, cucumber, celery, green pepper, tomato and a little Tabasco and Worcestershire sauce and process for just long enough to mix the ingredients.

Fill the tomatoes with the stuffing, return the caps on the tomatoes and serve chilled on large lettuce leaves.

Tomatoes Filled with a Salad of Salt Cod

If you can get them use the large, irregular Mediterranean tomatoes for this salad they look marvellous and have a more meaty flavour than our own varieties. This is my own variation of an excellent starter I first read about in one of Robert Carrier's books. I serve it as a summer main course salad dish.

For six people

6 large ripe tomatoes
1½ lb (675 g) dried salt cod
4 oz (100 g) cooked long grain rice
2 stalks of celery
½ pint (10 fl oz 300 ml) mayonnaise
  (see page 250)

2 cloves garlic
2 anchovy fillets
1 tablespoon capers
½ teaspoon dried tarragon
2 teaspoons lemon juice
Freshly ground black pepper

Soak the cod fillets overnight.

Cover the tomatoes with boiling water and leave them to stand for three minutes and then slide the skins off. Cut a slice from the top of the tomatoes and scoop out the flesh and core with a spoon (a grapefruit spoon is ideal for this job). Turn the tomatoes upside down and leave them to drain. Cover the salt cod with cold water in a saucepan, bring to the boil, drain, cover with more cold water, bring to the boil and cook gently for six minutes. Drain, cool, remove any skin and bones and flake the flesh. Peel and roughly chop the garlic. Soak the tarragon in the lemon juice for five minutes. Roughly chop the celery stalks.

Double-bladed knife Finely chop the celery and remove.

Process the garlic until finely chopped.

Add the anchovy fillets and capers and process until the anchovies and capers are coarsely chopped.

Add the mayonnaise, lemon juice and tarragon, season with pepper and process to mix well. Add the salt cod, celery and rice and process to mix the ingredients ...... do not overprocess.

Fill the tomatoes with the salt cod mixture, return the tops of the tomatoes and chill before serving.

Spinach Patties with Tomato Sauce

A sophisticated first course which is light and attractive to look at.

For four people

4 oz (100 g) cooked spinach
2 eggs
¼ pint (5 fl oz 150 ml) single cream
1 oz (25 g) butter
Salt and freshly ground black pepper

Pinch ground nutmeg
¼ pint (5 fl oz 150 ml) tomato sauce
  (see page 259)
4 tablespoons sour cream

Melt the butter in a frying pan. Add the spinach and cook over a medium heat until the butter is absorbed into the spinach.

Double-bladed knife Process the eggs and cream until smooth. Add the spinach, season with salt, pepper and a little ground nutmeg and process until the spinach is fairly finely chopped and the ingredients are well mixed.

Turn the mixture into four, well oiled, pattie tins or ramekins put them in a bain marie with enough hot water to come two thirds up the sides of the tins or ramekins and bake them in a moderately hot oven (350°F. 175°C. Reg. 4) for thirty minutes or until the mixture has risen and is coming away from the sides of the tins or ramekins (a needle plunged into the patties should come out clean). Turn out the patties on to four serving plates, spoon over the tomato sauce (this should be warm) and top with a spoonful of sour cream.

Chicken Liver Pâté

For four people

1 medium onion
1 clove garlic
1½ oz (40 g) butter or rendered chicken fat
8 oz (225 g) chicken livers
¼ pint (5 fl oz 150 ml) good chicken stock

1 hard boiled egg
2 teaspoons brandy
Good pinch mixed herbs
Salt and freshly ground black pepper

For garnishing
1 small onion
1 small green pepper

1 hard boiled egg
2 tablespoons finely chopped parsley
Quarters of lemon

To make the pâté
Peel and roughly chop the onion and garlic. Remove any fibres or discoloured flesh from the chicken livers. Roughly chop the hard boiled egg.

Double-bladed knife
Process the onion and garlic until finely chopped. Melt the butter in a heavy frying pan. Add the onion and garlic and cook over a low heat until the onion is transparent and absolutely soft. Raise the heat, add the chicken livers and cook over a high heat until the livers are browned on all sides. Add the stock and brandy, season with salt and pepper, mix in the herbs and cook over a high heat for about five minutes until most of the liquid has been absorbed and the livers though cooked are still slightly pink in the centre.

Double-bladed knife
Combine the chicken livers, onion, garlic, the juices from the pan and the egg and process until the mixture is smooth. Pile into a mound on a serving dish and chill well.

To make the garnish
Peel and roughly chop the onion. Remove the seeds and core from the pepper. Roughly chop the hard boiled egg.

Double-bladed knife
Process the egg until finely chopped and remove. Process the onion until finely chopped and remove. Process the pepper until finely chopped and remove. Dust the pâté with the parsley and surround with separate piles of the garnishing ingredients separated by lemon wedges.

Chicken Liver Terrine

For eight people

Small bunch parsley
1 lb (450 g) chicken livers
8 oz (225 g) sausage meat
8 oz (225 g) belly of pork with the skin removed
8 oz (225 g) streaky bacon with the rinds removed

4 tablespoons brandy
4 tablespoons port
3 cloves garlic (peeled)
Pinch thyme
Salt and freshly ground black pepper
Pinch ground nutmeg and mace
2 or 4 bay leaves

Double-bladed knife

Remove any fibres from the chicken livers and roughly chop the flesh. Roughly chop the belly of pork, process until coarsely chopped and remove. Process the parsley until finely chopped. Add the garlic and process until finely chopped. Add the chicken livers and process until the livers are coarsely chopped. Add the sausage meat and process to mix. Add the brandy, port and thyme, season generously with salt and freshly ground black pepper and lightly with a pinch of mace and ground nutmeg and process to mix.

Add the pork to the chicken livers and process to mix. In the standard Magimix you may have to do this in two batches.

Leave to marinate for 8 hours or overnight.

Stretch the bacon rashers with the back of a knife so that they become almost transparently thin and use threequarters of them to line a 1½ lb (675 g) terrine or loaf tin. Pack the meat into the lined tin pressing it down firmly, and banging it on a solid surface to make sure the ingredients settle down tightly in the tin. Top with remaining rashers of bacon and the bay leaves. Stand the tin in a bain marie or roasting tin half filled with nearly boiling water and cook, uncovered, for 1½ hours (at 350°F. 175°C. Reg. 4). Cool, cover with a piece of board wrapped in foil, weight down and refrigerate for at least 4 hours. Turn out and serve the terrine cut into slices with hot toast.

Pâté Casa

An unusual pâté of pig's liver and bacon with a flavouring of mushrooms. This is what I call a 'two step pâté'. I cook it, leave it to cool, and then process it until smooth adding more seasoning, some green peppercorns and some pistachio nuts to give texture.

Unlike so many pâtés it is relatively inexpensive to make.

1 shallot	Salt and freshly ground black pepper
2 cloves garlic	Piece of pork fat
8 oz (225 g) pig's liver	3 bay leaves
4 oz (100 g) streaky bacon	1 tablespoon brandy
4 oz (100 g) fat pork	2 oz (50 g) melted butter
4 oz (100 g) mushrooms	2 teaspoons green peppercorns
¼ pint (5 fl oz 150 ml) double cream	1 tablespoon pistachio nuts
Pinch mixed herbs	

Peel and roughly chop the shallot and garlic. Roughly chop the pig's liver, bacon and fat pork.

Double-bladed knife

Process the shallot and garlic until finely chopped. Add the bacon and fat pork and process until reduced to a fairly smooth paste and remove. Process the liver with the mushrooms until very finely chopped. Add the cream, herbs and seasoning and process until well mixed. Add the bacon and pork mixture and process to mix well.

You may have to do this in two batches if using the standard Magimix. Butter a 1 lb (450 g) terrine and press the pâté mixture firmly into the terrine. Top with the fat pork and bay leaves, cover tightly with three layers of foil. Place in a bain marie with enough hot water to come half way up the sides of the terrine. Bake in a moderate oven (325°F. 150°C. Reg. 3) for 1 hour. Press down, cool and then refrigerate until well chilled. Remove the fat pork and bay leaves. Break up the pâté with a fork.

Double-bladed knife   Process the pâté until smooth. Check seasoning add the brandy and process for just long enough to mix. Add the pistachio nuts and peppercorns and melted butter and process until these are fairly finely chopped.

Turn the mixture into a clean terrine and chill in a refrigerator until firm.

Note For special occasions I top pâtés like these with some tinned consommé to which I have added some gelatine, port and sherry, a touch of lemon juice and seasoning. I garnish the pâté with small bay leaves and pour over the consommé mixture allowing plenty of time for it to set before serving.

Rich Pâté in Pastry

This is a two stage pâté. You cook the pâté first in the normal way then process the pâté again add some pistachio nuts to give a lovely smooth texture and add some colour and when that is set firm you wrap it in pastry and come up with a stunning first course. It takes time (start a day ahead) but the results are well worth while.

For ten people

8 oz (225 g) pig's liver	Salt and freshly ground black pepper
8 oz (225 g) chicken livers	2 fl oz (60 ml) port
1 lb (450 g) fat belly of pork with the rind removed	1 fl oz (30 ml) brandy
1 small onion	3 oz (75 g) pistachio nuts
2 cloves garlic	4 rashers streaky bacon
1 small bunch parsley	2 bay leaves
½ teaspoon mixed herbs	1 packet (14 oz 400 g) frozen puff pastry
	1 egg

Roughly cut up the pig's liver. Pick over the chicken livers removing any tough fibres or yellow stained flesh. Peel and roughly chop the onion. Peel and roughly chop the garlic. Cut the belly pork into cubes.

Double-bladed knife   Process the parsley until finely chopped and remove to a bowl. Process the pig's liver until very finely chopped and add to the parsley. Process the chicken liver until finely chopped and add to the pig's liver. Process the onion and the garlic until finely chopped, add half the belly of pork and process until the belly of pork is very finely chopped. Add the pork belly to the livers and process the remaining belly until very finely chopped (if using the Grande Famille the pork belly can be processed in one batch). Add the finely chopped belly to the other ingredients with the herbs, season well with salt and pepper and mix in the port and brandy – the ingredients should be well mixed.

Remove the rinds from the bacon and stretch each rasher with the back of a knife. Line a small loaf tin with the rashers and pack in the pâté mixture. Top with the bay leaves, cover with foil and bake in a moderate oven (350°F. 175°C. Reg. 4) for 1½ hours. Leave to cool in the tin remove the bay leaves and break up with a fork.

Double-bladed knife Process the pâté until smooth. You will have to do this in two batches if using the standard Magimix. Check seasoning, add the pistachio nuts and process until the nuts are roughly chopped. Pack the pâté into a lightly oiled loaf tin and chill in a refrigerator for 1 hour. Turn out of the tin.

Roll out the pastry to about ¼ in. thickness and wrap it around the pâté neatly. Seal the edges well with water, cut an air vent and decorate the top with pastry leaves from the trimmings.

Double-bladed knife Process the egg with a little salt until smooth. Brush the pastry with the egg wash and bake in a hot oven (400°F. 200°C. Reg. 6) for 30 minutes until golden brown. Leave to cool and cut into slices.

Game and Liver Terrine

For eight people

1 shallot	Pinch mixed herbs
2 cloves garlic	Salt and freshly ground black pepper
4 oz (100 g) fat pork	Pinch mixed spice
1 pheasant	8 oz (225 g) fat bacon or barding fat
8 oz (225 g) pig's liver	1 tablespoon brandy
8 oz (225 g) cottage cheese	4 bay leaves
6 oz (175 g) cooked ham	

Peel and roughly chop the shallot and garlic. Roughly chop the fat pork. Skin the pheasant, cut off the breasts and then remove the meat from the legs and top of the wings. Roughly chop the pig's liver and the cooked ham.

Double-bladed knife Process the shallot and garlic until finely chopped. Add the fat pork and the meat from the legs and wings of the pheasant. Process until the mixture is reduced to a fine paste. Remove to a bowl. Process the pig's liver until smooth. Add the cottage cheese and continue to process until the ingredients are a smooth paste. Add the herbs, seasoning and spice and process to mix well. Add to the first ingredients. Process the pheasant breast and ham until coarsely chopped.

Mix all the ingredients with a wooden spoon, adding the brandy then fry a teaspoon of the mixture in a little butter to test for seasoning. Line a 1 lb terrine with stretched bacon or barding fat. Press in the terrine mixture. Top with more bacon or barding fat and the bay leaves. Cover tightly with two thicknesses of foil. Put the terrine into a bain marie with enough very hot water to come half way up the sides of the terrine and bake in a moderate oven (325°F. 150°C. Reg. 3) for 1 hour and 10 minutes. Remove from the bain marie. Press down with a heavy weight and leave to cool. Chill in a refrigerator for at least 8 hours before turning out and cutting into thick slices.

Game Terrine with Gammon

A simply made terrine that nevertheless has plenty of flavour. I like to serve it with a Cumberland sauce (see page 268) or a home made chutney on the side. One plump partridge, small wild duck or 2 woodcock can be used in place of the pheasant.

7 oz (200 g) uncooked gammon	Salt and freshly ground black pepper
4 oz (100 g) pig's liver	1 tablespoon brandy
1 pheasant	2 oz (50 g) melted butter
¼ pint (5 fl oz 150 ml) double cream	8 oz (225 g) bacon or barding fat
Pinch mixed herbs	3 bay leaves

Roughly chop the gammon and liver. Remove the skin from the pheasant and cut the meat off the bones, top of the wings and breasts.

Double-bladed knife
Combine the gammon and liver and process until reduced to a smooth paste and remove. Process the meat from the pheasant legs and wings until reduced to a paste and add the cream, herbs, seasoning, brandy and butter. Roughly chop the pheasant breast and add it to the other ingredients in the bowl. Process until the pheasant is fairly finely chopped. Add this mixture to the liver and gammon and mix well. Line a 1 lb (450 g) terrine with stretched bacon or thin barding fat, press the ingredients firmly into the terrine and top with three bay leaves and an extra piece of bacon or fat and cover tightly with three layers of foil. Stand in a bain marie with enough hot water to come half way up the sides of the terrine. Bake in a moderate oven (325°F. 150°C. Reg. 3) for 1 hour. Remove the top piece of fat, press down firmly and leave to cool. Chill in a refrigerator for at least 8 hours before serving. *Note* If you wish to be more tidy and sophisticated, turn it out of the terrine and remove the barding bacon and fat. Put a thin layer of consommé to which a little gelatine seasoning, port and lemon juice has been added with the bottom of the terrine down and leave to set until firm. Replace the trimmed terrine in the dish, pour over enough consommé to encase the sides and cover the top and leave in a refrigerator until set firm. Turn out and serve in thickish slices with hot toast.

Potted Hough

This is an old Scottish favourite and I was delighted to see, on a recent trip to Edinburgh that you can still buy cartons of homemade potted hough at good butcher's shops. It's delicious as a first course with a Cumberland sauce (see page 268) and plenty of hot toast and also makes an excellent and nourishing sandwich filling – ideal for packed lunches. The marrow from a beef marrow bone is essential to this dish for flavour and texture; most good butchers will supply you with marrow bones for only a few pence.

For six people	1½ lbs (675 g) beef shin	1 teaspoon mixed herbs
	1 marrow bone	Small glass red wine
	Salt and freshly ground black pepper	2 bay leaves
	Pinch ground nutmeg and mace	Small bunch parsley

Put the beef into a saucepan with the marrow bone. Cover with water and the wine. Season with salt, pepper and a mere pinch of ground nutmeg and mace, add the bay leaves, bring to the boil, cover and simmer for about 4 hours or until the meat is fork tender and will shred easily. Strain off the liquid, remove the bay leaves and the marrow bone scoop out the marrow from the bone.

Double-bladed knife — Process the parsley until finely chopped and remove. Process the meat and marrow until finely chopped but do not reduce to a paste. Combine the chopped meat with the cooking liquid, add the mixed herbs, season liberally with freshly ground black pepper and more salt if necessary and boil for 7 minutes. Cool, mix in the parsley, pack into a dampened mould (or small individual moulds) and chill in a refrigerator until set firm.

Savoury Pancakes with Spinach and Cheese

For eight people as a first course or four people as a main course	8 pancakes (see page 245)	2 chicken livers
	8 oz (225 g) cooked spinach (fresh or frozen)	3 oz (75 g) butter
	1 slice of white bread with the crusts removed	3 tablespoons flour
	4 oz (100 g) cream cheese	1 pint (600 ml) milk
	1 oz (25 g) grated Parmesan (Grate Parmesan cheese through the Parmesan grating disc)	¼ pint (5 fl oz 150 ml) single cream
		Salt and freshly ground black pepper
		Pinch ground nutmeg
		2 oz (50 g) Cheddar, or Mozzarella cheese

Double-bladed knife — Process the bread until reduced to fine crumbs and remove.

Coarse grating disc — Using a gentle pressure on the pusher grate the Cheddar, or Mozzarella cheese and remove.

Double-bladed knife — Process the spinach until roughly puréed and leave in the bowl. Melt 1 oz (25 g) of the butter in a small frying pan. Add the chicken livers and cook over a medium high heat until the livers are firm and browned on the outside but still pink in the centre. Add the livers to the spinach and process for long enough to chop the livers and mix the ingredients.

Melt the remaining butter in a saucepan, add the flour and mix well. Add the milk and stir over a medium high heat, until the sauce comes to the boil and is thick and smooth. Season the sauce with salt, pepper and nutmeg, add the Parmesan, cream and cream cheese and simmer gently for three minutes, stirring, until the cheese has melted and is incorporated into the sauce.

Add ⅓ of the sauce to the spinach and chicken livers and switch on and off to mix the ingredients.

Fill the pancakes with the spinach sauce and roll up neatly. Place them in a buttered, baking dish, pour over the remaining sauce and sprinkle over the breadcrumbs and grated cheese. Bake in a hot oven (400°F. 200°C. Reg. 6) for about 20 minutes until the pancakes are hot through and the topping is golden brown.

Ideas for filling savoury pancakes Pancakes make the most useful vessels for using up leftovers of all kinds. Make a fairly thick white sauce, season it well with salt, pepper and a little nutmeg and flavour the sauce with grated cheese. To ⅓ of the sauce add chopped lightly fried onions, leftover chopped chicken, ham, tongue or cooked fish. Fill the pancakes, pour over the remaining sauce, top with grated cheese and bake in a hot oven (400°F. 200°C. Reg. 6) for about 20 minutes until the pancakes are hot through and the topping is golden brown.

You can also fill the pancakes with some crab meat or other shellfish mixed with a white sauce flavoured with a little wine (top the filled pancakes with grated cheese), sliced, sautéed mushrooms with white sauce or crisply fried, chopped bacon and parsley with a fairly strongly flavoured cheesey white sauce.

Spinach and Cream Cheese Stuffed Pancakes

For six people

12 savoury pancakes (see page 245)
1 lb (450 g) spinach
8 oz (225 g) firm button mushrooms
1 oz (25 g) butter
3 oz (75 g) cream cheese

Salt and freshly ground black pepper
Pinch cayenne
4 tablespoons double cream
1 oz (25 g) Parmesan cheese

Wash the spinach and cook it in ½ inch boiling salted water until just tender. Drain well.

Double-bladed knife   Process the mushrooms until roughly chopped.

Melt the butter. Add the mushrooms and cook them over a medium heat until they are just tender (about 5 minutes).

Double-bladed knife   Combine the spinach and cream cheese, season with salt, pepper and cayenne and process until the ingredients are mixed (do not over process, the spinach should still have some texture).

Add the mushrooms and butter and switch the machine on and off to mix the ingredients. Spread the pancakes with the spinach mixture, roll them up neatly and arrange them in a shallow buttered, baking dish.

Parmesan grating disc   Process the Parmesan cheese and remove.

Plastic blade   Process the cream until thick. Add the Parmesan, season with a little salt, pepper and cayenne and switch the machine on and off to mix the ingredients. Spread the cream over the pancakes and bake in a hot oven (450°F. 240°C. Reg. 8) until the pancakes are hot through and the topping is golden and bubbling.

Potato and Bacon Pancakes with Sour Cream

This sounds rather mundane to serve as a first course and I have to admit I pondered for a while as to whether or not I should give it some high falutin name. In the end I decided it was so good in its own right that it didn't need dressing up. The only trouble is the pancakes must be made at the last minute so you want to serve them in one of those situations where you can be cooking in the kitchen while your guests congregate around you with their pre-dinner drinks.

For six people

12 oz (350 g) potatoes
½ green pepper
3 oz (75 g) streaky bacon with the rinds removed
1 small onion

¼ pint (5 fl oz 150 ml) sour cream
1 tablespoon finely chopped chives
1 large egg
Salt and freshly ground black pepper
Oil for frying

Peel the potatoes

Coarse grating disc
Process the potatoes, cover them at once with cold water and leave them to stand for at least twenty minutes. Remove the core and seeds from the green pepper. Roughly chop the pepper. Peel the onion.

Plastic blade
Process the sour cream until light and fluffy. Add the chopped chives, season with salt and pepper, process to mix well and remove.

Double-bladed knife and a clean bowl
Process the pepper with the bacon until the ingredients are fairly finely chopped and remove.

Coarse grating disc
Process the onion through the grating disc and remove. Strain the potatoes through a sieve and wash them (in the sieve) in cold water to remove the starch. Pat the potatoes dry with a clean kitchen towel.

Plastic blade
Process the egg until smooth and add the potatoes, bacon, pepper and onion. Season with salt and pepper and process to mix the ingredients. Heat the oil until a haze rises from it in a large heavy frying pan. Add the potato mixture in spoonfuls (do not overcrowd the pan) and cook over a high heat, pressing the pancakes flat with a spatula, for five minutes until they are firm and golden brown on the bottom, flip them over and cook on the other side until golden brown. Drain the pancakes well on kitchen paper and keep them warm.
Top each pancake with a dollop of the sour cream and serve at once.

Deep Fried Cheese Stuffed Pancakes

This makes a delicious and unusual first course. I had it with my sister-in-law the first time and then nagged her until I got the recipe. It is important to freeze the filled egg and breadcrumbed pancakes before cooking them so that the filling doesn't melt and explode through the pancakes.

For eight people	8 pancakes (see page 245)	Salt and freshly ground black pepper
	1½ oz (40 g) butter	Pinch cayenne
	3 tablespoons flour	1 egg
	½ pint (10 fl oz 300 ml) milk	2 slices white bread with the crusts
	1 egg yolk	removed
	6 oz (175 g) grated Gruyère cheese	Deep oil for frying
	1 oz Parmesan cheese	

Fine grating disc Grate the Gruyère cheese.
Parmesan disc Process the Parmesan.

Melt the butter in a saucepan, add the flour and mix well. Gradually add the milk, stirring continually over a medium high heat until the sauce is thick and smooth.

Double-bladed knife Combine the sauce and Gruyère and Parmesan cheese and process until well mixed. Season with salt, pepper and cayenne and with the motor running, drop in the egg yolk through the feed tube. Process until smooth. Leave the sauce to cool.

Double-bladed knife and a clean bowl Process the bread until reduced to fine crumbs and remove. Process the egg until smooth. Halve the pancakes. Place a tablespoon of the filling in the middle of each half pancake, fold both sides of the pancakes over to make a triangle and then fold over the rounded top to make a neat parcel. Press the edges together and then coat the parcels in beaten egg and breadcrumbs. Lay the finished pancakes out on a tray and freeze them until solid.

Heat the oil until very hot, drop in the frozen pancakes, a few at a time and cook until they are crisp and golden brown. Drain well on kitchen paper and keep warm while frying the rest of the pancakes.

Petites Fondues

Delicious circles of Gruyère flavoured thick cheese sauce, dipped in egg and breadcrumbs and deep fried.

The secret of this dish is to prepare it well in advance and then chill the cheese mixture in the deep freeze before frying. They must be cooked just before serving. I also serve them as a supper dish with garlic mayonnaise (see page 251) or tomato sauce (see page 259).

For four people	2 oz (50 g) butter	2 egg yolks
	4 tablespoons flour	1 egg
	¾ pint (15 fl oz 450 ml) milk	2 tablespoons milk
	4 oz (100 g) Gruyère cheese	4 oz (100 g) fresh bread with the crusts
	1 teaspoon mustard	removed
	Salt and freshly ground black pepper	Deep oil for frying
	Pinch ground nutmeg	

Fine grating disc Grate the Gruyère cheese.

Melt the butter in a saucepan, add the flour and mix well. Gradually add the milk stirring continually over a medium high heat until the sauce comes to the boil and is thick and smooth. Add the cheese, season with salt, pepper, mustard and nutmeg and simmer, stirring, for three minutes or until the cheese has melted.

Double-bladed knife Process the sauce for 30 seconds and, with the machine switched on add the egg yolks one at a time and process until the sauce is really thick and smooth. Transfer to a bowl and refrigerate for three hours until firm. Form the sauce into ½ in. (1·25 cm) thick circles about 2 in. (5 cm) in diameter.

Double-bladed knife and a clean bowl Process the bread until reduced to fine crumbs and remove. Process the egg with the milk until smooth. Dip the circles of cheese sauce in the egg, coat with breadcrumbs and freeze for at least 30 minutes. Heat the deep oil until smoking, add the cheese circles and cook until crisp and golden brown. Drain on kitchen paper and serve as soon as possible, piping hot.

Chinese Prawn Toasts

These are one of my passions. I serve them sometimes as a first course with a garlic mayonnaise and sometimes as an accompaniment to soup – either way they are delicious.

For four people

¾ inch piece fresh ginger root
Walnut-sized piece of peeled onion
1 egg
8 oz (225 g) peeled prawns
2 tablespoons cornflour
1 tablespoon dry sherry

3 slices white bread with the crusts removed
Salt and freshly ground black pepper
4 tablespoons sesame seeds
4 slices white bread
Oil for frying

Peel and roughly chop the ginger root.

Double-bladed knife Combine the ginger and onion and process until finely chopped. Add the egg, prawns, cornflour, sherry and the three slices of bread, season with salt and pepper and process until the mixture is reduced to a smooth paste.

Remove the crusts from the four slices of bread. Spread the bread generously and evenly with the prawn paste, cut into thick fingers (about 1 in. (2·5 cm) thick) and press the paste side into sesame seeds (lay them out on a shallow plate).

Heat about ¼ in. (0·75 cm) of oil until a haze rises from it in a large frying pan, add the fingers of bread and cook, paste side down, over a high heat until they are golden brown, turn over and cook until the other side of the bread is golden and crisp. Drain on kitchen paper and serve as soon as possible.

Variations I have made these toasts equally successfully with streaky bacon and with raw chicken – both are delicious.

Basle Cheese Toasts

Good open toasted cheese sandwiches with a topping of onion that makes them special.

For four people   4 thick slices white bread with the crusts   French Dijon mustard
 removed   1 medium onion
4 oz (100 g) Gruyère cheese   Paprika pepper
Butter

Peel and halve the onion. Remove any rind from the cheese.
Thin slicing disc   Slice the cheese through the disc.
Thinly butter the bread, and spread each slice with a thin skim of mustard. Top each slice neatly with the sliced cheese, place the slices on a baking sheet and toast them in a hot oven (400°F. 200°C. Reg. 6) until golden brown and bubbling (about 8 minutes).
Thin slicing disc   Process the onion through the slicing disc.
Melt ½ oz butter in a heavy frying pan. Add the onion and cook over a medium high heat until the onion is soft and golden brown. Place a heap of onion slices on top of the cheese sandwiches sprinkle with paprika and serve piping hot.

Anchovy Puffs

Easily made, finger sized, bites to serve as appetisers or with drinks.

6 oz (175 g) frozen puff pastry   3 oz (75 g) Cheddar cheese
6 anchovy fillets   Pinch cayenne pepper
Milk   1 egg

Soak the anchovy fillets in milk for 15 minutes, drain well and pat dry on kitchen paper.
Double-bladed   Process the egg until well mixed and remove. Cut the cheese into squares and
knife   process until reduced to fine crumbs. Add the anchovies and cayenne and process until the mixture is reduced to a paste.
Roll out the pastry to about ⅛ in. (0·25 cm) thickness and cut into fingers 1½ in. (3·75 cm) × 4 in. (10 cm) long. Spread the centre of half the fingers with the anchovy paste, damp the edges and cover with the remaining pastry pressing the edges firmly together with the back of a fork. Brush the tops with beaten egg and bake in a hot oven (400°F. 200°C. Reg. 6) for about 15 minutes until the pastry is puffed and golden brown. Serve at once.

Savoury Cheese Soufflé (Page 82)

Pizza

For eight people

1½ level teaspoons dried yeast
2 fl oz (60 ml) warm water
1 teaspoon sugar
14 oz (500 g) plain flour
2 oz (50 g) melted butter
2 tablespoons oil
½ teaspoon salt
2 onions

2 cloves garlic
2 tins tomatoes (15 oz 425 g)
1 teaspoon dried oregano
Salt and freshly ground black pepper
12 anchovy fillets
12 black olives
4 oz (100 g) Mozzarella cheese
1 oz (25 g) Parmesan cheese

Combine the blood warm water with the yeast and sugar and mix into a smooth paste. Cover and leave in a warm place for 5–10 minutes. Warm the flour in a low oven.

Double-bladed knife

Put the flour into the Magimix bowl with the salt. Add the yeast mixture and process to mix. Add the melted butter and 1 tablespoon oil and process until the dough forms a ball around the knife. Continue to process for 6 turns of the dough. Turn the dough onto a floured board, knead with the knuckles for about 30 seconds and then put in an oiled bowl. Cover with a damp cloth and leave in a warm place, draughtless, to rise for 60 minutes.

Peel the onions and garlic.

Medium slicing disc

Slice the onions and garlic and remove. Slice the Mozzarella cheese (without putting too much pressure on the pusher) and remove.

Parmesan grater disc

Grate the Parmesan cheese and remove. Heat the remaining tablespoon of oil in a heavy pan. Add the onions and garlic and cook over a moderately low heat until the onion is soft and transparent. Add the tomatoes and oregano, mix well, season with salt and pepper and cook, uncovered, for 35 minutes until the sauce is thick and reduced.

Punch down the dough and roll it out to about ¼ in. (0·75 cm) thickness. Trim into a neat rectangle, transfer to a baking sheet and slightly crimp up the edges. Spread the tomato sauce over the dough and decorate the top with strips of anchovies and halved stoned black olives. Spread over the slices of mozzerella, sprinkle with Parmesan cheese and bake the pizza in a hot oven (400°F. 200°C. Reg. 6) for 15–20 minutes until the dough is golden and the cheese has melted. Serve hot or warm.

Smoked Mackerel Filled Baking Powder Biscuit Thins

Oh these are good! The pastry is based on American style baking powder biscuits, thin, crisp and light and the inside is a good blend of smoked mackerel, seasonings, milk and oil. These can be served hot or cold and I have had a great success by serving them cold with a hot homemade tomato sauce (see page 259) at a summer buffet party. In any case, they make lovely things just to have around when anyone feels peckish, and they certainly go well with drinks.

Marinated Leg of Lamb (Page 110)

The pastry

Small sprig fresh sage (or a pinch dried
　　sage)
7 oz (200 g) plain flour
1 teaspoon baking powder
1 egg
Salt and pinch paprika
1 – 2 tablespoons cold water

Filling

1 egg
2 cloves garlic
8 oz (225 g) filleted smoked mackerel
　　without skin or bones
2 fl oz (60 ml) milk
2 fl oz (60 ml) sunflower oil
Salt and freshly ground black pepper
1/4 teaspoon lemon juice

To make the pastry

Double-bladed knife

Remove any coarse stalks from the sage.
Process the sage until finely chopped. Add the flour, baking powder and seasonings and process until well mixed. Add the egg and process until just mixed. With the machine running add enough cold water (about 1 1/2 tablespoons) to form a stiff dough around the blade. Stop the machine at once. Wrap the dough in a cloth and chill in a refrigerator for 30 minutes before rolling out. On a well floured board roll out the pastry very thinly and cut into rounds with a 2 in. (5 cm) cutter.

To make the filling

Plastic blade
Double-bladed knife and a clean bowl

Process the egg until beaten and remove. Wipe the bowl with kitchen paper. Place the garlic in the Magimix bowl and process until finely chopped. Add the mackerel and process until the mackerel is reduced to a fine paste. Add the lemon juice and season with salt and freshly ground black pepper. With the machine switched on add the milk mixed with the oil, a little at a time through the feed tube in the same way as though you were making mayonnaise.

Damp the edges of half the pastry circles and place a heaped teaspoon of the mackerel filling on each one. Cover with a second undampened piece of pastry, press the edges firmly together; crimp the edges together with the back of a fork and cut a small vent in the centre of each pastry. Brush with the beaten egg and bake in a hot oven (425°F. 220°C. Reg. 7) for about 10 minutes until golden brown. Sprinkle while hot with salt and white pepper.

Quiche Lorraine

For six people

1 10 in. (25 cm) quiche case
　　(see page 240)

Filling
1 medium onion
Small bunch parsley
3 leeks
1 oz (25 g) butter or margarine
4 oz (100 g) cooked ham
3 eggs
4 oz (100 g) cream cheese

1/4 pint (5 fl oz 150 ml) single cream
3 oz (75 g) Cheddar cheese
Salt, freshly ground black pepper, pinch
　　cayenne and ground nutmeg

Topping
2 slices white bread with the crusts
　　removed
1 oz (25 g) grated Cheddar cheese
1/2 oz (13 g) grated Parmesan cheese

Peel the onion. Roughly chop the ham. Wash and trim the leeks.

To make the topping

Double-bladed knife Process the bread with the Cheddar and Parmesan cheese until the mixture is reduced to fine crumbs and remove.

To make the filling

Double-bladed knife Process the parsley until finely chopped and remove. Process the ham until finely chopped and remove.

Thin slicing disc Process the onion and leeks through the slicing disc. Heat the butter or margarine in a saucepan. Add the onion and leeks and cook over a low heat, stirring, until they are soft and transparent.

Roughly chop the Cheddar cheese.

Double-bladed knife Process the Cheddar cheese until reduced to fine crumbs. Add the eggs with the cream cheese and cream, season with salt, pepper, cayenne and nutmeg and process until the ingredients are well mixed. Add the parsley and switch on and off to mix the ingredients. Place the ham, onions and leeks in the chilled quiche case, pour over the custard mixture and sprinkle over the breadcrumbs. Bake in a moderately hot oven (350°F. 175°C. Reg. 4) for 40 minutes until the filling is set and the topping and pastry are golden brown.

Serve hot, warm or cold.

Petites Quiches Lorraines

Quiche Lorraine has come to be thought of as a quiche with cheese and bacon. Originally it was just bacon with a custard filling – very subtle and very good.

For six people

Special pastry dough (see page 238) or pâté brisee (see page 239)
¼ lb (100 g) sliced streaky bacon (Canadian bacon is excellent for this)
3 eggs

¼ pint (5 fl oz 150 ml) double cream
2½ oz (65 g) butter
Salt and freshly ground black pepper, ground nutmeg and cayenne

Roll out the pastry to ⅛ in. (0·5 cm) thickness and line twelve tartlet tins. Lightly prick the bottom of the pastry cases with a fork.

Double-bladed knife Process the bacon until coarsely chopped. Blanch the bacon in boiling water for 3 minutes and drain well. Divide the bacon between the pastry cases. Dot the butter over the bacon in small pieces.

Double-bladed knife or plastic blade Combine the eggs and cream and process until smooth. Season with salt, pepper and a small pinch of nutmeg and cayenne. Process to mix and pour the filling into the tarts. Bake in a hot oven (400°F. 200°C. Reg. 6) for 20 – 30 minutes until just set.

A Quiche of Mixed Vegetables

This is always popular with vegetarians since it provides a substantial and attractive main course without using meat or poultry. This recipe makes a lot of filling and you may find it easier to use two 7 in. (18 cm) quiche cases rather than one very large one. However, don't be put off it is delicious.

For eight people

1 11 in. (27·5 cm) quiche case
  (see page 240)
1 large onion
2 tomatoes
2 courgettes
1 small aubergine
1 oz (25 g) butter
1 tablespoon oil
3 eggs
2 oz (50 g) Cheddar cheese
4 oz (100 g) cream cheese

¼ pint (5 fl oz 150 ml) single cream
Pinch oregano, or mixed herbs
Salt and freshly ground black pepper
Nutmeg and cayenne

Topping
2 slices white bread with the crusts
  removed
1 oz (25 g) Cheddar cheese
½ oz (13 g) Parmesan cheese

To make the topping

Double-bladed knife

Process the bread with the roughly chopped Cheddar and Parmesan cheeses until it is reduced to fine crumbs and remove.

To make the filling

Peel the onion. Cover the tomatoes with boiling water, leave to stand for three minutes and slide off the skins.

Thin or medium slicing disc

Slice the onion and remove.

Chipper disc
Coarse grating disc

Process the tomatoes through the chipper disc and remove.
Grate the courgettes and aubergine and remove.

Double-bladed knife

Process the Cheddar cheese until reduced to crumbs. Add the eggs, cream cheese and cream, season with salt, pepper, nutmeg and cayenne, add the oregano and process until the ingredients are well mixed.

Heat the butter with the oil in a frying pan. Add the onion and cook over a low heat, stirring, until it is soft and transparent. Add the courgettes, aubergine and tomatoes and continue to cook over a medium heat until the vegetables are soft (about 5 minutes).

Arrange the vegetables in the chilled flan case, pour over the custard and sprinkle with the topping. Bake in a moderately hot oven (350°F. 175°C. Reg. 4) for about 40 minutes or until the filling is set firm and the topping and pastry are golden brown.

Tarte Paysanne

This is a mixture I am extremely fond of; anchovies and onion together, to my mind, produce one of the simplest and most satisfactory of flavourings.

For six to eight people

1 10 inch (25 cm) quiche case
   (see page 240)
2 large onions
3 oz (75 g) Gruyère cheese
3½ oz (115 g) butter

4 anchovy fillets
2 eggs
Freshly ground black pepper, pinch of
   cayenne and nutmeg

Peel and halve the onions to fit into the feed tube.

Fine grating disc
Grate the Gruyère cheese and remove.

Use the medium slicing disc
Slice the onions.

Melt the butter in a heavy frying pan.

Add the onions and cook over a low heat, stirring to prevent sticking, until the onions are soft and transparent.

Double-bladed knife
Combine the drained anchovies and eggs and process until the eggs are smooth.

Season with pepper, cayenne and nutmeg and process to mix.

Arrange the onions in the chilled quiche case, pour over the egg mixture sprinkle with the cheese and bake in a moderately hot oven (375°F. 190°C. Reg. 5) for about 30 minutes or until the filling is set and the pastry is golden brown.

EGGS

Eggs Eugenie

An exceptional and inexpensive first course or light main course that is best made in the spring when the spinach or chard are young and fully flavoured.

For four people

4 hard boiled eggs
12 oz (350 g) young spinach or Swiss chard
2 rashers streaky bacon
2 tomatoes
2 oz (50 g) mushrooms
½ oz (13 g) butter

2 tablespoons sunflower oil
1 tablespoon white wine vinegar
Salt and freshly ground black pepper
Pinch ground cumin
¼ pint (5 fl oz 150 ml) mayonnaise made with a whole egg (see page 253)
1½ teaspoons curry paste

Wash the spinach or chard and cook it in a little boiling salted water for five minutes. Drain well. Remove the rinds from the bacon and roughly chop the rashers. Cook the rashers in a frying pan without extra fat until they are crisp and drain on kitchen paper. Cover the tomatoes with boiling water, leave for three minutes and then slide off the skins. Discard the cores and seeds.

Medium slicing disc
Slice the mushrooms. Melt the butter in a saucepan, add the mushrooms and cook over a high heat for 2 minutes.

Double-bladed knife
Process the tomato flesh until finely chopped. Add the bacon, oil and vinegar, season with salt, pepper and cumin and process until well mixed. Add the spinach and process for just long enough to roughly chop the spinach. Turn into a bowl, add the mushrooms and toss lightly to mix. Arrange the spinach on a serving dish and top with the hard boiled eggs cut into halves.

Double-bladed knife or plastic blade
Combine the mayonnaise with the curry paste and process until well mixed. Coat the eggs with the curry mayonnaise.

Curried Eggs

Serve this hot or cold as part of a curry or as a first course; accompany the eggs with crisply fried poppadums, some mixed chopped tomato and onion with a little vinegar, toasted desiccated coconut and some sliced banana laced with lemon juice. Fresh coriander can be found in Indian grocery shops throughout the summer and has a wonderful, aromatic flavouring.

For four people

6 hard boiled eggs
Small bunch coriander
2 green chillies (or use one dried red chilli)
4 cloves garlic
2 large onions
4 tablespoons sunflower oil

2 tablespoons Vindaloo or hot curry paste
½ pint (10 fl oz 300 ml) water
¼ pint (5 fl oz 150 ml) yoghurt
½ teaspoon cornflour
2 oz (50 g) sultanas
Salt

Remove the seeds from the chillies (wash your hands after doing this as the seeds are fiery hot). Peel and roughly chop the garlic. Peel and halve the onions.

Double-bladed knife
Process the coriander until finely chopped and remove. Process the garlic and chillies until finely chopped and remove.

Thin slicing disc
Process the onions through the slicing disc and remove.

Double-bladed knife
Combine the yoghurt and cornflour and process for 1 minute. Turn the yoghurt into a saucepan and stir clockwise over a low heat until the mixture comes to the boil and has thickened slightly (this stabilizes the yoghurt and prevents it from separating when cooked). Heat the oil in a large frying pan. Add the garlic, chillies and onions and cook over a low heat for five minutes. Add the curry paste and mix well. Cook over a medium heat for two minutes then add the water and yoghurt. Stir well and simmer for 10 minutes or until the onions are really soft. Season with salt and stir in the sultanas. Peel and halve the eggs and place them cut side down in the sauce, spooning the sauce over the eggs so that they are well coated. Simmer for ten minutes and scatter over the coriander before serving.

Stuffed Curried Eggs with Poppadums and Tomato Salad

Without shame I admit that I pinched this idea from my favourite restaurant The Horn of Plenty in Gunnislake, Devon. Sonia Stevenson's stuffed eggs have a different flavour from mine but the marks for presentation are entirely for her.

For four people	7 hard boiled eggs	3 firm, ripe, tomatoes
	1 tablespoon smoked cod's roe	½ cucumber
	2 teaspoons curry powder	2 spring onions chopped
	4 tablespoons double cream	1 teaspoon French Dijon mustard
	2 oz (50 g) cream cheese	¼ teaspoon tarragon
	2 teaspoons peach or mango chutney	1 tablespoon white wine vinegar
	4 poppadums	3 tablespoons olive or sunflower oil
	2 potatoes	Salt and freshly ground black pepper

Halve six of the hard boiled eggs lengthwise and remove the yolks. Roughly chop the remaining hard boiled egg.

Double-bladed knife   Combine the hard boiled egg yolks and whole chopped egg with the smoked cod's roe, curry powder, cream, cream cheese and chutney, season with salt and pepper and process until smooth scraping down the sides if necessary. Fill the halved egg whites with the yolk mixture rounding it up neatly. Chill the eggs while preparing the rest of the dish. Fry the poppadums until crisp, fold them slightly in half while they are still warm and leave them to drain on kitchen paper.

Peel the potatoes and cucumber.

Chipper disc   Process the potatoes through the chipper disc and remove.

Cook the potatoes in salted water until *just* tender, refresh in cold water and drain well.

Chipper disc   Process the tomatoes.

Thin slicing disc   Process the cucumber. Remove the tomatoes and cucumber and mix with the potatoes.

Double-bladed knife   Combine the mustard, tarragon, vinegar, oil and spring onions, season with salt and pepper, process to mix well.

Pour the dressing over the potatoes, tomatoes and cucumber, toss lightly and chill. Place each slightly folded poppadum on a serving plate and place three halved stuffed eggs inside the fold. Divide the tomato salad along the other side of the plate.

OEUFS EN COCOTTE

These savoury baked egg dishes always seem to provide a popular first course or light lunch or supper dish for everyone whatever their age, and with the help of your Magimix any number of exciting savoury flavourings can be added to the eggs with very little trouble. The secret in baking the eggs is not to overcook them, while at the same time making sure that they are *evenly* cooked. The best results are obtained by baking the eggs in ramekins set in a roasting pan or *bain marie* of hot water – the eggs are cooked when the whites have just become opaque. I keep a number of different sized collections of ramekin or *cocotte* dishes so that I can serve one or two eggs in each one and, in some cases, quite a substantial savoury nest for the eggs to nestle in.

Oeufs en Cocotte Tartare

For six people

6 eggs
6 oz (175 g) fillet or rump steak
Salt and freshly ground black pepper
Few drops Worcestershire and Tabasco
   sauce

2 oz (50 g) butter
6 tablespoons home made tomato sauce
   (see page 259)

Roughly chop the meat.

Double-bladed knife

Process the meat until finely chopped (ground), season with salt and pepper, add a few drops of Worcestershire sauce and Tabasco sauce and switch on and off to mix. Make a ring of meat in the bottom of six ramekin dishes and break the eggs into the centre of the rings. Melt the butter and pour it over the eggs and place the ramekins in a *bain marie* with enough hot water to come halfway up the sides of the ramekin dishes. Bake in a preheated very hot oven (425°F. 220°C. Reg. 7) for about 8 minutes until the eggs are just set. Pour a tablespoon of warm tomato sauce over each egg and serve at once.

Oeufs en Cocotte à la Lyonnaise

Eggs and onions combined together produce the most sophisticated taste from what are basically two of the more humble ingredients.

*For four people
as a first course*

1 medium onion
4 eggs
1½ oz (40 g) butter

Pinch sugar
Salt and freshly ground black pepper
4 tablespoons single cream

Peel the onion and cut it into half to fit into the feed tube of your Magimix.
Butter 4 ramekin dishes.

Thin slicing disc

Process the onion into thin slices.
Heat the butter in a shallow saucepan, add the onion, sprinkle with a pinch of sugar and cook over a medium high heat, stirring every now and then to prevent sticking, until the slices are really soft and lightly browned. Season them with salt and freshly ground black pepper. Divide the cooked onion and the juice between the ramekin dishes. Break an egg into each dish, top with a tablespoon of single cream and bake as above.

Oeufs à la Vichy

Another ludicrously simple starter that gets a meal going to a delicious start.

For six people

1 lb (450 g) carrots
1 oz (25 g) sugar
2 oz (50 g) butter
Small bunch parsley

6 eggs
Salt and freshly ground black pepper
6 tablespoons single cream

Butter six ramekin dishes. Peel the carrots. Remove the coarse stalks from the parsley.

Double-bladed knife

Process the parsley until finely chopped and remove.

Julienne or Coleslaw disc

Process the carrots.

Melt the butter, add the carrots, sprinkle over a pinch of sugar and season with salt and pepper. Cook the carrots over a low heat, stirring and sprinkling over a teaspoon of water every now and then to prevent burning, until they are tender. Divide the carrots between the ramekin dishes and break an egg into each dish. Top each egg with a tablespoon of cream, sprinkle with the parsley and some freshly ground black pepper, then bake as above.

Other ideas for Oeufs en Cocotte Spread the bottom of the ramekin dishes with some ham finely chopped with the double-bladed knife; top with cream. Chop some leftover vegetables with the double-bladed knife, heat them through with a little butter, season well and use the mixture as a base for the baked eggs.

Place some ratatouille made in the Magimix (see page 167) in the bottom of the ramekin dishes, season well and top with an egg and cream.

Usé some home made tomato sauce (see page 259) as a base for the eggs and top with cream.

Make duxelles in your Magimix (a delicious mushroom sauce base flavoured with herbs and lemon juice) (see page 270). Place a generous tablespoon of duxelles in the bottom of four buttered ramekin dishes, break an egg into each dish and pour a tablespoon single cream over each egg. Dust with a little freshly ground black pepper and bake as above.

SIMPLE OMELETTES

A good omelette is one of the quickest and most satisfactory recipes to knock up in a hurry so why is it that so few of them ever seem to turn out well. In books about the French and especially about French lovers the principal characters seem to me to be tossing up the lightest and most succulent of omelettes almost any time of the night or day, but get the same kind of fare in an English or American kitchen and it seems my lot to be served up with a thin, rubbery, mess. My own omelettes, I hasten to say, seem to turn out well on the whole and so do those of my girl Fridays, Rosa and Jenny, but in cafés, pubs, small restaurants and, sometimes, even the better hotels, ask for an omelette and UGH! Part of the trouble is undoubtedly the omelette pan itself. No self respecting French woman would be without her omelette pan, kept expressly for that purpose and wiped out with a cloth or kitchen paper rather than being washed between omelettes. I have a nice, well used, Le Creuset pan I use both for omelettes and for pancakes but not for anything else; it is heavy and it browns evenly. Then there is the mixing – over-mix and you flatten the ingredients and make them rubbery; and, of course, the cooking itself, overcook the ingredients and again they turn tough and rubbery – the omelette should be moist and almost runny in the centre and just lightly cooked on the outside. Finally there is the heat at which you cook the omelette – the flame should be medium high, strong but not fierce, the butter should just be beginning to foam when the eggs are added and the medium high heat should be maintained during cooking time.

Very last of all, when talking about any sort of omelettes, they should be served as soon as they are cooked (with a few exceptions which include those omelettes which are designed to be served cold).

Making Omelettes with your Magimix or Grande Famille

Follow the normal rules for making omelettes but pay particular attention to the rule that the egg mixture should not be over mixed. To avoid this, when having added the eggs to any other ingredients in the bowl switch the machine on and off for two or three times to mix the eggs rather than keeping the machine running and thereby risking over-processing.

Work out the order in which ingredients should be processed so that your bowl will not have to be washed up in between processing steps.

Experiment with fillings for omelettes that are made from small quantities of this and that leftover in your refrigerator in order to be able to produce inexpensive and delicious omelette dishes in a matter of moments.

Serve omelettes with hot French bread, butter and a salad to make a delicious, attractive, quick and satisfying meal, at any time of the day or night.

Classic French Plain Omelette

For two people

4 eggs
Salt and freshly ground black pepper
1½ oz (40 g) butter

Roughly chop ½ oz (13 g) butter.

Double-bladed knife

Combine the eggs and chopped butter in the Magimix bowl, add a little salt and pepper and switch on and off two or three times so that the eggs are just broken and mixed together.

In a clean, dry, frying pan melt the remaining butter over a low heat swirling it around to cover the bottom of the pan with a thin film of melted butter. As soon as the butter has melted, raise the heat and at the moment at which the butter begins to foam pour in the eggs. As the eggs begin to set on the bottom lift up the omelette with a spoon or spatula and let the runny egg from the top pour down onto the base of the pan. Continue to lift the omelette until the bottom is *just* firm but the top is still shining with moisture although no longer definitely runny. Slide the omelette onto a warm serving dish, folding it in half as you slide it onto the dish.

Cheese Omelette

For two people	4 eggs	1½ oz (40 g) butter
	Salt and freshly ground black pepper	1 oz (25 g) grated Cheddar cheese

Roughly chop ½ oz (13 g) butter.

Fine grating disc   Grate the cheese into the Magimix bowl. Remove the grating disc and replace with the double-bladed knife, making sure the blade is firmly pressed down in the bowl.

Double-bladed knife   Add the eggs, chopped butter and seasoning to the cheese and process by switching the machine on and off until the eggs are just broken up and mixed.

Cook the Omelette in the same way as the Classic French Omelette (see page 75).

Fresh Herb Omelette

Choose only fresh herbs for this omelette; the classic combination is parsley, chervil and chives but a very little fresh sage and thyme or some oregano can also be added. The flavour of the herbs should not be overdone.

For two people	4 eggs	3 chives
	2 sprigs parsley	1½ oz (40 g) butter
	1 sprig chervil	Salt and freshly ground black pepper

Remove any tough stalks from the herbs. Make sure the herbs are dry.
Chop ½ oz (13 g) butter into small pieces.

Double-bladed knife   Process the herbs until they are finely chopped. Add the eggs, chopped butter and season with a little salt and pepper. Switch the machine on and off to process the eggs until they are just broken up and mixed.

Cook the Herb Omelette in the same way as the Classic French Omelette, (see page 75).

Bacon and Potato Omelette

For two people   2 thin rashers streaky bacon   1½ oz (40 g) butter
1 small cooked and skinned potato   Salt and freshly ground black pepper
4 eggs

Remove the rinds from the bacon, and roughly chop the rashers.

Chipper disc   Process the potato through the disc, and remove from the bowl.
Chop ½ oz (13 g) butter.

Double-bladed knife   Process the bacon until finely chopped. Remove the bacon and cook it in a small frying pan over a medium heat, stirring to prevent browning, for two minutes. Drain the bacon on kitchen paper.

Double-bladed knife   Break the eggs into the bowl, add the chopped butter, season with salt and pepper and switch on and off twice to break up the eggs. Add the bacon and potato and switch the machine on and off again so that the ingredients are just mixed. Cook the Omelette in the same way as Classic French Omelette on page 75.

Mushroom Omelette

For two people   4 eggs   Salt and freshly ground black pepper
1½ oz (40 g) butter   2 oz (50 g) firm button mushrooms

The problem with a mushroom omelette is allowing the mushrooms to become grey, flabby and unattractive. Solve this problem by not washing them (or if you absolutely must, making sure they are quite dry before processing them), choosing really fresh and firm button mushrooms rather than large open mushrooms and by tossing them lightly in the hot butter you are to cook your omelette in before adding the eggs.

Chop ½ oz (13 g) butter.

Medium slicing disc   Process the mushrooms through the slicing disc and remove. Wipe out the bowl with kitchen paper.

Double-bladed knife   Combine the eggs, chopped butter and seasoning in the Magimix bowl and switch on and off three times to break up and mix the eggs.

Heat the butter over a medium heat in the omelette pan. Add the mushrooms and stir them over the medium heat until they are golden brown. Raise the heat so that the butter foams, pour in the egg mixture and continue to cook in the same way as the French Classic Omelette, (see page 75).

Kidney Omelette

A delicious richly filled omelette which has a filling of kidneys in a savoury sauce in its succulent middle.

For two people

Small bunch parsley
2 lambs or sheeps kidneys
½ small onion
½ oz (13 g) fat, lard or dripping
2 teaspoons plain flour

3 fl oz (90 ml) stock
1 tablespoon red wine
Salt and freshly ground black pepper
4 eggs
1½ oz (40 g) butter

Remove any tough stalks from the parsley. Peel and coarsely chop the onion. Remove any outer skin and fat from the kidneys, slice each kidney, remove the core and roughly chop the flesh.

Double-bladed knife
Process the parsley until finely chopped and remove. Process the onion till finely chopped and remove. Process the kidneys until fairly finely chopped and remove. Wipe the bowl and knife with kitchen paper.

Heat the fat, lard or dripping in a small saucepan. Add the onion and cook over a low heat until the onion is soft and transparent. Add the kidney and cook for a minute, stirring. Sprinkle over the flour, mix well and gradually blend in the stock and wine, stirring all the time until the sauce is thick and smooth. Season with salt and pepper and simmer uncovered for five minutes stirring every now and then. Cover the sauce and keep warm.

Double-bladed knife
Combine the eggs with ½ oz (13 g) butter cut into small pieces in the Magimix bowl and switch on and off two or three times to break up and mix the eggs. Cook the omelette as for the Classic French Omelette, on page 75, when the omelette is just cooked spread the kidney filling over the top and slide the omelette onto a serving dish folding it in half as it slides from the pan. Sprinkle over the chopped parsley and serve at once.

Ham Omelette

Another simple omelette which uses up a little remaining cooked ham, with the addition of some tomato and chives as a filling ..... so easy and yet so very good for a quick and cheap main dish for an informal occasion.

For two people

1 ripe tomato
1 dessertspoon finely chopped chives
1 dessertspoon olive or sunflower oil
Salt and freshly ground black pepper
Pinch oregano

1 tablespoon red wine
4 eggs
1½ oz (40 g) butter
2 oz (50 g) ham

Chipper disc Remove any stalk from the tomato and process (without putting pressure on the pusher) through the chipper disc. Remove the chipper disc and tomato from the bowl and wipe out the bowl with kitchen paper.

Heat the oil in a small saucepan. Add the tomato, chives, oregano and red wine and season with salt and pepper. Bring to the boil, stir well and cook, uncovered, stirring every now and then, for 15 minutes, keep warm.

Roughly chop the ham. Chop ½ oz (13 g) butter.

Double-bladed knife Place the ham in the Magimix bowl and process until coarsely chopped. Add the eggs and chopped butter, season with salt and pepper and switch the machine on and off two or three times to break up the eggs and mix the ingredients.

Cook the omelette according to the instructions for the Classic French Omelette on page 75. Spread the tomato sauce over the centre of the omelette and slide it, folding in half, as you ease the omelette out of the pan onto a warmed serving dish.

SPANISH OMELETTES

Another omelette to make if you have a good range of leftovers in the refrigerator and especially if they tend to be of the vegetable nature. Almost any cooked vegetable can go into a Spanish omelette or, when necessary, you can start from scratch. I am including two recipes in this book, one for a cooked vegetable Spanish omelette made from leftovers and one made from scratch with small quantities of raw vegetables and cooked meat. Both made excellent quick dishes to serve with crusty bread and a crisp salad. The Spanish omelette is also a good dish to serve cold for a buffet or to take on a picnic.

Spanish Omelette with Cooked Vegetables

For four people

Small bunch parsley
12 oz (350 g) cooked vegetables (potatoes, onions, celery, chopped peppers, carrots, peas, French beans etc.)

6 eggs
1 oz (25 g) butter, lard or dripping
Salt and freshly ground black pepper

Note For this omelette you will need a large pan and it is easier to use a non-stick one.

Double-bladed knife Remove the tough stalks from the parsley and discard them. Process the parsley until finely chopped. Add the cooked vegetables and switch the machine on and off two or three times until the vegetables are fairly finely chopped. Heat the butter, lard or dripping, add the vegetables, seasoning well with salt and pepper, and cook, stirring, until the vegetables are hot through and golden brown. While the vegetables are cooking process the eggs in the Magimix bowl with the double-bladed knife (there is no need to wash the bowl after chopping the vegetables) and switch on and off two or three times to break up the eggs. Pour the eggs over the vegetables and cook (without stirring) until the eggs are lightly set on the bottom. Put the pan under a grill or in a moderately hot oven to cook the top of the omelette until it is just set. Slide from the pan onto a warm serving dish.

Spanish Omelette with Uncooked Vegetables

For four people

1 small bunch parsley
1 medium potato
1 small onion
2 small carrots
2 oz (50 g) shelled peas
4 oz (100 g) topped and tailed French
  beans

1 tomato
Pinch bicarbonate of soda
6 eggs
Salt and freshly ground black pepper
1 tablespoon sunflower oil
½ oz (13 g) butter

Remove any tough stalks from the parsley. Peel the potato. Peel and roughly chop the onion. Peel and wash the carrots.

Double-bladed knife
Process the parsley until finely chopped and remove.

Chipper disc
Process the potato, onion and carrot through the chipper disc and remove. Process the tomato through the disc and remove.

Thick slicing disc
Carefully position the beans in the feed tube and process the beans. Heat the oil and butter in a large pan over a low to medium heat, add the potato, carrots and onion and cook over a low heat, covered, stirring every now and then until the potatoes and carrots are soft. Cook the peas and beans in boiling salted water to which a small pinch of bicarbonate of soda has been added for about six minutes until tender and drain well. Add the peas and beans to the other vegetables, season with salt and pepper, add the tomato and mix well. Cook for two minutes while preparing the eggs.

Double-bladed knife and the same bowl
Break the eggs into the bowl, add the parsley, and switch the machine on and off to break up the eggs and mix lightly. Pour the eggs over the vegetables and cook over a medium high heat until the bottom is lightly set. Transfer the pan to the grill or into a moderately hot oven (350°F. 180°C. Reg. 4) for about five minutes or until the top of the omelette is just set. Slide onto a warm serving dish, folding in half as the omelette slides from the pan.

SOME SPECIAL OMELETTES

Some of these are made in exactly the same way as the Classic French Omelette recipe on page 75. These, however, benefit from especially exotic or exciting fillings which set them apart from the ordinary, run of the mill omelettes. Others are made into soufflés, light to the touch and interesting to the palate, still others, like the Omelette Arnold Bennett are omelettes which are the triumphs of great chefs and well tried delights for the discerning.

Serendipity Omelette

This omelette (or not exactly this one but something very like it) was one I had for the first time at a combined shop restaurant in New York called "Serendipity", a lovely avant garde sort of place with feather boas, way out clothes and a few tables serving simple but excellent lunchtime food. This is what a friend of mine describes as "poem" food, it looks fantastic and it tastes even better than it looks. Again, this is not party food because it must be served as soon as it is ready.

For two people

4 eggs
1½ oz (40 g) butter
2 oz (50 g) cottage cheese
2 tablespoons sour cream

1 tablespoon finely chopped chives
Salt and freshly ground black pepper
½ medium jar red caviar

Cut ½ oz (13 g) butter into small pieces.

Double-bladed knife

Combine the cottage cheese and sour cream in the Magimix bowl and process until the mixture is smooth. Add the chives, season with salt and pepper and process to mix. Remove from the bowl.

Use the same bowl into which you break the eggs, add the chopped butter, season with salt and pepper and switch the machine on and off two or three times to break up the eggs.

Heat the remaining butter in the omelette pan and cook the omelette as for the Classic French Omelette on page 75.

When the omelette is *just* cooked spread the cream mixture over the centre of the omelette, top with the red caviar and fold the omelette in half as you slide it out of the pan and onto a warm serving dish.

Omelette with Swiss Chard

If you are fortunate enough to have your own vegetable garden and you produce this delicious and versatile vegetable which seems to flourish under the most adverse of conditions try making this lovely variation of the omelette theme. Swiss Chard (or seakale beet as it is sometimes called) produces two vegetables in one, the dark, slightly crinkly leaves and the thick white stalks. This recipe only uses the green leaves but the white stalks, cut into ¼ in. (0.75 cm) lengths and cooked like asparagus, make a good vegetable to go with the omelette in the place of a salad. If you cannot get Swiss Chard large spinach leaves can be used in its place.

For two people

4 eggs
1 medium onion
1 clove garlic
1½ lb (675 g) Swiss chard
1 small bunch parsley

2 tablespoons olive or sunflower oil
1½ oz (40 g) Parmesan cheese
Salt and freshly ground black pepper
1½ oz (40 g) butter

Peel and roughly chop the onion and garlic. Cut out the white stalks of the Swiss chard (I do this with a pair of kitchen scissors). Remove the tough stalks of the parsley.

Parmesan grating disc

Process the Parmesan and remove.

Double-bladed knife   Process the onion and garlic until finely chopped and remove.
Heat the oil in a saucepan large enough to contain the chard leaves. Add the onion and garlic and cook over a medium low heat until the onion is soft and transparent. Add the chard leaves and parsley and continue to cook for about four minutes or until the chard is just soft. Refresh with cold water and drain in a sieve pressing out any excess water.
Chop ½ oz (13 g) butter.

Double-bladed knife   Process the chard and onion etc. in the Magimix bowl until the leaves are fairly finely chopped. Add the eggs, chopped butter and Parmesan cheese, season with salt and pepper and process for just enough to mix the ingredients.
Melt the remaining butter in an omelette pan and proceed exactly as for the Classic French Omelette on page 75.

Savoury Cheese Soufflé

Illustrated on page 63

For four people

1 tablespoon finely grated Parmesan cheese	Freshly ground black pepper
4 oz (100 g) Cheddar cheese	Pinch cayenne
2 oz (50 g) butter	4 egg yolks
1½ oz (40 g) flour	5 egg whites
½ pint (10 fl oz 300 ml) milk	Pinch salt
½ teaspoon celery salt	Pinch of cream of tartar
3 sage leaves	

Butter a 2½ pint (1·5 litre) soufflé dish and sprinkle the Parmesan cheese around the inside.

Coarse grating disc   Break the Cheddar cheese into pieces and grate through the grating disc. Remove the cheese.

Double-bladed knife   Melt the butter in a saucepan, add the flour and mix well. Cook the roux over a low heat, stirring occasionally, for 3 minutes. Gradually blend in the milk, stirring over a medium high heat until the sauce is thick and smooth. Transfer the sauce to the bowl and add the celery salt, sage leaves, a good twisting of freshly ground black pepper and a pinch of cayenne. With the machine running, add the egg yolks, one at a time, through the feed tube and process until the mixture is smooth. Add the grated cheese, reserving one tablespoonful, and process until the cheese is mixed in.
Beat the egg whites until foaming, add a pinch of salt and a pinch of cream of tartar and continue beating until the egg whites are really stiff. Add a quarter of the egg whites to the mixture in the Magimix bowl and switch the machine on and off quickly to mix the ingredients.
Fold the mixture from the Magimix bowl into the remaining egg whites and pour into the prepared soufflé dish. Sprinkle the reserved tablespoon of grated cheese on top and place the dish in the centre of a hot preheated oven (400°F. 200°C. Reg. 6). After 5 minutes turn the oven down to medium (375°F. 190°C. Reg. 5) and cook for a further 20–25 minutes. Serve at once.

Spinach Soufflé

For four people

6 oz (175 g) spinach
1½ oz (40 g) Cheddar cheese
1 oz (25 g) finely grated Parmesan
  cheese
1 small onion
2 oz (50 g) ham
2½ oz (65 g) butter
Pinch salt

1½ oz (40 g) flour
½ pint (10 fl oz 300 ml) boiling milk
Freshly ground black pepper
Pinch cayenne pepper and ground
  nutmeg
4 egg yolks
5 egg whites
Pinch cream of tartar

Note on spinach — If you are using fresh spinach, blanch it for 5 minutes in boiling water and then drain thoroughly and chop. If using frozen spinach it should be thawed and then chopped if necessary.

Coarse grating disc

Break the Cheddar cheese into pieces and grate through the disc. Remove the Cheddar from the bowl.

Double-bladed knife

Butter a 2½ pint (1·5 litre) soufflé dish and sprinkle the Parmesan cheese around the inside of the dish, shaking it well to distribute the cheese evenly.

Peel and quarter the onion. Process the onion until finely chopped. Remove the onion. Roughly chop the ham and process until well chopped. Remove the ham from the bowl. Melt ½ oz (13 g) butter in a saucepan and cook the onion and ham for 3 minutes over a low heat. Turn the heat up under the saucepan to medium high and add the spinach and a pinch of salt. Stir the mixture until as much moisture as possible has been evaporated and the spinach is nearly dry. This will take longer if you use frozen spinach. Remove the pan from the heat.

Melt 2 oz (50 g) butter in another pan and stir in the flour. Cook for about 2 minutes but do not let it brown. Transfer the roux to the Magimix bowl and add the boiling milk, process until smooth. Add a seasoning of salt, pepper, cayenne and nutmeg. With the motor still running, add the egg yolks one at a time allowing each one to be mixed in. Process until well mixed.

Add the egg yolk mixture to the spinach and mix well.

Beat the egg whites with a pinch of salt. When the eggs are foaming, add a pinch of cream of tartar and continue beating until the egg whites are really stiff.

Stir a quarter of the egg whites into the spinach mixture. Add all but a tablespoon of the grated cheese and mix well. Carefully fold in the remainder of the egg whites, turning the mixture over lightly.

Turn the mixture into the prepared soufflé dish and sprinkle the remaining cheese on top. Place the dish in the centre of a hot preheated oven (400°F. 200°C. Reg. 6). After 5 minutes turn the oven down to medium (375°F. 190°C. Reg. 5) and cook for a further 20–25 minutes. Serve at once.

Marinated Sea Bass

I first had an example of this dish, which I consider to be one of the most delicious fish dishes in the world, made with salmon. Finding salmon so outrageously expensive I tried making something similar with sea bass – if anything it was even better at about quarter of the cost. Don't be put off by the thought of the fish being raw because in fact the action of the acid in the lemon juice and the wine have the effect of cooking it. The fish is extremely rich and you can serve it as a main course summer dish with an accompanying salad and some new potatoes.

For six to eight people

1 sea bass 2½ lb (1·2 kg) approximately	Juice of one lemon
1 small onion	8 green peppercorns
4 sprigs coriander (or use 1 teaspoon coriander seeds)	1 teaspoon sea salt
	½ teaspoon dry mustard
4 sprigs dill (or use 1 teaspoon dried dill)	4 tablespoons sunflower oil
	¼ pint (5 fl oz 150 ml) dry white wine

Ask your fishmonger to fillet and skin the sea bass. Chill the sea bass in a deep freeze for 20 minutes and then cut each fillet into four thick slices along the length of the fillets. Cut each strip diagonally into three inch (7·5 cm) lengths and lay them in a shallow dish.
Peel the onion.

Thin slicing disc Slice the onion and remove from the bowl.
Double-bladed knife Combine the fresh coriander, dill, mustard, lemon juice, salt, peppercorns and oil in the Magimix bowl, and process for about 1 minute. (If you use coriander seeds process these first to break them up a little before adding to the other ingredients). Add the wine and onion and switch on and off to mix. Pour the marinade over the fish, cover with polythene film and refrigerate for 4–8 hours.
Drain off the marinade and serve the fish on lettuce leaves with hot French bread. A garlic mayonnaise (see page 251) can be served on the side.

Serbian Fish Salad

The perfect dish for a summer luncheon. It looks cool and elegant and it tastes superb. Serve with a mixed green and a potato salad.

For six people

1 lb (450 g) halibut or cod
3 carrots
2 stalks celery
4 oz (100 g) French beans
1 egg
½ teaspoon dry English mustard
Small pinch salt
1 teaspoon lemon juice

¾ pint (15 fl oz 450 ml) sunflower oil
1 teaspoon anchovy essence
Few drops Worcestershire sauce
Few drops Tabasco sauce
1 tablespoon drained capers
3 hard boiled eggs
Watercress for garnishing

Steam the halibut or cod until just cooked and leave to cool.
Remove any skin and bones and separate the fish into large flakes.
Peel the carrots. Trim the celery stalks and the French beans.

Chipper disc Process the carrots and celery, and remove.
Thick slicing disc Process the beans and remove.

Cook the carrots and celery in boiling salted water until just tender but still crisp, and drain well. Cook the beans in boiling salted water for a few minutes only until tender but crisp, rinse immediately in cold water and drain well.

Double-bladed knife Combine the egg and mustard and process for 30 seconds. With the motor running gradually add half the lemon juice and then the oil in a very light stream until the oil is emulsified into the egg and the sauce is very thick and smooth. Add the remaining lemon juice, a small pinch salt, anchovy essence, Worcestershire sauce, Tabasco sauce and capers and process for just long enough to mix. Taste for seasoning.

Roughly chop the hard boiled eggs.
Add half the mayonnaise sauce to the fish, eggs and cooked vegetables and mix lightly (it is important not to overmix the ingredients so that they break up) mound them into a loaf shape on a serving dish.
Mask the loaf with the remaining sauce and garnish with watercress.
Chill before serving.

Fish and Spinach Salad

A surprisingly delicious salad of spinach, tomatoes, raw mushrooms and cooked flaked fish. Serve the salad as a first course on lettuce leaves and take great care not to overcook the spinach.

For two people	12 oz (350 g) picked over young spinach	¼ teaspoon dried mustard
	2 oz (50 g) firm button mushrooms	1 tablespoon white wine vinegar
	4 small firm tomatoes	½ teaspoon Garam masala or curry
	10–12 oz (275 g-350 g) firm white fish	powder
	(coley, pollock, hake etc.)	1 tablespoon tomato ketchup
	Court bouillon (or use 1 chicken stock	Pinch mixed salad herbs
	cube with water, onion, carrot and	Salt and freshly ground black pepper
	bouquet garni)	2 spring onions
	3 tablespoons olive or sunflower oil	Crisp lettuce leaves

Cover the fish with the court bouillon, bring gently to the boil and simmer until the fish has turned opaque. Drain, remove any bones and skin, leave to cool, coarsely flake the flesh and put in a bowl. Cook the spinach in a very little boiling salted water for about 3 minutes until it is just tender and drain well.

Chipper disc   Process the tomatoes through the chipper disc without putting any pressure on the pusher. Add the tomatoes to the fish.

Thin slicing disc   Process the mushrooms through the thin slicing disc and add them to the fish and tomatoes.

Double-bladed knife   Process the spinach until coarsely chopped and add it to the fish, tomatoes and mushrooms.

Double-bladed knife   Combine the mustard, oil, vinegar, herbs, tomato ketchup, curry powder and seasoning in the Magimix bowl and process until the dressing is well mixed. Pour the dressing over the salad ingredients and toss lightly to mix.

Arrange the salad on lettuce leaves and chill before serving with slices of buttered brown bread. Garnish with finely sliced spring onions.

Fish Mousse in a Spinach Casing

An attractive pale yellow mousse made from a mixture of smoked haddock and white fish encased in spinach leaves.

For six to eight people	1 lb (450 g) large spinach leaves	2 eggs, separated
	6 oz (175 g) smoked haddock fillets	Salt and freshly ground black pepper
	8 oz (225 g) white fish fillets	Few drops Tabasco and Worcestershire
	1 oz (25 g) butter	sauce
	1 packet (½ oz 13 g) gelatine powder	¼ pint (5 fl oz 150 ml) single cream
	2 tablespoons hot water	¼ pint (5 fl oz 150 ml) mayonnaise
	Juice ½ lemon	(see page 250)

Remove the stalks from the spinach leaves and blanch the leaves for two minutes. Drain well, separate the leaves carefully and leave them to dry on kitchen paper. Line a circular or lightly oiled round mould with the spinach leaves arranging them with the top of the leaves at the bottom of the mould and the stalk ends overhanging the sides of the mould.

Place the fish in a buttered steamer, dot with butter and steam for about eight minutes until just tender. Leave to cool. Soften the gelatine in the hot water and mix in the lemon juice.

Double-bladed knife   Process the fish until reduced to a purée. Add the egg yolks and process well to mix. Add the gelatine mixture, cream and mayonnaise, season with salt and pepper, Tabasco and Worcestershire sauce and process to mix the ingredients.

Whip the egg whites until stiff. Lightly fold the fish mixture into the egg whites and turn the mixture into the prepared mould. Fold over the tops of the spinach leaves and chill in a refrigerator until set firm.

Turn on to a serving dish and pour over a little vinaigrette dressing made with lemon juice just before serving.

Variations A little finely chopped and blanched red pepper can be added to the mixture to give more colour or you can add some peeled, cored, and seeded and chopped tomato to give the same effect.

Smoked Haddock and Egg Mousse

A light summery mousse which can be served as a light main course for a summer luncheon. I sometimes put this mousse into a ring mould and fill the centre with watercress dipped into a vinaigrette dressing.

For six people

1 lb (450 g) smoked haddock or cod
½ pint (10 fl oz 300 ml) double or
  whipping cream
1 tin consommé (14 oz 400 g)
1 packet gelatine powder (½ oz 13 g)
3 hard boiled eggs

Freshly ground black pepper
Few drops Tabasco sauce
1 tablespoon finely chopped parsley
¼ pint (5 fl oz 150 ml) mayonnaise
  (see page 250)

Steam the fish until just tender, cool and remove any skin and bones.

Soften the gelatine in a little consommé over a warm heat until it has dissolved. Add the gelatine mixture to the rest of the consommé.

Roughly chop the hard boiled eggs.

Double-bladed knife   Combine two thirds of the consommé with the cooked haddock, hard boiled eggs and parsley, season with freshly ground black pepper, add a few drops of Tabasco and process for just long enough to coarsely chop the eggs and flake the haddock. Turn into a bowl and refrigerate until the mixture is just beginning to set.

Plastic blade   Process the cream until thick (do not put the pusher in the feed tube while whipping the cream) and remove.

Fold the mayonnaise and cream into the setting mousse and turn into a soufflé dish. Top with the remaining consommé and chill in a refrigerator until set firm.

Note If you are using a ring mould the consommé should be set in the bottom of the mould before the mousse is added.

Tuna Mousse with Cucumber

For four people

1 cucumber
1 clove garlic
1 tin tuna (10 oz 275 g)
2 teaspoons gelatine powder
2 tablespoons water
¼ pint (5 fl oz 150 ml) mayonnaise
  (see page 250)

Juice ½ lemon
Salt and freshly ground black pepper
Worcestershire and Tabasco sauce
¼ pint (5 fl oz 150 ml) double cream
1 teaspoon white wine vinegar

Peel the cucumber. Peel and roughly chop the garlic. Soften the gelatine in two tablespoons hot water. Drain the oil from the tuna.

Coarse grating disc or the Julienne disc

Process the cucumber, place it in a colander, sprinkle with salt and leave to sweat for 30 minutes.

Double-bladed knife

Process the garlic until finely chopped.

Plastic blade

Add the tuna to the garlic and process until the tuna is reduced to a paste. Add the mayonnaise, gelatine and lemon juice, season with salt and pepper and a few drops of Tabasco and Worcestershire sauce. Whip the cream until thick and lightly fold in the tuna mixture. Put the mousse into a lightly oiled mould and refrigerate until set. Unmould onto a serving dish. Press the cucumber to remove excess liquid and pat dry on kitchen paper. Sprinkle the cucumber with vinegar and arrange it around the tuna mousse.

Summer Fish Quiche

A delicious filling of tuna and prawns which is as delicious cold as it is hot. All you need to accompany the quiche is a bowl of fresh summer salad.

For six to eight people

10 in. (25 cm) chilled quiche case
  (see recipe and preparations on
  page 240)
2 onions
1 tin tuna (7 oz 200 g)
4 oz (100 g) peeled prawns
4 anchovy fillets
1 oz (25 g) butter
Small bunch parsley

1 tablespoon oil
1 carton (4 oz 100 g) cottage cheese
3 eggs
¼ pint (5 fl oz 150 ml) single cream
Salt and freshly ground black pepper
Pinch cayenne
3 oz (75 g) Cheddar cheese
2 slices white bread with the crusts
  removed

Peel the onions. Remove the stalks from the parsley. Drain the tuna and anchovy fillets.

Double-bladed knife Process the bread until reduced to fine breadcrumbs and remove. Process the parsley until finely chopped and remove.

Fine grating disc Grate the cheese through the disc and remove.

Thin slicing disc Process the onions through the disc and remove. Melt the butter with the oil, add the onions and cook over a low heat until the onions are soft.

Double-bladed knife Process the cottage cheese until smooth. Add the cream and eggs, season with salt, pepper and a pinch of cayenne and process until smooth and well mixed. Add two thirds of the cheese, the anchovies and parsley and switch on and off to mix.

Spread the onions over the base of the chilled pastry case and cover with the tuna broken up with a fork, spread the prawns evenly on top, then pour over the cheese custard mixture and top with the breadcrumbs mixed with the remaining grated cheese. Bake in a moderately hot oven (375°F. 190°C. Reg. 5) for about 35 minutes or until the pastry is crisp and golden and the topping is golden brown.

Smoked Salmon or Smoked Haddock Quiche with Spinach

For six to eight people

1 10 in. (25 cm) quiche case
  (see page 240)
1 large onion
4 oz (100 g) smoked salmon (or use 8 oz
  (225 g) cooked smoked haddock)
8 oz (225 g) cooked spinach
3 eggs
4 oz (100 g) cream cheese
¼ pint (5 fl oz 150 ml) single cream

Salt, freshly ground black pepper, pinch
  ground nutmeg and cayenne

Topping
2 slices white bread with the crusts
  removed
1 oz (25 g) grated Cheddar cheese
½ oz (13 g) grated Parmesan cheese

Peel and roughly chop the onion.

Double-bladed knife Process the bread with the Cheddar and Parmesan cheese until reduced to fine crumbs and remove.

Process the onion until finely chopped and remove. Process the smoked salmon until coarsely chopped and remove. Process the spinach until fairly finely chopped and remove. Process the eggs, cream cheese and cream together, then season with salt, pepper, nutmeg and cayenne and process until the ingredients are well mixed. Heat the butter in a frying pan. Add the onion and cook over a low heat, stirring to prevent sticking, until the onion is soft and transparent. Spread the onion, smoked salmon and spinach in the chilled quiche case, pour over the custard and stir gently with a fork so that the custard seeps through the other ingredients. Sprinkle over the breadcrumb mixture and bake in a moderately hot oven (350°F. 175°C. Reg. 4) for about 40 minutes until the filling is just set and the topping and pastry are golden brown.

Serve hot, warm or cold.

Fish Croquettes

A good way of using coley, hake, huss or any relatively inexpensive white fish from the fishmonger.

For four people

4 slices white bread
1 lb (450 g) white fish (huss, coley, hake, pollock etc.)
1 onion
1 egg
Salt and freshly ground black pepper

Pinch mace and cayenne
1 teaspoon lemon juice
1 bunch parsley
1 beaten egg
Dried breadcrumbs

Steam or poach the fish, and when cool enough to handle remove any skin and bones, and cut fish into pieces. Peel and roughly chop the onion. Discard any tough stalks from the parsley.

Double-bladed knife
Process the parsley until finely chopped and remove. Cut the crusts off the bread and process until reduced to fine crumbs. Add the onion and fish and continue to process until the onion is very finely chopped and the fish is reduced to a coarse paste. Add the egg, season with salt, pepper, mace and cayenne and the lemon juice. Add the parsley and process for just long enough to mix into the other ingredients. Chill for one hour in the refrigerator and then shape into sausage shaped croquettes.
Dip each croquette into beaten egg and coat in dried breadcrumbs.
Fry the croquettes in shallow or deep oil for about 10 minutes until well crisped and golden brown. Drain on kitchen paper and serve with tartare sauce and sprigs of crisply fried parsley.

Sole Florentine

A classic way of serving fish which never ceases to appeal. Lemon juice and nutmeg added to the spinach helps to bring out the flavour of the leaves.

For four people

4 large or 8 small fillets of Dover or lemon sole.
Fish or chicken stock.
1 lb (450 g) fresh spinach
1 small onion
1 teaspoon lemon juice
Salt and freshly ground black pepper
Pinch ground nutmeg

2½ oz (65 g) butter
3 tablespoons flour
¼ pint (5 fl oz 150 ml) milk
¼ pint (5 fl oz 150 ml) single cream
1 egg yolk
3 oz (75 g) Cheddar cheese
Pinch paprika pepper

Place the fillets in a shallow pan, cover them with cold stock, bring them gently to the boil and poach them gently for about 5 minutes until they are just cooked.

Remove the fillets at once and reserve the stock.
Cook the spinach in a little boiling salted water for about six minutes until just tender and drain well.
Peel and roughly chop the onion.

Double-bladed knife Process the onion until finely chopped. Melt ½ oz (13 g) of butter in a small frying pan, add the onion and cook over a low heat until the onion is soft and transparent.

Double-bladed knife Combine the onion, the juices from the pan, the spinach and the lemon juice, season with a little salt, pepper and ground nutmeg and process for just long enough to chop the spinach coarsely.

Arrange the spinach in a buttered baking dish and place the fish fillets on top.

Coarse grating disc Grate the cheese, and remove 2 tablespoons from the bowl. Melt the remaining butter in a saucepan, add the flour and mix well. Gradually blend in the milk, ¼ pint (5 fl oz 150 ml) of the stock and the cream stirring continually over a medium high heat until the sauce comes to the boil and is thick and smooth.

Double-bladed knife Combine the sauce and cheese and process until smooth and well mixed. Season the sauce with salt and pepper and with the machine running add the egg yolk through the feed tube. Process until the ingredients are well mixed. Pour the sauce over the fish, sprinkle over the 2 tablespoons of cheese and bake in a hot oven (425°F. 220°C. Reg. 7) for 10 minutes to heat dish through and brown the top. Sprinkle with a little paprika pepper before serving.

Haddock Pie

An unusual way of using smoked haddock which I find very successful.

For four to six people

1¼ lb (525 g) smoked haddock or cod
1 lb (450 g) potatoes
3 sticks celery
3 large onions
2 tablespoons sunflower oil
¼ pint (5 fl oz 150 ml) chicken stock
1 tablespoon finely chopped parsley
Salt and freshly ground black pepper

3 oz (75 g) Cheddar cheese
2½ oz (65 g) butter
3 tablespoons flour
½ pint (10 fl oz 300 ml) milk
Pinch of nutmeg and cayenne
4 tablespoons double cream
2 egg yolks

Steam the haddock until just tender. Cool, remove any skin and bones and very roughly flake the flesh. Peel the potatoes. Trim the celery stalks. Peel and halve the onions.

Chipper disc Process the potatoes and remove.
Thin slicing disc Process the onions and celery.
Heat the oil with ½ oz (13 g) of the butter in a saucepan or large frying pan, add the potatoes, celery and onions and cook, stirring over a low heat until the oil and butter have been absorbed. Add the stock, season with pepper and simmer until the vegetables are tender and most of the liquid has been absorbed.

Arrange the vegetables in a buttered baking dish, top with the fish and sprinkle over the parsley.

Coarse grating disc Grate the cheese.

Melt the remaining butter in a saucepan. Add the flour and mix well. Gradually blend in the milk stirring continually over a medium high heat until the sauce is thick and smooth. Add half the cheese, season with salt, pepper, nutmeg and a small pinch of cayenne and stir until the cheese has melted.

Double-bladed knife Process the egg yolks and cream until smooth.

Add the egg and cream mixture to the sauce and stir until the ingredients are well mixed – do not allow to boil. Pour the cheese sauce over the other ingredients, top with the remaining grated cheese and bake in a moderately hot oven (375°F. 190°C. Reg. 5) for about 20 minutes until the dish is hot through and the top is a golden brown.

Quenelles of White Fish with Egg and Wine Sauce

For six to eight people

½ pint (10 fl oz 300 ml) milk
8 oz (225 g) softened butter
2 oz (50 g) flour
8 oz (225 g) white fish fillets with the
  skin removed

Salt and freshly ground black pepper
Pinch nutmeg
1 egg white
6 eggs
Chicken stock

Combine the milk with 2 oz (50 g) butter, bring to the boil and when the butter has melted, pour in all the flour at once. Beat vigorously over a low heat until the mixture is thick and smooth and then cook for about fifteen minutes, stirring every now and then to get rid of excess moisture. Cool and refrigerate until cold.

Double-bladed knife Process the fish until reduced to a paste. Season with salt and pepper and nutmeg, add the egg white and remaining butter process until well mixed. Add the thick sauce mixture and the eggs and process until the mixture is smooth. Chill in a refrigerator for 30 minutes.

Using a dampened tablespoon shape the mixture to resemble large eggs (they should weigh about 4 oz (100 g) each). Poach the quenelles in hot, not boiling, stock a few at a time until they are set firm and remove with a slotted spoon.

Note Quenelles can be made in advance and reheated in a sauce.

Egg and Wine Sauce

1 onion
2 oz (50 g) butter
2 tablespoons flour
½ pint (10 fl oz 300 ml) chicken stock
¼ pint (5 fl oz 150 ml) dry white wine

Salt and freshly ground black pepper
Pinch dried tarragon
1 teaspoon Dijon mustard
3 hard boiled eggs
¼ pint (5 fl oz 150 ml) double cream

Peel and roughly chop the onion. Roughly chop the hard boiled eggs.

Double-bladed knife

Process the onion until finely chopped.

Melt the butter in a saucepan, add the onion and cook over a low heat until the onion is soft and transparent. Add the flour and mix well. Gradually blend in the stock and wine, stirring continually, over a medium high heat until the sauce comes to the boil and is thick and smooth. Season with salt and pepper, mix in the mustard and tarragon and simmer for five minutes.

Double-bladed knife

Plastic blade

Process the eggs until coarsely chopped. Add the eggs to the sauce and stir lightly to mix.

Process the cream until thick.

Just before serving fold in the cream. Pour the sauce over the quenelles and heat through in a moderately hot oven (350°F. 175°C. Reg. 4) for 15 minutes before serving.

Variations Coat the quenelles with a rich, velvety Mornay sauce sprinkle over some grated Gruyère cheese and reheat under a hot grill. Coat the quenelles with a tomato sauce into which some double cream has been mixed and reheat in a moderately hot oven.

Trout with Bacon and Fennel

Lovely succulent baked trout with bacon, an irresistable country fresh combination.

For four people

4 trout 12 oz (350 g) each
1 medium fennel bulb (that is Florentine fennel)
Flour
6 thin rashers streaky bacon

Salt and freshly ground black pepper and a pinch of cayenne
¼ pint (5 fl oz 150 ml) single cream
2 oz (50 g) sliced white bread with the crusts removed

Gut and clean the the trout or ask your fishmonger to do this for you.

Trim and halve the fennel bulb. Remove the rinds from the bacon rashers.

Double-bladed knife

Thin slicing disc

Process the bread until reduced to fine crumbs and remove.

Process the bacon until roughly chopped and remove.

Process the fennel bulb through the slicing disc. Thinly coat the trout with flour seasoned with salt, pepper and a little cayenne. Arrange the trout in a well buttered baking dish.

Blanch the fennel slices in boiling water for four minutes and drain well. Slip the slices into the cavities of the trout. Scatter over the bacon, cover with foil and bake in a moderately hot oven (350°F. 175°C. Reg. 4) for about 20 minutes until they are just cooked through. Remove the trout on to a serving dish.

Pour the cream over the fish, sprinkle over the breadcrumbs, dot with butter and brown under a hot grill for about four minutes.

Grilled Fish with Cream and Mushrooms

I like my fish dishes to be simple since all too often the very flavour of a delicate fish can be drowned by too much seasoning or too many other ingredients.

For four people

4 trout fillets, small whiting fillets or large sole fillets
Salt and freshly ground black pepper
2 oz (50 g) melted butter

6 oz (175 g) firm button mushrooms
¼ pint (5 fl oz 150 ml) chicken stock
¼ pint (5 fl oz 150 ml) double cream

Medium slicing disc

Plastic blade

Season the fillets with salt and pepper.
Slice the mushrooms.
Cook the mushrooms for three minutes in the stock and drain well. (the stock can be used again for soups or sauces.)
Process the cream until thick, season it with a little salt and pepper, add the mushrooms and process for just long enough to mix the ingredients.
Brush the fish fillets with melted butter and grill them under a hot grill for about three minutes a side until just cooked. Transfer the fish to a hot serving dish, spoon over the cream and mushroom sauce and serve at once.

Salmon Steaks with Cucumber and Cream

Good salmon is such an exquisite fish that, in my book, it is criminal to spoil its own delicate flavour with anything too strong. Cucumber cooked with the fish makes an attractive and subtle dish.

For four people

4 salmon steaks
1 small cucumber
¼ pint (5 fl oz 150 ml) single cream
3 fl oz (90 ml) dry white wine

1 oz (25 g) butter
1 teaspoon finely chopped fresh dill
    (or use ¼ teaspoon dried dill)
Salt and freshly ground black pepper

Chipper disc

Season the fish with salt and pepper.
Peel the cucumber, cut it in half lengthwise and remove the seeds.
Process the cucumber through the chipper disc. Combine the cream with the wine, add the dill, season and mix well. Arrange the steaks in a well buttered dish, surround the fish with the cucumber and pour over the cream and wine mixture. Dot with butter, cover tightly with foil and bake in a moderately hot oven (375°F. 190°C. Reg. 5) for 20-30 minutes depending on the thickness of the steaks until the fish is just cooked.
Serve the dish with new potatoes and young green peas or broad beans.

Oriental Spiced Fish

An interesting idea for those who tend to find fish too bland and unexciting. Compare prices and buy a reasonably priced firm white fish. The final sprinkling of sugar provides a sweet/sour effect.

For six people   2 lb (900 g) firm white fleshed fish fillets (coley, cod, pollock, huss, monk fish etc.)
1½ pints (30 fl oz 900 ml) water
1 tablespoon white wine vinegar
1 walnut sized piece of fresh ginger root, peeled
2 cloves garlic
Pinch ground saffron
1 teaspoon dry mustard

¼ teaspoon ground coriander
3 teaspoons curry powder
1 tablespoon tomato purée
2 onions
Salt and freshly ground black pepper
2 green peppers
2 tablespoons olive oil
2 spring onions, thinly sliced
Caster sugar

Remove the skin from the fish and cut the fillets into approximately 4 in. × 2 in. (10 cm × 5 cm) pieces. Place the fish in a shallow pan, cover with the water, add the vinegar, season with salt and pepper and bring slowly to the boil. Cover and simmer for 6 minutes. Strain off cooking liquid and reserve.

Double-bladed knife   Combine, the garlic, ginger, saffron, mustard, coriander and curry powder in the Magimix bowl and process until the garlic and ginger are very finely chopped, scraping down the sides of the bowl if necessary. Add the tomato purée, switch on the motor, add 4 teaspoons of the cooking liquid and process until the ingredients are reduced to a paste. Spread the paste over the cooked fish and leave to stand in a cool place for one hour. Peel the onions. Halve the peppers and remove the cores and seeds.

Thin slicing disc   Thinly slice the onions and peppers.
Heat the oil in a heavy frying pan. Add the onions and peppers and cook over a low heat, stirring every now and then, for six minutes. Add the fish and continue to cook for a further 10 minutes turning the pieces of fish carefully once during the cooking time. Turn on to a serving dish, sprinkle with sugar and the spring onions and serve with rice and a mixed salad.

Curried Coley

It always surprises me that curried fish dishes are not more popular in this country – they have a lot going for them and their flavour, provided the curry seasoning is not overdone, can be very delectable.

For six people   1 ½ lb (675 g) coley fillets (or other firm fleshed white fish)
1 in. (2 cm) fresh ginger root
1 green pepper
1 teaspoon turmeric
Pinch chilli powder
½ pint (10 fl oz 300 ml) low fat natural yoghurt

Salt and freshly ground black pepper
2 bay leaves
2 small onions
1 teaspoon garam masala (mixed curry spices) or medium hot curry powder
4 tablespoons oil
1 tablespoon fresh coriander leaves or celery leaves

Cut the fish into 2 in. (5 cm) squares. Peel the ginger root and chop it roughly. Remove the core and seeds from the green pepper. Peel the onions.

Double-bladed knife   Finely chop the coriander or celery leaves and set aside. Combine the ginger with the turmeric and salt and process until the ginger is finely chopped (you may have to scrape the sides of the bowl during the processing). Add pepper, chilli powder and the yoghurt and process until well mixed. Pour the mixture over the fish and leave to marinate for at least one hour.

Thin slicing disc   Slice the onions through the slicing disc, remove and divide into rings.
Slice the green pepper through the slicing disc.
Heat the oil in a deep frying pan. Add the onion and pepper and cook over a low heat, stirring every now and then, until the onion is soft and transparent. Add the bay leaves and garam marsala and stir until the bay leaves have turned brown. Add the fish and yoghurt mixture, cover the pan tightly and cook over a low heat for about 15 minutes until the fish has turned opaque and the sauce is thick and rich. Remove the bay leaves then sprinkle the coriander or celery leaves over the dish and serve with wedges of lemon on the side, some fluffy boiled rice and a selection of curry side dishes (see page 273).

Curried Fish Puffs

1 packet frozen puff pastry (14 oz 400 g)
12 oz (350 g) cooked white fish (cod, hake etc.)
1 small onion
1 oz (25 g) butter

1 tablespoon of curry powder
Salt and freshly ground black pepper
1 ½ tablespoons flour
¼ pint (5 fl oz 150 ml) milk
Deep oil for frying

Peel and roughly chop the onion.
Double-bladed knife   Process the onion until finely chopped.
Melt the butter in a saucepan. Add the onion and cook over a low heat until the onion is soft and transparent. Add the curry powder and stir for a couple of minutes. Add the flour and mix well. Gradually blend in the milk stirring continually over a medium high heat until the sauce is thick and smooth.
Double-bladed knife   Combine the sauce and fish in the Magimix bowl, season with salt and pepper and process until the ingredients are mixed. Leave to cool. Roll out the pastry to about

⅛ in. (0·5 cm) thickness and cut into two rectangles. Drop small tablespoons of the fish mixture onto the pastry 1¼ in. (3 cm) apart. Brush with cold water in between the mounds of fish. Cover with the remaining pastry pressing firmly between the mounds with the fingertips and cut the pastry into squares around the fish with a pastry wheel. Make sure the edges of the pastry are firmly stuck together. Chill the squares in the refrigerator for 30 minutes.

Fry the pastry squares in very hot, deep oil and cook until they are golden and crisp – do not cook too many squares at one time. Drain on kitchen paper and serve, piled onto a napkin with wedges of lemon and some crisply fried sprigs of parsley.

Sole en Croute with Julienne of Vegetables

Such an easy starter to make yet one that looks professional enough to have come from the kitchen of a four star restaurant.

For six people

14 oz (400 g) puff pastry, thawed
3 small fillets sole with the skin
   removed
1 medium carrot
1 onion
1 stick celery

1 small green pepper
3 oz (75 g) butter
4 tablespoons of white wine
¼ pint (5 fl oz 150 ml) double cream
Salt and freshly ground black pepper
1 egg

Roll the pastry out very thinly and cut into twelve thick fingers about 6 in. × 4 in. (15 cm × 10 cm). Peel the carrot and the onion. Trim the celery. Remove the core and seeds of the green pepper.

Julienne disc   Process the vegetables through the julienne disc using a firm pressure on the pusher.

Heat the butter in a heavy frying pan, add the vegetables and cook over a medium low heat, stirring until the vegetables are soft. Add the wine and cook for a further five minutes. Stir in the cream, season with salt and pepper and mix well. Remove from the heat and leave to cool. Damp the edges of the pastry 'fingers' and place half a fish fillet in the centre of each one. Top with the vegetable mixture and cover with a second layer of pastry, press the edges of the pastry firmly together and crimp them with the back of a fork.

Double-bladed knife   Process the egg with a little salt until well beaten. Brush the pastry with the beaten egg and cook in a moderately hot oven (375°F. 190°C. Reg. 5) for about 20 minutes until the pastry is puffed and golden brown. Serve at once.

Note If you have some of the vegetable mixture left over you can process it to a rough purée and serve it separately with the Sole en Croute.

MEAT

Chilli Beefsteaks

Do not be put off by the idea of chilli. When the meat is cooked these have a delicious, but not searingly hot, flavour and the chilli has the effect of tenderizing the meat.

For four people

2 lb (900 g) topside or chuck steak cut into 4 steaks
3 tablespoons sunflower or cooking oil
1 large onion
1 tin (15 oz 425 g) tomatoes
2 small green peppers

Salt and freshly ground black pepper
1 tablespoon chilli powder
¼ teaspoon oregano
1 tablespoon tomato purée
1 tablespoon wine vinegar

Beat the steaks with a mallet to stretch and tenderize them. Rub the steaks with the chilli powder. Halve the onion.

Thin slicing disc   Slice the onion through the disc and remove.

Remove the core and seeds from the peppers, and roughly chop the flesh.

Double-bladed knife   Process the peppers until finely chopped. Add the tomatoes, season with salt and pepper, add the oregano, tomato purée and vinegar and process until the tomatoes are well chopped. Heat the oil in a frying pan, add the onion and cook over a low heat until the onion is soft and transparent. Remove the onion with a slotted spoon. Raise the heat, add the steaks and sear until browned on both sides. Remove the steaks to a shallow casserole with a slotted spoon, spread over the onion and then pour in the tomato sauce. Cover tightly and bake in a moderate oven (300°F. 150°C. Reg. 3) for 1½ hours or until the steaks are fork tender.

Tournedos Chasseur

For four people

4 thick fillet steaks	4 oz (100 g) mushrooms
4 slices white bread	1 tablespoon dry white wine
Small bunch parsley	1 tablespoon cornflour
Oil for frying	½ pint (10 fl oz 300 ml) chicken stock
1 shallot	½ teaspoon French Dijon mustard
2 oz (50 g) butter	Salt and freshly ground black pepper

Cut the bread into cubes about the same size as the steaks and fry the bread until crisp in hot oil. Drain on kitchen paper. Peel and roughly chop the shallot. Remove any tough stalks from the parsley.

Double-bladed knife Process the parsley until finely chopped and remove. Process the shallot until finely chopped and remove. Process the mushrooms until finely chopped and remove. Rub a heavy frying pan with a thin film of oil and heat until a haze rises. Add the steaks and fry until the steaks are sealed on one side. Turn over and cook for about 2 minutes. Place the steaks on top of the bread on a serving dish and keep warm. Add the butter to the juices in the pan and mix in the shallot. Cook over a medium heat, stirring until the shallot is soft. Add the mushrooms and mix well. Sprinkle over the cornflour and mix well until the flour has browned. Gradually stir in the wine and stock stirring continually over a medium high heat until the sauce comes to the boil and is thick and glossy. Add the parsley, season with salt, pepper and mustard and boil until reduced by half. Pour the sauce over the steaks and serve at once.

Hacienda Steaks

All of us who are enthusiastic cooks can do well to look towards the cooking of the third world countries for inspiration. In this dish 14 oz of chuck steak is turned into four appetising portions and is cooked in a casserole to make an easy dish with a whole meal in the one casserole – as a result there is little washing up and surely nobody could complain about that!

For four people

1 medium onion	2 sticks celery
14 oz (400 g) chuck steak	1 tin (15 oz 425 g) tomatoes
Salt and freshly ground black pepper	2 tablespoons dry Vermouth
½ teaspoon ground chilli powder	4 oz (100 g) frozen peas
1 tablespoon cooking oil	1½ lb (675 g) mashed potatoes
1 large green pepper	Cornflour

Peel and roughly chop the onion. Cut the steak into cubes. Trim the celery. Remove the seeds and core of the green pepper.

Double-bladed knife Process the onion until finely chopped. Add the meat and process until very finely chopped. Add a seasoning of pepper and the chilli powder and process to mix. On a board sprinkled with cornflour, shape the meat into four ¼ in. (0·75 cm) thick patties.

Heat the oil in a heavy pan until a haze rises from the oil, add the patties of meat and cook them over a high heat until they are well browned on both sides. Lift the patties from the pan to a casserole dish with a slotted spoon or spatula.

Chipper disc Process the green pepper and the celery through the disc, putting only a light pressure on the pusher. Drain the tomatoes and process them through the chipper disc.

Add the peppers, celery and tomatoes to the juices in the frying pan, stir well, season with salt and pepper, bring to the boil, mix in the Vermouth and pour the vegetables over the steaks, cover tightly and cook in a moderate oven (350°F. 175°C. Reg. 4) for 1 hour. Mix in the peas, cover with the potatoes and cook uncovered in a hot oven (400°F. 200°C. Reg. 6) for a further 20 minutes.

Chilli Pepper Steak

Mexico's answer to the French *steak au poivre*. If you like food with a bit of bite to it you will certainly like this way of cooking steak.

For two people

1 lb (450 g) rump or entrecôte in two steaks
1 clove garlic

2 tablespoons chilli powder
2 tablespoons wine vinegar
Butter

Peel and roughly chop the garlic.

Double-bladed knife Combine the garlic, vinegar and chilli powder in the Magimix and process until the mixture is smooth (you may need to scrape down the sides of the bowl during the processing).

Pour the mixture over the steaks and rub it into each side with the back of a wooden spoon. Leave the steaks to marinate for three hours.

Heat a heavy frying pan until very hot, rub it with a thin film of butter, add the steaks and cook over the highest possible heat, turning them once, until they are done as you like them.

Serve with baked potatoes and a salad.

Swedish Steaks

A Scandinavian form of hamburger which has added beetroot to give it both flavour and colour. I like to top these with slices of lemon, anchovy fillets and capers in the way you would an escalope of veal.

For four people	Small bunch parsley
	1¼ lb (550 g) chuck steak
	2 medium potatoes
	2 egg yolks
	4 tablespoons double cream

2 pickled beetroot
Salt and freshly ground black pepper
Pinch paprika
2 oz (50 g) butter
1 tablespoon oil

Remove any tough stalks from the parsley. Cut the meat into cubes. Roughly chop the beetroot. Peel the potatoes and cook them until tender but still firm.

Double-bladed knife Process the parsley until finely chopped. Add the meat and process until finely chopped (ground). Add the beetroot and process until finely chopped. Add the egg yolks and cream, season with salt, pepper and paprika and process until the ingredients are well mixed.

Remove all the ingredients to a bowl.

Coarse grating disc Process the cooked potatoes through the grating disc. Add the potatoes to the other ingredients and mix lightly.

Shape into four cakes about ¼ in. (0·75 cm) thick and fry in the combined oil and butter for about 4 minutes on each side. Pour over the juices in the pan.

Mexican Hamburgers

Half beef and half sausagemeat hamburgers gently cooked in a spiced tomato sauce. A dish that can be made in advance and reheated, and one which I find popular with teenagers as well as their parents.

For four to five people

1 lb (450 g) chuck steak
1 lb (450 g) belly of pork with the skin removed
Salt and freshly ground black pepper
3 tablespoons oil
1 medium onion

2 cloves garlic
1 green pepper
1 tin (15 oz 425 g) tomatoes
2 teaspoons chilli powder
Pinch ground cumin
4 tablespoons water or red wine

Cut the meat into cubes. Peel and halve the onion. Peel the garlic. Remove the core and seeds from the green pepper.

Medium slicing disc Slice the onion, garlic and pepper and remove.

Double-bladed knife Process the beef until fairly finely chopped and remove. Process the pork until fairly finely chopped and remove. If using the Grande Famille you can process the beef and pork together. Combine the beef and pork in a bowl, season with pepper and mix well. Shape into ⅓ in. (1 cm) thick hamburgers. Rub a large heavy frying pan with a thin film of oil and heat until a haze of heat rises from the pan. Add the hamburgers and cook quickly until brown and sealed on both sides. Remove the hamburgers and lower the heat.

Add the remaining oil, heat through and add the onion, garlic and pepper. Cook over a moderate heat, stirring, until the onion is soft. Pour off excess oil, add the tomatoes, chilli and cumin, season with salt. Add 4 tablespoons water or red wine, mix well, bring to the boil and simmer for 10 minutes.

Place half the hamburgers in a shallow, heat-proof casserole, pour over half the sauce; cover with the remaining hamburgers and with the remaining sauce. Cover tightly and cook in a moderately low oven (275°F. 140°C. Reg. 1) for one hour or until the meat is tender. Serve with baked potatoes and a salad.

Aubergine and Meat Pudding

Not an impressive title but a most delicious dish. I had to try this out about three times until I finally got the formula right; once I did it became a firm favourite amongst our family. When aubergines are relatively inexpensive it makes one of the best ways to use up leftover lamb or beef that I know.

For six people

3 medium aubergines	Salt and freshly ground black pepper
8 oz (225 g) cooked lamb or beef	1 teaspoon dried oregano
2 large onions	3 tablespoons oil
2 cloves garlic	2 eggs
10 oz (275 g) cooked rice	4 oz (100 g) cream cheese
1 tin (15 oz 425 g) tomatoes	4 tablespoons yoghurt
2 tablespoons tomato purée	1½ oz (40 g) Parmesan cheese

Roughly chop the lamb or beef. Peel and roughly chop the onions and garlic.

Double-bladed knife
Process the onion and garlic until fairly finely chopped.

Cut the skin off the aubergines in thin slices.

Medium slicing disc
Slice the aubergine flesh, place the slices in a colander, sprinkle with salt and leave to stand for 30 minutes. Pat dry on kitchen paper.

Heat the oil in a large frying pan. Add the aubergine skin and fry until soft. Remove with a slotted spoon. Add the sliced aubergines to the oil in the pan and fry until the slices are soft. Remove with a slotted spoon. Add the onions and garlic to the oil in the pan and cook over a medium heat until the onions are soft and transparent. Raise the heat, add the meat and cook until well browned, stirring. Add the tomatoes, tomato purée, rice and oregano and season with salt and pepper. Cook over a high heat, stirring every now and then until the mixture is fairly dry and the tomato juice has been absorbed.

Double-bladed knife
Process the eggs with the cream cheese and the yoghurt until smooth. Line a baking dish or pudding basin (I use a soufflé dish) with the aubergine skins and then with a layer of the aubergine slices. Place half the meat mixture in the lined dish, cover with the remaining aubergine slices and with half the egg and cream mixture (the meat should be pressed firmly into the dish). Finish with the remaining meat mixture and the remaining egg custard.

Parmesan disc Grate the Parmesan through the parmesan disc and sprinkle over the top. Cover tightly with foil and bake in a moderate oven (350°F. 175°C. Reg. 4) for 1¼ hours. Turn out the dish (you may have to loosen it around the sides but it should turn out easily enough) onto a circular platter and serve with green vegetables.

Note I have also served this dish cold and it is very successful indeed. A home made tomato sauce (see page 259) can be served with the pudding.

Bobotie

An extremely good South African dish which makes excellent use of minced beef. It is similar to a moussaka but with a more exciting flavour.

For six people

1 lb (450 g) chuck steak or lean lamb	1 tablespoon curry powder
1 slice white bread, crusts removed	2 tablespoons peach chutney
½ pint (10 fl oz 300 ml) milk	1 tablespoon blanched almonds
2 onions	2 tablespoons raisins
1 cooking apple	1 tablespoon vinegar
1 aubergine	Salt and freshly ground black pepper
2 firm ripe tomatoes	2 eggs
½ oz (13 g) butter	Ground nutmeg
1½ tablespoons oil	4 bay leaves

Soak the bread in the milk. Cube the meat. Peel and roughly chop the onions. Peel, core and roughly chop the apple.

Double-bladed knife Process the almonds until finely chopped and remove. Process the meat until fairly finely ground and remove. Process the onion and apple together until fairly finely chopped and remove.

Chipper disc Process the aubergine and tomatoes.

Heat the butter with the oil in a large heavy frying pan. Add the onion, apple, aubergine and tomatoes and cook over a medium heat, stirring, until the onion and aubergine are soft. Raise the heat, add the meat and stir until the meat has browned. Add the curry powder and mix well. Mix in the chutney, almonds, raisins and vinegar and season with salt and pepper. Squeeze the milk from the bread and add the bread to the meat mixture stirring with a fork to mix in the bread. Spread the meat mixture in a buttered baking dish.

Double-bladed knife Combine the eggs with the milk in the Magimix bowl and season with salt, pepper and a little ground nutmeg. Process to mix well. Pour the custard over the meat, top with the bay leaves and bake in a moderate oven (350°F. 175°C. Reg. 4) for 40 minutes.

Savoury Meat Loaf wrapped in Pancakes

Another variation on the meat loaf theme but this time wrapped in pancakes which go satisfyingly crisp and keep the flavour of the loaf in the confines of its wrappings. Serve it with the sharp onion sauce below.

For four to six people

12 oz (350 g) chuck steak
Small bunch parsley
2 slices white bread with the crusts removed
1 small onion
1 clove garlic
2 eggs
Salt and freshly ground black pepper
Pinch ground nutmeg and ground mace
Pinch dried herbs
4 pancakes (see page 245)

1 oz (25 g) butter

For the sauce
½ small onion
1 clove garlic
1 fl oz (30 ml) white wine vinegar
½ pint (300 ml) water
1 teaspoon sugar
2 cartons (½ pint: 10 fl oz 300 ml) sour cream
Salt, pepper and a pinch of paprika

Cut the meat into cubes. Peel and roughly chop the garlic and onion. Remove the stalks from the parsley.

Double-bladed knife

Process the parsley until finely chopped and remove. Process the bread until reduced to fine crumbs and remove. Process the onion and garlic until finely chopped, add the beef and continue to process until the beef is finely chopped. Add the bread, parsley and eggs, season with salt and pepper and a little mace and nutmeg, add the herbs and process until the ingredients are well mixed.

Line a buttered loaf tin with four pancakes leaving the top of the pancakes to hang out over the edge of the tin. Fill with the meat mixture pressing it down firmly, and fold over the tops of the pancakes. Dot with butter, cover with foil and bake in a moderately hot oven (375°F. 190°C. Reg. 5) for 1¼ hours. Turn upside down on to a serving dish and keep warm while making the sauce. To make the sauce:— Peel and roughly chop the onion and garlic.

Double-bladed knife

Process the onion and garlic until finely chopped. Combine the onion, garlic, vinegar, water and sugar in a small saucepan, bring to the boil and cook over a high heat until the liquid is reduced by two thirds and the onion is thoroughly soft. Add the sour cream, season with salt, pepper and paprika and stir over a low heat until the sauce is hot through and thick. Pour the sauce over the loaf before serving.

Stacked Pancakes with Meat and Yoghurt Sauce

For eight people

8 pancakes (see page 245)
1 lb (450 g) chuck steak
Small bunch parsley
2 rashers streaky bacon with the rinds removed
1 large onion
1 clove garlic
1 stick celery
2 tablespoons oil
2 teaspoons flour

½ pint (10 fl oz 300 ml) good stock
4 tablespoons red wine
1 tablespoon tomato purée
Pinch dried oregano
Salt and freshly ground black pepper
½ oz (13 g) Parmesan cheese
1 oz (25 g) Cheddar cheese
½ carton (2½ fl oz 75 ml) natural yoghurt
½ carton (2½ fl oz 75 ml) sour cream
Pinch cayenne

Cut the meat into cubes. Remove the tough stalks from the parsley. Peel and roughly chop the onion and garlic. Roughly chop the celery.

Double-bladed knife
Process the parsley until finely chopped and remove. Process the meat and bacon until finely chopped and remove. Process the onion, garlic and celery until finely chopped and remove.

Heat ¼ teaspoon salt in a heavy frying pan, add the oil and when very hot add the meat and bacon and cook over a high heat until the meat is browned. Remove the meat with a slotted spoon and add the onion, garlic and celery to the juices in the pan. Cook over a medium low heat, stirring, until the onion is soft. Add the meat, stir in the flour and mix well. Gradually blend in the stock, tomato purée, wine and oregano, season with pepper and simmer for 20 minutes or until the meat is tender. Add the parsley and check the seasoning.

Parmesan disc
Process the Parmesan cheese.

Fine grating disc
Grate the Cheddar cheese.

Double-bladed knife
Combine the cheeses, yoghurt and sour cream, season lightly with salt and a pinch of cayenne and process to mix well. Spread the pancakes with the meat sauce and stack them neatly.

Spoon over the cheese sauce and bake in a hot oven (400°F. 200°C. Reg. 6) for about 10 minutes until the cheese sauce is bubbling and golden brown.

Beef Loaf

A relatively inexpensive dish which makes a good summer lunch dish.

For four people

2 oz (50 g) brown bread without crusts
1 lb (450 g) chuck steak
1 small onion
1 egg
Salt and freshly ground black pepper

Pinch mixed herbs
Few drops Tabasco and Worcestershire sauce
4 fl oz (120 ml) stock (or water and stock cubes)

Double-bladed knife

Cut the meat into cubes. Peel and roughly chop the onion.
Process the bread until reduced to crumbs. Add the onion and process until the onion is finely chopped. Add the beef and process until the meat is fairly finely ground. Add the egg, herbs, Tabasco and Worcestershire sauces, seasoning and stock and process for just long enough to mix the ingredients. Turn into an oiled 1 lb loaf tin, cover tightly with two thicknesses of foil and bake in a moderately hot oven (400°F. 200°C. Reg. 6) for 1¼ hours. Leave to cool and then refrigerate until well chilled. Turn out and serve in slices with jacket potatoes and a salad.

Chilli Con Carne

This is, in fact, a dish invented by the Americans and not the Mexicans, but it has become so identified as 'hot Mexican' that you are sure to find it on the menu of any Mexican restaurant. Chilli con Carne can be as hot or as mild as you care to make it and should be served with sliced avocados on the side and 'tortillas' (see page 233). I also accompany the chilli with a crisp green salad.

For four people

1 lb (450 g) chuck steak
¾ teaspoon salt
1 large onion
2 cloves garlic
1 tin (15 oz 425 g) tomatoes
1 large tin (1 lb 11 oz 750 g) red kidney beans

1½ teaspoons chilli powder
1 tablespoon tomato purée
1 teaspoon dried oregano
½ teaspoon dried cumin
1 bunch fresh coriander (this can be bought from better greengrocers or Indian grocery shops in the summer)

Double-bladed knife

Roughly cut up the meat. Peel and roughly chop the onion and garlic.
Process the meat until fairly finely ground and remove. Process the onion and garlic until fairly finely chopped and remove.
Heat the salt in a large heavy frying pan over a moderately high heat. Add the meat and cook, stirring without extra fat until browned. Add the onion and garlic and cook over a moderate heat until the onion is soft. Mix in the tomatoes with a fork to break them up, add the kidney beans and the liquid from the tin, the chilli powder, tomato purée, oregano and cumin. Simmer, uncovered stirring every now and then for about 30 minutes or until the meat is really tender.

Double-bladed knife and a clean dry bowl

Remove the coarse stems from the coriander and process the leaves until they are coarsely chopped. Sprinkle the coriander over the chilli just before serving.

Sailor's Stew

A good basic beef stew made with well flavoured shin beef, onions and potatoes layered and ending up as a good savoury hearty dish.

For six to eight people

1 small bunch parsley
2 lb (900 g) shin beef
2½ oz (65 g) butter
1 tablespoon oil
Salt and freshly ground black pepper

3 medium onions
1½ lb (675 g) potatoes
¼ pint (5 fl oz 150 ml) beef stock
¾ pint (15 fl oz 450 ml) dark ale

Remove any tough stalks from the parsley. Cut the shin beef into ¼ in. (0·6 cm) thick slices and beat them well to tenderize the meat. Peel the onions. Peel the potatoes.

Double-bladed knife

Process the parsley until finely chopped, and remove.

Medium slicing disc

Slice the onions and remove.

Slice the potatoes and keep in a bowl of cold water. Heat 1½ oz (40 g) butter with the oil in a large, heavy, frying pan. Add the meat and cook over a high heat until browned on both sides. Add the onions and continue to cook, stirring, until the onions are soft and transparent. Add the parsley, stock and beer to the meat and onions and season with salt and pepper.

Using kitchen paper pat the potatoes dry and arrange half of them in a well buttered baking dish, cover with the meat and onions and top with the remaining potatoes.Season with a little more salt and pepper, dot with the remaining butter. Cover tightly with foil and bake in a moderate oven (350°F. 175°C. Reg. 4) for 1½ hours. Remove the cover and continue to cook for a further 30 minutes until the potatoes are brown and the meat is tender.

Beef Tokany

A rich beef stew with onions, mushrooms and peppers flavoured with sour cream and paprika both of which also have the attributes of tenderizing the meat.

For six people

2 lb (900 g) chuck steak
2 onions
4 oz (100 g) firm button mushrooms
1 green pepper
Salt

1 teaspoon paprika pepper
2 oz (50 g) butter
Small bunch parsley
1 carton ¼ pint (5 fl oz 150 ml) sour
    cream

Cut the meat into very thin slices and then into very thin strips. Peel and roughly chop the onions. Remove the core and seeds from the pepper.

Double-bladed   Process the onions until fairly finely chopped and remove.
knife
Medium slicing   Slice the green pepper and mushrooms.
disc   Heat the butter in a heavy frying pan. When the butter is foaming, add the meat and
brown over a high heat on all sides. Add the onion and cook over a medium heat,
stirring, until the onion is soft. Add the pepper and mushrooms, season with salt
and paprika and stir over a medium heat for two minutes. Transfer to a casserole,
cover tightly with foil and cook in a moderate oven (350°F. 175°C. Reg. 4) for 1½
hours or until the meat is fork tender.
Double-bladed   Remove any tough stems from the parsley and process until finely chopped. Add
knife and a clean   the sour cream and process until smooth and light. Pour the cream and parsley over
dry bowl   the meat and vegetables, mix well, check seasoning and turn onto a heated serving
dish.

Chinese Stir Fried Beef with Vegetables

The beef should be crisp and almost crunchy and the vegetables still very crisp
when this dish is served. Accompany it with rice and have all the ingredients ready
when you start cooking.

For four people   1 lb (450 g) rump steak   1 piece root ginger about ¾ inches
1 small egg   (2 cm) long
1 teaspoon cornflour   1 tablespoon soy sauce
1 stalk celery   ½ teaspoon brown sugar
1 carrot   2 tablespoons chicken stock
2 inches (5 cm) cucumber   ¾ pint (15 fl oz 450 ml) sunflower or
1 small red dried chilli pepper   ground nut oil
2 cloves garlic   Salt

Cut the meat against the grain into very thin slices and then into matchstick strips.
Trim the celery and cut it to fit the feed tube lengthwise. Peel the carrot and cut it to
fit the feed tube lengthwise. Peel the cucumber and cut it to fit the feed tube
lengthwise. Remove the seeds from the red pepper (wash your hands after you have
done this as the seeds are fiery hot). Peel and roughly chop the garlic and ginger.
Mix together the soy sauce, sugar, salt and chicken stock.
Julienne disc   Process the celery, carrot and cucumber through the julienne disc and remove.
Double-bladed   Process the garlic, ginger and pepper until very finely chopped and remove.
knife   Process the egg with the cornflour.
Combine the beef strips with the egg and cornflour mixture in a shallow plate and
mix until the meat is coated with the egg and cornflour mixture. Heat the oil in a
wok or large, heavy frying pan until a haze rises from the oil. Add a quarter of the
beef strips and cook them over the highest possible heat until the meat is tender and
slightly crisp on the outside. Remove the meat with a slotted spoon and drain on
kitchen paper. Fry the rest of the meat in batches.

Pour off all but 1 tablespoon of the oil in the pan. Add the garlic, ginger root and chilli and stir over a high heat for 1 minute. Add the vegetables and stir over a high heat for two minutes. (It is important to stir the ingredients all the time). Add the meat to the ingredients, pour over the soy sauce mixture and stir for a further minute to mix the ingredients.
Serve at once.

Lamb Cutlets en Chemise

Savoury lamb cutlets baked with a stuffing inside a puff pastry case. Buy some paper frills from a stationery shop to decorate the ends of the cutlets.

For four people

8 small lamb cutlets chined
Oil
1 small bunch mint
2 oz (50 g) mushrooms
4 oz (100 g) sausage meat
2 oz (50 g) ham

Salt and freshly ground black pepper
1 tablespoon tomato purée
1 packet (14 oz 400 g) frozen puff
  pastry, defrosted
1 beaten egg

Double-bladed knife

Remove any tough stalks from the mint. Roughly chop the ham. Process the mint until finely chopped. Add the ham and mushrooms and process until they are fairly finely chopped. Add the sausage meat and tomato purée, season with salt and freshly ground black pepper and process to mix the ingredients. Trim off any excess fat from the cutlets. Heat a thin film of oil in a heavy frying pan until a heat haze rises from the pan, add the cutlets and cook them over a high heat for just long enough to brown them on both sides. Remove the cutlets and leave to cool on a rack. Roll out the pastry to about ⅛th inch (0·5 cm) thickness and cut into eight triangles large enough to encase the meaty part of the cutlets. Place a cutlet on each triangle, top with some of the stuffing and fold over the pastry. Dampen the edges, crimp them together (cut off any excess pastry if necessary) and brush with beaten egg.
Bake in a hot oven (400°F. 200°C. Reg. 6) for about 20 minutes until the pastry is puffed and golden brown.

Lamb and Mint Pies

Deliciously savoury individual pies filled with lamb which can be served hot or cold for picnics or outdoor eating. I use the knuckle end of the lamb as it seems to have more flavour.

For six people	Hot water crusty pastry
	(see page 243)
	1½ lb (675 g) leg of lamb off the bone
	1 large onion
	2 cloves garlic
	1 tablespoon lard
	½ teaspoon oregano

Salt and freshly ground black pepper
Pinch mixed spice and ground nutmeg
¼ pint (5 fl oz 150 ml) good strong
  stock or gravy
1 tablespoon tomato purée
1 tablespoon finely chopped mint
1 egg

Cut the meat into cubes. Peel and roughly chop the onion and garlic.

Double-bladed knife Process the onion and garlic until finely chopped. Heat the lard in a saucepan, add the onion and garlic and cook over a medium heat until the onion is soft. Process the meat until finely chopped (ground). Raise the heat to high and when the onions begin to brown stir in the meat and brown quickly. Add the oregano, mixed spice and nutmeg, season with salt and pepper and mix in the stock or gravy, tomato purée and mint. Simmer for 15 minutes.

Reserve one third of the pastry and roll the rest out to about ¼ in. (0·75 cm) thickness. Line six oiled muffin or patty tins with the pastry, fill with the meat and then roll out the remaining pastry to make lids. Damp the edges of the pastry with water and press them firmly together (it is important that the pies are well sealed).

Double-bladed knife Process the egg with a little salt until smooth. Brush the top of the pies with the egg wash, cut a slit in the centre of each pie to allow the air to escape during the cooking time and bake in a hot oven (400°F. 200°C. Reg. 6) for 20 minutes until the pastry is beginning to brown. Lower the heat to moderate (350°F. 175°C. Reg. 4) and continue to bake for a further 25 minutes until the pastry is golden brown. Serve the pies hot or cold.

Marinated Leg of Lamb   Illustrated on page 64

Lamb, especially if it is imported, can be a slightly insipid dish. Marinate your leg of lamb in this way and the results will not only be deliciously tender but also very tasty.

For six people	1 leg of lamb
	2 cloves garlic
	1 piece fresh root ginger about 1 inch
	(2·5 cm) long
	Salt and freshly ground black pepper

1 tablespoon Provençal herbs
2 tablespoons olive or sunflower oil
1 teaspoon French Dijon mustard
2 tablespoons tomato ketchup
Grated rind and juice of 1 orange

Peel and roughly chop the garlic and root ginger.

Double-bladed knife Process the garlic and ginger until very finely chopped scraping down the sides of the bowl if necessary. Add the remaining ingredients and process until well mixed and smooth. Spread the mixture all over the lamb, cover the dish with cling film and refrigerate (basting every now and then with the marinade) for two days.

Place on a spit and barbecue the lamb or roast the lamb in a pre-heated hot oven (425°F. 225°C. Reg. 7) for 10 minutes then lower the heat to moderate (350°F. 175°C. Reg. 4) and continue to roast for a further 1¼ hours basting every now and then.
Note If you like your lamb well cooked add a quarter of an hour on to the cooking time.

If cooked in the oven serve this gravy with the meat.

1 small onion or shallot
2 tablespoons flour
1 tablespoon tomato purée

2 tablespoons red wine
Scant ½ pint (10 fl oz 300 ml) stock

Peel and roughly chop the onion.
Double-bladed knife Process the onion until finely chopped. Remove the meat onto a warm serving dish and keep warm. Remove the surface grease from the juices in the pan.
Place the roasting pan with the juices over a low heat. Add the onion and stir until the onion has softened. Add the flour and mix well until the flour turns a nutty brown. Add tomato purée and the wine, then gradually blend in the stock stirring continually over a medium high heat until the sauce comes to the boil and is thick and smooth. Strain and serve with the meat.

Mexican Leg of Lamb

In Mexico this method of cooking a leg of lamb is called "barbecued" but in fact it is braised in the oven. The flavour when the meat is cooked has surprising overtones and while the dish is to be highly recommended when it is served hot, it is also delicious cold – something you don't always find when a leg of lamb is served the day after it has been roasted. Next time you decide to cook a leg of lamb try this recipe it really is great!

For eight people
1 leg lamb
3 rashers streaky bacon
3 cloves garlic
2 large green and 1 large red pepper
Salt and freshly ground black pepper

2 teaspoons chilli powder
¼ teaspoon each ground cloves, cumin, cinnamon, oregano and thyme
2 bay leaves

Peel and roughly chop the garlic.
Parboil the peppers in boiling, salted water for 20 minutes, drain well and leave to cool.
Double-bladed knife Combine the bacon and garlic and process until the mixture is reduced to a paste. Using a sharp pointed knife make nicks all over the lamb to about ⅓ in. (1 cm) depth. Stuff the nicks with the bacon mixture. Remove the cores and seeds from the cooled peppers.

Double-bladed knife   Combine the peppers, herbs and spices in the Magimix bowl and season with salt and pepper. Process until reduced to a paste.

Lay the meat on a clean damp tea towel. Spread it all over with the spiced paste and make a neat parcel with the cloth. Wrap the lamb in a second damp cloth. Place it in a heavy casserole with a tight fitting lid (or cover with a double layer of foil), and cook in a moderately low oven (275°F. 140°C. Reg. 1) for 3 hours. Unwrap, cut into thin slices and serve with avocados steeped in lemon juice and a salsa verde (see page 258).

Leg of Lamb Steaks with Carrots and Onions

For six to eight people

Small boned leg of lamb (about 3½ lb 1·5 kg)
1 tablespoon flour
A pinch of salt, ground black pepper, cayenne and paprika
3 tablespoons sunflower oil
2 lb (900 g) carrots
1½ lb (675 g) onions

2 cloves garlic
1 small tin (8 oz 225 g) tomatoes
1 teaspoon mixed herbs
¼ pint (5 fl oz 150 ml) dry white wine
6 bay leaves
1½ tablespoons flour
4 tablespoons stabilized yoghurt (see page 15)

Cut the lamb into ½ in. (1·25 cm) thick slices across the leg. Place the slices between two sheets of greaseproof paper and beat them with a mallet to tenderize and stretch the meat. Lightly coat the slices with flour, salt, pepper, cayenne and paprika.

Peel and halve the onions. Peel the carrots and garlic.

Medium slicing disc   Slice the carrots and remove. Slice the onions.

Double-bladed knife   Process the garlic until finely chopped. Add the tomatoes and process until smooth. Add the mixed herbs and the wine and process until well mixed.

Heat the oil in a large heavy frying pan. Add the meat steaks and brown over a high heat on both sides. Remove the slices from the pan with a slotted spoon to remove excess oil.

Arrange half the onions in a lightly oiled baking dish. Cover with the carrots, season with salt and pepper, lay the meat on top and top with the remaining onions and carrots. Pour over the tomato sauce, top with the bay leaves, cover tightly with foil and bake in a moderately low oven (300°F. 150°C. Reg. 2) for three hours. Remove the bay leaves and strain off the juices.

Double-bladed knife   Combine the flour with ¼ pint (5 fl oz 150 ml) of the strained liquid and 4 tablespoons stabilized yoghurt (see page 15) and process until smooth. Pour into a small saucepan, add the remaining liquid and stir over a moderately high heat until the sauce comes to the boil and is thick and smooth, check seasoning and pour the sauce over the meat and garnish with finely chopped parsley or celery leaves before serving.

Lancashire Hot Pot

For four people

2 lb (900 g) middle neck lamb chops
2 large potatoes
3 onions
2 carrots

Salt and freshly ground black pepper
Pinch mixed herbs
¼ pint (5 fl oz 150 ml) beef stock
2 oz (50 g) butter

Trim most of the fat from the chops. Peel the onions, carrots and potatoes and cut the potatoes to fit the feed tube.

Medium or thick slicing disc

Slice the onions and remove. Slice the carrots and remove.
Slice the potatoes, and remove.

Place a layer of potatoes in the bottom of a well buttered fireproof casserole. Layer the chops, onions and carrots in the dish seasoning the layers with salt and sprinkling them with herbs. Finish with a neat, overlapping, layer of the potatoes and pour over the stock.

Melt the butter, pour it over the potatoes and bake, uncovered, in a medium oven (350°F. 175°C. Reg. 4) for one hour or until the potatoes are golden brown and the chops are tender.

Stuffed Best End of Lamb

For six to eight people

3 lb (1·3 kg) best end of lamb (ask your butcher to bone the lamb)
4 lb (1·8 kg) fat belly of pork with the rind removed
Small bunch parsley
3 slices white bread with the crusts removed
2 oz (50 g) chopped suet

Pinch mixed herbs
Salt and freshly ground black pepper
1 oz (25 g) dripping or lard
1 tablespoon apple purée
1 tablespoon chestnut purée } if available

Cut the pork into cubes. Remove the stalks from the parsley.

Double-bladed knife

Process the parsley until finely chopped. Process the bread until reduced to fairly fine crumbs and remove. Process the pork until very finely chopped (ground), add the parsley, bread, suet, herbs, apple purée and chestnut purée, season with salt and pepper and process to mix well.

Spread out the lamb with the cut side up and spread the stuffing over the meat, roll it up loosely to allow the stuffing to expand and tie in a roll. Season the outside of the joint with salt and pepper. Heat the dripping in a hot oven (425°F. 220°C. Reg. 7), add the meat and cook for 25 minutes to the pound and 25 minutes over.

Serve with gravy made from the juices in the pan and redcurrant and mint jelly.

Stuffed Breast of Lamb

For six people

2 boned breasts of lamb
1 slice white bread with crusts removed
Small bunch parsley
1 onion
1 clove garlic
1 stick celery
2 oz (50 g) ham
4 oz (100 g) sausage meat
½ teaspoon grated orange rind

Juice of an orange
1 small egg
Salt and freshly ground black pepper
2 tablespoons medium dry sherry
2 tablespoons sunflower oil
2 teaspoons flour
1 tablespoon redcurrant jelly
¼ pint (5 fl oz 150 ml) stock
2 tablespoons yoghurt or sour cream

Peel and roughly chop the onion and garlic. Roughly chop the celery. Roughly chop the ham.

Double-bladed knife

Process the bread until reduced to fine crumbs and remove. Process the parsley until finely chopped. Add the celery, onion and garlic and process until the onion is fairly finely chopped. Add the bread, sausage meat, ham, orange rind, juice of ½ orange and the egg, season with salt and freshly ground black pepper and process to mix well.

Place one of the breasts of lamb skin side down on a board and spread with the stuffing. Top with the second breast of lamb skin side up.

Heat the oil in a roasting tin in a hot oven (400°F. 200°C. Reg. 6). Place the lamb carefully in the hot oil, pour over the sherry and return to a hot oven. Cook for about 1½ hours, basting every 30 minutes and covering the meat with foil if it browns too much on the top (remove the foil for the last ten minutes of cooking time). Carefully remove the cooked meat onto a serving dish and keep warm.

Transfer the roasting tin with the juices to the top of the stove and stir in the flour over a medium heat, stirring until the flour has browned. Stir in the stock, remaining orange juice and redcurrant jelly and stir until the gravy comes to the boil and is thick and smooth. Season with salt and pepper if necessary and strain through a fine sieve. Put into a small saucepan, whisk in the yoghurt or sour cream and heat through.

Carve the breast into thin fingers and serve the gravy separately. The joint can be garnished with bunches of watercress and halves of grilled tomatoes.

Keema with Spinach

Keema is one of the classic, simple, Indian curry dishes that comes in many forms and a wide variety of flavourings. In this version it is combined with spinach rather than the more traditional peas making a delicious dish to serve with rice and perhaps another curry dish.

For four people

1 lb (450 g) boned shoulder lamb
1 lb (450 g) spinach
4 medium ripe tomatoes
2 medium onions
3 tablespoons sunflower oil
3 green chilli peppers (or use 1 dried red
   chilli pepper)
4 cloves garlic
4 cloves

¾ in. (2 cm) piece fresh root ginger
1–2 in. stick cinnamon
½ teaspoon ground turmeric
1 teaspoon ground coriander
1 teaspoon Madras curry powder
Small bunch parsley or fresh coriander
Salt and freshly ground black pepper
1 teaspoon Garam Masala

Cut the lamb into cubes. Wash the spinach and cook it in a little boiling salted water for 5 minutes until just tender and drain well. Cover the tomatoes with boiling water, leave them to stand for 3 minutes and then drain the tomatoes and slide off the skins. Discard the tough core and seeds of the tomatoes. Peel and roughly chop the onions. Remove the seeds from the chillis (be careful to wash your hands after this as the seeds are searing hot). Peel and roughly chop the garlic and ginger.

Double-bladed knife
Process the coriander or parsley until finely chopped and remove. Process the onions until finely chopped and remove. Process the chillis, garlic and ginger until finely chopped and remove. Process the tomatoes until fairly finely chopped and remove. Process the meat until fairly finely chopped (ground).

Heat the oil in a large, heavy frying pan. Add the onions, cinnamon and cloves and cook over a moderate heat stirring for four minutes. Add the garlic, ginger, chilli, turmeric, coriander and curry powder and cook for three minutes. Raise the heat, add the meat and cook over a high heat, stirring until the meat is well browned. Lower the heat and cook, stirring for five minutes. Add the tomatoes, bring to the boil and simmer for 20 minutes or until the meat is tender. The mixture should be fairly dry – if it begins to stick stir in a little water.

Double-bladed knife
Process the spinach until coarsely chopped.
Add the spinach to the meat, season with salt and pepper and cook for five minutes. Stir in the Garam Masala and the coriander or parsley and serve the dish with rice.

Minced Lamb Kebabs

These kebabs make a perfect main dish for a barbecue and benefit from being prepared in advance. Cook them over a high heat so that the outside of the meat is dark and crusty while the inside is still slightly pink.

For four people

1 lb (450 g) lean lamb
4 fl oz (120 ml) yoghurt
1 tablespoon porridge oats
¾ in. (2 cm) fresh root ginger
2 cloves garlic
Salt and freshly ground black pepper

½ teaspoon ground cumin, coriander
   and cardamon
Pinch ground cloves
1 medium onion
Wedges of lemon or lime

Double-bladed knife

Cut the meat into cubes. Cook the oats in a dry frying pan over a high heat until they are lightly browned. Peel and roughly chop the root ginger and garlic. Peel the onion.

Process the garlic and ginger until finely chopped. Add the meat and process until the meat is very finely chopped and almost reduced to a paste. Season with salt and pepper and add the oats, spices and yoghurt. Process into a smooth paste.

Using damp hands work the meat around barbeque skewers into sausage shapes about ½ in. (1·25 cm) thick, roll them on an oiled surface to consolidate and smooth the meat. Brush the kebabs with oil and cook under a high grill or over a barbecue until the surface is dark and crusty and the inside is tender but still slightly pink.

Fine slicing disc

Slice the onion and serve the kebabs garnished with thinly sliced onion and lemon or lime wedges.

Cooked Lamb Cakes

An alternative to shepherd's pie to use up your leftover lamb. Serve the cakes with a home-made tomato sauce (see page 259) or with the sauce below.

For four people

12 oz (350 g) cooked lamb
1 onion
1 small clove garlic
1 tablespoon tomato purée
1 egg

Cornflour
Salt and freshly ground black pepper
2 fl oz (60 ml) good stock
Oil for frying

Double-bladed knife

Peel and roughly chop the onion. Peel and chop the garlic. Cut the meat into cubes. Process the onion and garlic until finely chopped. Add the meat and process until the meat is finely chopped. Add the egg, tomato purée and stock, season with salt and pepper and process until well mixed.

Shape into four flat cakes on a board sprinkled with cornflour. Fry the cakes in ⅛ in. (0·5 cm) oil until crisp and golden brown and cooked through (about 5 minutes on each side). Remove the cakes onto a warm serving dish with a slotted spoon.

For the sauce
½ oz (13 g) butter
1 clove garlic, crushed
1 teaspoon dried rosemary

1 teaspoon lemon juice
1 oz (25 g) cornflour
½ pint (10 fl oz 300 ml) chicken stock
3 tablespoons soured (or double) cream

Add the butter and garlic to the juices in the pan and mix well. Mix in the rosemary, lemon juice, and cornflour, gradually blend in the stock, stirring continually over a medium heat until the sauce comes to the boil and is thick and smooth. Season with salt and pepper, lower the heat and whisk in the sour cream or double cream. Heat the sauce through without boiling.

Pancakes with Meat and Spinach Filling

Make small pancakes for this dish and serve it as a first course before a light main course or as a summer lunch or supper dish, with salad.

For four people

12 small pancakes. (see 'savoury pancakes' page 245)
4 oz (100 g) cooked beef or lamb
2 oz (50 g) cooked ham
1 small onion
2 tablespoons oil
1 lb (225 g) spinach

½ oz (13 g) butter
2 egg yolks
Salt, freshly ground black pepper and a pinch of nutmeg
½ pint (10 fl oz 300 ml) tomato sauce (see page 259)
2 oz (50 g) Parmesan cheese

Peel and roughly chop the onion. Roughly chop the meat and ham. Wash the spinach and cook it in ½ in. (1·25 cm) boiling salted water for about 5 minutes until just tender and drain well.

Double-bladed knife Process the onion until finely chopped and remove. Process the meat and ham together until finely chopped and remove. Heat the oil in the frying pan, add the onion and cook over a medium heat until the onion is soft and transparent. Raise the heat, add the meat and cook over a high heat until the meat is browned on all sides. Add 2 tablespoons of the tomato sauce, season with pepper and simmer for 20 minutes until the meat is really tender.

Double-bladed knife Process the spinach until roughly chopped. Season with salt and nutmeg add the butter, meat and egg yolks and process until the ingredients are well mixed. Spread the filling in the pancakes, roll them up neatly and arrange them in a buttered baking dish. Spread over the remaining tomato sauce.

Parmesan cheese grating disc Process the Parmesan cheese.
Sprinkle the Parmesan over the tomato sauce and bake in a hot oven (425°F. 220°C. Reg. 7) until the pancakes are hot through and the top is golden brown.

Pork Chops Sebastian

An aromatic and mouthwatering combination of pork chops flavoured with rosemary and cooked with a sauce of onions, carrots and celery in consommé. The pork chops are flamed with Calvados and the sauce is sharpened with yoghurt and a final finish is given by an apple sauce lightly flavoured with Calvados.

For four people

4 pork chops
1 medium onion
3 stalks celery
3 medium carrots
1½ tablespoons sunflower oil
1 tin consommé

1 teaspoon rosemary
¼ pint (5 fl oz 150 ml) yoghurt
Salt and freshly ground black pepper
3 tablespoons Calvados
3 medium cooking apples
1½ oz (40 g) butter

Thin slicing disc Peel and halve the onion. Trim the celery. Peel the carrots.
Slice the onion and remove. Slice the celery.

Julienne disc Cut the carrots to fit the feed tube lengthwise and process them through the julienne disc.

Combine the carrots and celery and consommé, bring to the boil and cook over a high heat, without covering for ten minutes. Heat the oil in a large, heavy frying pan. Add the onion and stir over a medium heat until the onion is soft. Remove the onion with a slotted spoon, raise the heat, add the rosemary and brown the pork chops quickly on both sides. Add 2 tablespoons Calvados, set alight to the Calvados and shake the pan gently until the flames die down. Spread the onion over the chops and spoon over the carrots, celery and reduced consommé. Cover the pan and simmer gently for 20 minutes or until the chops are tender and cooked through. Add the yoghurt and season with salt and pepper. Peel, core and roughly chop the apples and cook them with two tablespoons water until they are tender.

Double-bladed knife Combine the apples, butter and remaining Calvados and process until smooth. Transfer the chops to a heated serving dish, pile on the vegetables, top with the apple sauce and serve with potatoes and a green vegetable.

Paprika Pork Chops with Cabbage

A dish with Hungarian origins which is both subtle and satisfying.

For four people

4 pork chops	8 tablespoons dry cider
1 large onion	Salt
1 oz (25 g) lard	1 teaspoon paprika pepper
2 oz (50 g) firm button mushrooms	1 carton (5 fl oz 150 ml) sour cream
1 small Savoy cabbage	Chopped parsley

Peel and roughly chop the onion.

Double-bladed knife Process the onion until fairly finely chopped and remove.

Medium or thick slicing disc Slice the mushrooms and remove.
Slice the cabbage.

Heat the lard in a frying pan. Add the onion and cook over a medium high heat until the onion is soft. Remove the onion to a casserole with a slotted spoon, raise the heat and fry the pork chops over a high heat until browned on both sides. Place the pork chops on top of the onion. Stir the cider into the juices in the pan and season the liquid with salt and paprika. Pour the juices over the chops, cover the dish tightly with foil and cook in a moderately hot oven (350°F. 175°C. Reg. 4) for 45 minutes or until the chops are tender.

Cook the shredded cabbage in a little boiling, salted, water for six minutes, add the mushrooms and cook for a further two minutes or until the cabbage is just tender. Drain well, add the sour cream and season with salt and pepper. Arrange the cabbage and mushrooms in a serving dish, top with the onions and chops and pour over the liquid from the casserole. Sprinkle with chopped parsley just before serving.

Roast Stuffed Belly of Pork

Boned belly of pork stuffed with an aromatic mixture of prunes and apples. I like this joint just as much cold as hot.

For six people

4 lb (1·8 kg) boned belly of pork
8 oz (225 g) prunes
2 slices white bread with the crusts removed
1 small onion
¼ teaspoon dried sage
Pinch mixed spice

Salt and freshly ground black pepper
1 small cooking apple
1 oz (25 g) flour
½ pint (10 fl oz 300 ml) chicken stock
¼ teaspoon sage
2 tablespoons redcurrant jelly

Soak the prunes in tea overnight, drain and remove stones. Trim off 4 oz (100 g) of the pork with the skin removed. Roughly cut up this meat. Peel and roughly chop the onion. Peel, core and quarter the apple.

Double-bladed knife

Process the bread until reduced to fine breadcrumbs and remove.

Thin or medium slicing disc

Slice the apple and remove.

Double-bladed knife

Process the onion until finely chopped.

Add the roughly chopped pork and process until it is finely chopped (ground). Add the bread and sage, season with salt, and pepper and add the mixed spice and prunes and process until the prunes are finely chopped and the ingredients are well mixed. Spread the prune mixture over the cut side of the belly and top with the sliced apple. Roll up lightly and tie loosely with a piece of string. Place the joint, seam side down, on a rack in a roasting tin. Roast in a moderate oven (350°F. 175°C. Reg. 4) for 30 minutes then pour over the stock and continue to roast for 1¼ hours, basting occasionally, or until the meat is cooked. Remove the meat onto a serving dish. Remove excess fat from the gravy, add the flour, redcurrant jelly and sage to the juices in the pan and stir over a high heat on the top of the stove until the gravy is thick.
Strain the gravy through a fine sieve.

Mexican Estofade

A marvellously ethnic dish, rich, aromatic and nourishing. A perfect rich main course to follow a light and sophisticated starter. This dish has its origins in Spain but its final finesse comes from a mixing of half a dozen civilizations and cuisines. Serve with rice and with a good green or mixed salad. The stew should be dry, not slumpy, when it is finished.

For eight people

3 lb (1·3 kg) lean pork
3 tablespoons sunflower or cooking oil
3 large onions
3 cloves garlic
3 teaspoons chilli powder
3 bay leaves

1 teaspoon salt
1 teaspoon mild curry powder
1 teaspoon dry mustard
¼ teaspoon ground cumin
Freshly ground black pepper
8 fl oz (240 ml) medium sherry

Double-bladed knife

Cut the meat into 1 in. (2·5 cm) cubes. Peel and roughly chop the onions and garlic. Coarsely chop the onions and garlic and remove. Combine the sherry, spices and seasonings, except for the bay leaves, in the Magimix bowl, and process until well mixed.

Heat the oil in a fireproof earthenware cast iron or enamelled casserole and when a film of heat rises from the oil add the meat and brown quickly on all sides. Lower the heat, add the onions, garlic and bay leaves and cook, stirring to prevent sticking, until the onions are soft and golden. Add the liquid from the Magimix bowl, cover tightly and cook for 2½ hours in a low oven (250°F. 125°C. Reg. ½). Remove the bay leaves before serving. (*Note* the stew, like so many of the South American and Mexican dishes benefits from being left overnight and reheated).

Pork Stew with Runner Beans

A good dish to make in the summer when runner beans are cheap. This dish freezes well too.

For four to six people

2 lb (900 g) lean pork
1 tablespoon flour
2 onions
1 lb (450 g) ripe tomatoes
2 lb (900 g) runner beans

2 oz (50 g) lard or dripping
¼ pint (5 fl oz 150 ml) red wine
Salt
1 teaspoon paprika

Cut the pork into cubes and dust lightly with flour. Peel and roughly chop the onions. Top and tail the beans and trim them to fit sideways in the feed tube. Cover the tomatoes with boiling water, leave for three minutes, drain and slide off the skins.

Double-bladed knife — Process the onions until fairly finely chopped and remove.

Medium slicing disc — Carefully place the beans sideways in the feed tube and process to slice, remove from bowl.

Chipper disc — Process the tomatoes through the chipper disc using only a light pressure on the pusher.

Heat the dripping in a heavy frying pan. Add the onions and cook over a medium heat until the onions are soft. Remove the onions to a casserole with a slotted spoon. Raise the heat, add the meat and brown over a high heat on all sides. Remove the meat with a slotted spoon and add it to the onions with the runner beans and tomatoes. Add the wine to the juices in the pan, mix well and season with salt and paprika. Pour the sauce over the meat and vegetables, cover tightly with foil and cook in a moderate oven (300°F. 150°C. Reg. 2) for about 1½ hours or until the meat is fork tender.

Note A carton of sour cream can be mixed into the stew and it can be garnished with finely chopped parsley.

Barbecued Spareribs with a Tangy Sauce

Barbecued spareribs are delicious and cheap but they can, in my opinion, be over-sauced. The sauce in this variation on the sparerib theme is hot and tangy but not cloying.

For four people

2 racks spareribs (about 4 lb 1·8 kg)	1 tablespoon brown sugar
Water	1 tablespoon vinegar
2 chicken stock cubes	1 tablespoon tomato ketchup
Freshly ground black pepper	2 tablespoons soy sauce
¼ teaspoon mixed herbs	1 teaspoon Worcestershire sauce
1 large onion	1 teaspoon chilli sauce
2 cloves garlic	Salt
1 teaspoon ground ginger	

Divide the spareribs into individual ribs. Place them in a saucepan, cover them with cold water, add the stock cubes, season with pepper and add the herbs. Bring slowly to the boil, skimming off the scum as it rises to the surface and simmer the ribs for 45 minutes. Drain them well (the stock can be used to make soup).

Peel and roughly chop the onion and garlic.

Double-bladed knife — Process the onion and garlic until finely chopped, add the remaining ingredients and process until the sauce is almost smooth.

Place the ribs in a roasting tin, pour over the sauce and bake them in a hot oven (400°F. 200°C. Reg. 6) for 40 minutes basting the ribs every now and then and turning them over twice during the cooking time.

Savoury Meat Loaf

A good savoury meat loaf made from a combination of veal and pork and served with a rich gravy flavoured with redcurrant jelly.

For six people

10 oz (275 g) lean pork
10 oz (275 g) pie veal
2½ medium thick slices brown bread
1 small onion
2 eggs
1 teaspoon salt
Freshly ground black pepper
Pinch mixed herbs
3 tablespoons single cream

4 oz (100 g) bacon fat
2 oz (50 g) butter
8 tablespoons beef stock
½ pint (10 fl oz 300 ml) single cream
1½ tablespoons plain flour
2 tablespoons soy sauce
1 tablespoon tomato purée
1 tablespoon redcurrant jelly

Cut the meat into cubes. Remove the crusts from the bread. Peel and roughly chop the onion. Cut the bacon fat into small squares.

Double-bladed knife

Process the bread until reduced to coarse crumbs and remove. Process the pork until finely chopped (ground) and remove. Process the onion until finely chopped, add the veal and process until the veal is finely chopped (ground), add the eggs, season with salt and pepper, add the herbs and cream and process until well mixed. Combine all the processed ingredients in a bowl and mix well.

Form into a loaf shape in a roasting tin and press the bacon fat over the surface. Dot with knobs of butter and bake in a hot oven (400°F. 200°C. Reg. 6) for 15 minutes. Pour over the stock and cream and continue to cook for a further 20 minutes. Pour off the juices from the pan.

Double-bladed knife

Combine the juices from the pan, the flour, soy sauce, redcurrant jelly and tomato purée, and season with salt and pepper. Process to mix well. Pour into a saucepan and cook over a medium high heat, stirring continually, until the sauce comes to the boil and is thick and smooth (thin with a little extra stock if necessary).

Pour the sauce over the meat loaf and cut into thick slices.

Stuffed Peppers

For four people

4 peppers
8 oz (225 g) lean beef
4 oz (100 g) rice
2 oz (50 g) bacon
1 onion
2 cloves garlic
1 slice white bread
2 oz (50 g) Cheddar cheese
2 tablespoons oil

1 tin (15 oz 425 g) tomatoes
1 tablespoon raisins
¼ teaspoon turmeric
Pinch ground cardamon and coriander
Pinch mixed herbs
Salt and freshly ground black pepper
½ tablespoon tomato purée
1 oz (25 g) butter

Double-bladed knife

Cut the meat into cubes. Cook the rice in boiling salted water until tender and drain well. Remove the rinds from the bacon and roughly chop the rashers. Peel and roughly chop the onion and garlic. Drain and reserve the juice from the tomatoes. Process the bread with the cheese until reduced to fine crumbs and remove. Process the onion and garlic until finely chopped and remove. Process the meat and bacon until finely chopped (ground) and remove.

Heat the oil in a frying pan. Add the onion and garlic and cook over a low heat until the onion is soft and transparent. Raise the heat, add the meat and bacon and cook over a high heat, stirring, until the meat has browned. Add the drained tomatoes, raisins, spices and herbs and season with salt and pepper. Mix in the tomato purée, bring to the boil and cook, stirring every now and then with a fork to break up the tomatoes until the meat is tender and most of the liquid from the tomatoes has been absorbed. Add the rice and check seasoning.

Cut slices from the stalk end of the peppers and remove the cores. Stand the peppers in a baking dish, fill them with the meat mixture and top with the crumbs and cheese. Dot with butter, pour around the tomato juice and bake in a moderately hot oven (400°F. 200°C. Reg. 6) for 45 minutes or until the pepper cases are soft.

Savoury Sausage and Apple Cakes

Serve these for a late Sunday breakfast, for children's supper or for a snack meal. They can be accompanied by the home made tomato sauce on page 259.

For four to five people

1 small onion
1 small, crisp, eating apple
1 lb (450 g) pork belly with the skin
    removed (or use sausage meat)
2 slices white bread
Salt and freshly ground black pepper

¾ teaspoon dried sage
Pinch allspice
Flour
½ oz (13 g) butter
1 tablespoon sunflower or cooking oil

Double-bladed knife

Peel and roughly chop the onion. Peel and roughly chop the apple. Cut the pork into 1 in. (2·5 cm) cubes. Remove the crusts from the bread.

Process the bread until reduced to coarse breadcrumbs. Add the pork and process until fairly finely chopped. Add the onion and apple, sage and allspice and season with salt and pepper. Process until pork, apple and onion are finely chopped.

Using hands well floured with seasoned flour shape the mixture into four or five ½ in. (1·25 cm) thick flat, round, cakes. Heat the butter with the oil in a large heavy frying pan, add the sausage cakes and cook over a medium low heat for eight minutes on each side until the cakes are crisp and golden brown.

Casserole of Sausages in Wine

There are a lot more things to do with sausages than just fry them.
The quality of this dish will, of course, depend to a great extent on the quality of the sausages you use. I either buy them from a butcher who makes his own or use the herb flavoured sausages sold in Marks and Spencers.

For eight people

2 lb (900 g) pork sausages
2 tablespoons olive or sunflower oil
3 onions
2 cloves garlic
1 aubergine

1 green pepper
1 tin (15 oz 425 g) tomatoes
¼ pint (5 fl oz 150 ml) red wine
Salt and freshly ground black pepper
Pinch dried oregano

Heat the oil in a heavy pan, add the sausages and cook them over a low to moderate heat, shaking the pan every now and then to turn the sausages until they are well browned on all sides.
Peel the onions and garlic. Remove the core and seeds from the green pepper.

Medium slicing disc
Slice the onions and garlic and remove.

Chipper disc
Process the aubergine and green pepper through the disc. Remove the sausages from the pan with a slotted spoon. Add the onions, garlic, aubergine and pepper and cook over a medium heat, stirring, until the onions are soft and transparent. Add the tomatoes and mix with a fork to break them up. Add the wine, season with salt and pepper and mix in the oregano. Add the sausages, bring to the boil, cover and cook for 30 minutes.

Crisp Breaded Grilled Kidneys

For four people

12 lamb's kidneys
2 oz (50 g) white bread with the crusts removed
1 teaspoon French Dijon mustard
Salt and freshly ground black pepper

Few drops Worcestershire and Tabasco sauce
Juice of ½ lemon
2 oz (50 g) melted butter

Halve the kidneys sideways leaving them hinged at the rounded side. Open them out and cut away the core with kitchen scissors.

Double-bladed knife
Process the bread until reduced to coarse crumbs.
Add the mustard, season with salt and pepper, put in a little Worcestershire sauce and Tabasco and the lemon juice and melted butter. Process until the ingredients are well mixed and the crumbs are fine. Spread the mixture over the cut sides of the kidneys and cook them under a hot grill for about 6 minutes (the kidneys should still be a little pink in the centre) and serve with grilled tomatoes, mashed potatoes and crisply cooked French beans.

Forcemeat Stuffed Roast Poussins (Page 133)

Devilled Kidneys

Originally this was an Edwardian breakfast dish and it still causes a sensation if served for a country style Sunday breakfast. Devilled kidneys also make a quick supper dish or, for a more grand occasion, a savoury.

For four people

8 lamb's kidneys
2 oz (50 g) butter
2 teaspoons mango chutney
1 teaspoon dry English mustard

1 teaspoon curry powder
2 teaspoons lemon juice
Few drops Worcestershire sauce
Salt and freshly ground black pepper

Remove the core and any fat or skin from the kidneys and split them ⅘ of the way through so that they lie flat without cutting all the way through.

Double-bladed knife
Combine the butter, chutney, mustard, curry powder, lemon juice and Worcestershire sauce in the Magimix bowl, season with salt and pepper and process (scraping down the sides of the bowl every now and then if necessary) until the ingredients are well mixed.

Spread the devil sauce on the uncut side of the kidneys and grill them under a hot grill for 3 minutes, turn the kidneys over, continue to grill for a further 2 minutes. Serve the kidneys on buttered rounds of toast and pour over any juices from the pan.

Roulade with Kidneys and Collared Greens

One of the most sensational of dishes and also an extremely versatile one. A roulade (or in plain English a 'soufflé roll') resembles a mouth-melting Swiss roll soufflé; it can be filled with any number of savoury mixtures and although the dish always looks spectacular it is not really all that difficult to make. According to the filling used a roulade can be served as a first or light main course. This first filling is one that I am particularly fond of but I have followed it with a number of ideas for alternative combinations.

For eight people

For the filling
4 lamb's kidneys
2 cloves garlic
1 medium onion
8 oz (225 g) curly kale or collared greens
Pinch bicarbonate of soda
2 oz (50 g) butter
Salt and freshly ground black pepper
4 tablespoons of single cream

1 tablespoon French Dijon mustard

For the Roulade
2 oz (50 g) Parmesan cheese
1 oz (25 g) butter
2 tablespoons flour
7 fl oz (210 ml) milk
6 eggs (separated)
Salt and freshly ground black pepper

Tagliatelle Verde with Tomatoes, Olives and Basil (Page 157)

To make the filling

Remove any skin and fat from the kidneys. Cut them in half lengthways and remove the cores. Peel and roughly chop the onion and garlic.

Cook the curly kale or collared greens in ½ in. (1·25 cm) boiling water, to which a pinch of bicarbonate of soda has been added, for 5 minutes. Refresh under cold running water and squeeze out excess water.

Double-bladed knife

Process the onion and garlic until finely chopped and remove.

Process the kidneys until coarsely chopped and remove.

Process the curly kale or collared greens until fairly finely chopped and remove. Heat the butter in a frying pan. Add the onion and garlic and cook over a medium low heat until the onion is soft and transparent. Raise the heat, add the kidneys and cook over a high heat stirring for 2 minutes. Add the kale and continue to stir for 2 minutes. Lower the heat and mix in the cream and mustard. Season with salt and pepper, remove from the heat but keep warm.

To make the roulade

Parmesan disc and a clean bowl

Process the Parmesan cheese and leave it in the bowl. Melt the butter in a saucepan, add the flour and mix well. Gradually add the milk, stirring continually over a medium high heat until the sauce comes to the boil and is thick and smooth. Leave to cool for five minutes.

Double-bladed knife

Add the white sauce to the Parmesan cheese. With the motor running add the egg yolks, one at a time through the feed tube, processing after each addition of egg until the egg yolk has been well mixed into the sauce. Season with salt and pepper and process to mix.

Oil an 18 in. × 12 in. (45 cm × 30 cm) Swiss roll tin and line it with Baco non-stick paper.

Beat the egg whites until stiff. Transfer the egg yolk mixture to a large bowl, mix in one third of the egg whites and then very lightly fold in the remainder of the egg whites. Spread the egg mixture evenly over the Swiss roll tin and bake in a moderate oven (350°F. 175°C. Reg. 4) for about 15 minutes until the roulade has just set. Turn the roulade upside down onto a slightly dampened tea towel, peel off the paper and spread over the kidney filling. Using the tea towel to roll up the roulade lightly into a Swiss roll shape and slide it on to a warm serving dish. Garnish the top of the roulade with chopped parsley.

Note Sometimes the roulade will crack a little when it is being rolled up. To disguise this I have successfully spread over the top a mixture of single cream and a little finely grated Cheddar cheese and put the roulade under a hot grill for a minute before serving.

Alternative fillings for a roulade

1   Cottage cheese and ham with tomato sauce

Spread the roulade with 8 oz (225 g) cottage cheese mixed with 4 oz (100 g) chopped ham and top it with home made tomato sauce on page 259.

2   Duxelles

Follow the recipe for duxelles on page 270 and use this to fill the roulade. Garnish with chopped watercress.

3   Haddock and cream cheese

Fill the roulade with a mixture of 12 oz (350 g) cooked flaked haddock, 6 oz (175 g) cream cheese and 4 tablespoons sour cream, season with salt and pepper and a touch of cayenne and top it with ¼ pint (150 ml) single cream mixed with 3 oz (75 g) Cheddar cheese. Brown under a hot grill just before serving.

4 Use the Serendipity omelette filling on page 80.

Croquettes de Ris de Veau

2 calf's sweetbreads
4 eggs
1 egg yolk
1 oz (25 g) butter
1 tablespoon flour
7 fl oz (210 ml) milk
2 slices fresh white bread

Small bunch parsley, stalks removed
Salt and white pepper
Pinch nutmeg and cayenne
Few drops of Worcestershire and
   Tabasco sauce
Oil for frying

Soak the sweetbreads in cold water for 1 hour and remove any blood and tough membranes. Blanch the sweetbreads in boiling salted water for 15 minutes. Refresh in cold running water, drain, pat dry and chop roughly.

Double-bladed knife
Process the parsley until finely chopped and remove. Melt the butter in a saucepan. Add the flour and stir well. Add the milk, stirring continuously over a medium high heat until the sauce is thick and smooth.

Double-bladed knife
Transfer the sauce to the Magimix bowl. Add two eggs and the egg yolk and process until thick and smooth. Add the sweetbreads and parsley, season with salt and pepper, add a little ground nutmeg, cayenne, Worcestershire sauce and Tabasco and process for just long enough to break the sweetbreads into small pieces. Return to the saucepan and stir gently over a moderate heat until the mixture comes to the boil. Remove from the heat, cool and then spread on a greased baking sheet about 1 in. (2·5 cm) thick. Chill for two hours and then cut into fingers 1 in. (2·5 cm) wide and 2 in. (5 cm) long.

Double-bladed knife and a clean bowl
Cut the crusts off the bread and process until reduced to fine crumbs. Remove the crumbs to a shallow dish.

Process the remaining two eggs until well beaten. Dip the fingers of croquettes into the beaten egg and then into the breadcrumbs and fry in deep oil until golden brown. Drain on kitchen paper and serve with bunches of deep fried parsley.

Creamed Brains with Ham on Toast

A sophisticated supper dish to have in front of the tele. (or perhaps, better still, in front of the video), in bed when you are feeling not quite the thing or after the cinema or theatre. It is light, creamy and delicious.

For two to four people

2 sets sheep's or calve's brains
1 medium onion
1 tablespoon vinegar
1 small bunch parsley
4 oz (100 g) ham

Juice of ½ a lemon
4 tablespoons cream
4 thick slices bread, toasted
2 oz (50 g) butter
Salt and white pepper

Soak the brains in cold water, salted, for 1 hour and rinse well in running water, remove skin. Peel and quarter the onion.

Combine brains, vinegar and onion in a saucepan with enough water to cover, bring to the boil and simmer gently for 10 minutes. Strain and refresh in cold water, drain well.

Remove the stalks from the parsley.

Double-bladed knife

Process the parsley until finely chopped and remove. Process the ham until coarsely chopped. Add the brains and process for just long enough to fairly finely chop them. Heat the butter in a frying pan, add the brains and ham, season with salt and pepper, and cook over a high heat, stirring lightly, for four minutes. Add the lemon juice and cream, stir in the parsley and spread at once on buttered hot toast. Serve at once.

Lamb's Liver with Browned Sauce

The secret of this dish lies in, first of all, the sauce which is made of a mixture of julienned carrots and thinly sliced leeks. The other trick is either to have a butcher who really will cut the liver into very, very, thin slices or to do it yourself with a properly sharpened carving knife.

1½ lb (675 g) lamb's liver in one piece
   or cut into *very* thin slices.
Milk
8 oz (225 g) carrots
2 leeks
2 oz (50 g) butter
2 tablespoons flour
Salt and freshly ground black pepper

¾ pint (15 fl oz 450 ml) chicken or beef
   stock (or water and stock cubes)
2 teaspoons freshly chopped sage (or
   use 1 teaspoon dried sage)
¼ pint (5 fl oz 150 ml) sherry
¼ pint (5 fl oz 150 ml) single cream
Flour
Oil for frying

Peel the carrots. Trim and clean the leeks if necessary. Cut the liver into very thin slices against the grain removing any tough fibres or tubes soak in milk and drain well.

Julienne disc

Cut the carrots to fit the feed tube sideways and process them with a firm pressure on the pusher.

Thin slicing disc

Cut the leeks to fit the feed tube and process the leeks with a firm pressure on the pusher. Heat the butter in a heavy pan. Add the carrots and leeks and cook over a low heat, stirring every now and then until the vegetables are soft. Add the flour and mix well. Season with salt and pepper and gradually blend in the stock and add the sage. Mix in the sherry and simmer for 10 minutes. Add the cream and check seasoning.

Coat the liver slices in flour seasoned with salt and pepper. Heat the oil in a large frying pan add the coated liver slices and cook over a high heat, turning once until the slices are golden brown on the outside and still faintly pink on the inside. Remove on to a serving dish, warmed, with a slotted spoon or tongs and pour over the vegetable sauce.

Serve at once.

Special Toad in the Hole

There are toad in the holes and toad in the holes – you can be as simple or as ingenius about them as you like. This is my special, invented for this book, and although I say it myself, it is very good indeed. There is more action than the regular toad in the hole and a lot more flavour. To my mind it is essential that the "toads" in "toad in the hole" should be cooked until nicely browned before the batter is poured over; if this is not done the sausages (toads) come out looking rather like fat pink pigs. I add herbs, garlic sausage and fried onions to the basic mixture.

For six to seven people

2 lb (900 g) sausages
3 large onions
1 tablespoon cooking oil
4 oz (100 g) garlic sausage
4 oz (100 g) plain flour
¼ teaspoon mixed herbs

Salt and freshly ground black pepper
1 egg
½ pint (10 fl oz 300 ml) mixed milk and water
2 tablespoons dripping, lard or cooking oil

Cook the sausages over a medium low heat, without extra fat, until they are well browned on all sides. Remove with a slotted spoon and drain on kitchen paper. Peel and halve the onions.

Thin slicing disc

Slice the onions. Fry the onions in 1 tablespoon oil over a medium low heat until they are really soft and transparent. Remove the onions from the oil with a slotted spoon.

Roughly chop the garlic sausage.

Double-bladed knife

Process the garlic sausage until fairly finely chopped. Add the flour, egg, herbs, milk and water and salt and pepper and process until the batter is smooth (the garlic sausage should, by then, be finely chopped). Heat the dripping, lard or 2 tablespoons oil, in a roasting dish in a hot oven (425°F. 220°C. Reg. 7) spread the onions over the bottom, place the sausages on top and pour over the batter. Bake in a hot oven (425°F. 220°C. Reg. 7) for 40 minutes or until risen and golden brown. Serve at once with cabbage and mashed potatoes.

I like to serve a gravy on the side.

POULTRY & GAME

Smothered Poussins

I find delectable small, mini, chickens (now easy to get from good supermarkets and Marks and Spencers) quick to cook and an easy answer to 'what to cook for an unexpected supper party'. In this recipe I smother them with a mixture of seasoned cottage cheese and butter which not only keeps the birds moist as they cook but also adds a delicious flavour to the tender flesh and provides an excellent in built sauce.

For four people

2 spring chickens or poussins
4 oz (100 g) cottage cheese
2 cloves garlic
1 teaspoon dried mixed herbs

1 tablespoon green peppercorns in brine (drained)
3 oz (75 g) butter
Salt and a pinch of paprika

Halve the chickens along the breast and backbone using a pair of kitchen scissors. Peel and roughly chop the garlic.

Double-bladed knife

Process the garlic until finely chopped. Add the cottage cheese, peppercorns, butter and seasoning and process until the mixture is reduced to a smoothish paste.
Spread the chicken with the cheese paste on the skin side and lay them, cut side down, in a roasting dish. Roast the chicken halves in a hot oven (400°F. 200°C. Reg. 6) for forty minutes, basting them frequently with the juices in the pan. When the chicken halves are cooked remove them to a warm serving dish and spoon over the juices from the pan.
Serve with sauté potatoes and a green vegetable or salad.

Forcemeat Stuffed Roast Poussins

Illustration on page 125

Such elegant little birds poussins but they do need the additional flavouring of a stuffing or sauce. In this recipe the birds are stuffed with a savoury veal mixture and finished off with lemon juice and browned breadcrumbs.

For eight people

4 medium 14 oz (400 g) poussins
9 oz (250 g) minced veal
5 slices white bread with the crusts
   removed
1 teaspoon grated lemon peel
9 oz (250 g) streaky bacon with the rinds
   removed
2 eggs

Small bunch parsley
Sprig thyme
Salt and freshly ground black pepper
Pinch cayenne
1 tablespoon brandy
2 teaspoons lemon juice
4 oz (100 g) butter

Remove the giblets from the poussins and roughly chop the livers. Remove the coarse stalks from the parsley and thyme.

Double-bladed knife

Process the parsley and thyme until finely chopped and remove.
Process 3 slices of bread until reduced to fine crumbs, add the bacon and process until the bacon is very finely chopped. Add the veal and poussin livers and process until the mixture is reduced to a coarse paste. Add the eggs, half the lemon juice, season with salt, pepper and cayenne and process until well mixed.
Add the herbs, lemon rind and brandy and process for just long enough to mix the ingredients.
Stuff the poussins with the veal forcemeat and place them in a roasting tin. Brush the birds with 2 oz (50 g) melted butter and roast in a hot oven (425°F. 220°C. Reg. 7) for 15 minutes then lower the heat to moderate (350°F. 175°C. Reg. 4) and continue to roast for a further 30 minutes or until the birds are cooked through.

Double-bladed knife

Process the remaining 2 slices of bread until they are reduced to fairly fine breadcrumbs. Fry the crumbs in 2 oz (50 g) melted butter until crisp and golden brown. Brush the cooked birds with the remaining lemon juice and sprinkle over the crisp crumbs just before serving.

Stuffed Chicken Breasts

Although this is an excellent dish to serve hot (it looks good and tastes even better) it is also good left to get cold and then cut into thin slices. The cold breasts, served with baked potatoes and a good mixed salad, are enough for six servings – the hot dish is less economical.

For four people

1 in. (2·5 cm) piece of fresh ginger root, peeled
4 chicken breasts (boneless)
3 oz (75 g) streaky bacon
1 chicken liver
4 oz (100 g) garlic sausage

3 slices white bread
1 oz (25 g) salted peanuts
Salt and freshly ground black pepper
Pinch mixed herbs
Small pinch of ground cumin and nutmeg
4 rashers of streaky bacon

Double-bladed knife

Remove the skin from the chicken breasts and pull off the fillets. Remove the rinds from the bacon and the crusts from the bread. Roughly chop the chicken fillets, liver and the garlic sausage.

Combine the 3 oz bacon, chicken liver, chicken fillets, garlic sausage, ginger root and bread in the Magimix bowl and process until reduced to the texture of sausagemeat. Add peanuts and process until peanuts are coarsely chopped. Season with salt and pepper and add herbs and spices and process for just long enough to mix in the seasonings. Beat the chicken breasts in between two sheets of greaseproof paper to stretch and tenderize them. Divide the forcemeat between the fillets, spread it out over the fillets and roll up neatly. Place the rolls in a baking dish, top with the bacon rashers (or wrap the rashers around the rolls) and cook in a moderate oven (350°F. 175°C. Reg. 4) for about 30 minutes basting every few minutes to prevent the breasts drying out.

Marinated Chicken Breast Kebabs

Another delicious dish for a barbecue. Chill the chicken breasts in the deep freeze for about thirty minutes to enable you to cut very, very thin slices.

For four people

12 oz (350 g) chicken breast cut into very thin horizontal strips
1 tablespoon lemon juice
1 teaspoon salt
¾ in. (2 cm) piece fresh ginger root

2 cloves garlic
4 tablespoons yoghurt
1 tablespoon Madras curry powder
Sunflower oil
Lemon wedges

Double-bladed knife

Marinate the chicken in lemon juice and salt for 30 minutes. Peel and roughly chop the ginger and garlic.

Process the garlic and ginger until very finely chopped. Add the yoghurt and curry powder and process until the ingredients are well mixed.

Pour the yoghurt mixture over the chicken and leave to stand in a cool place for three hours turning the chicken pieces every now and then to make sure they are well coated. Thread the chicken pieces on thin bamboo skewers stretching the flesh out along the skewers. Brush them with a little oil and grill them under a high heat or over a charcoal until cooked through and slightly crisp at the edges. Serve with lemon wedges.

Note I sometimes serve these as an appetiser with a curry sauce (see page 266).

Chicken Thighs Paprika

Packets of chicken thighs can be bought from Marks and Spencer and some other supermarkets. Used in this way they make an elegant and inexpensive main course.

For four to five people

4 or 5 chicken thighs	2 slices of white bread with the crusts removed
2 oz (50 g) chicken livers	
4 oz (100 g) ham	5 tablespoons medium sherry
Small bunch parsley	½ pint (10 fl oz 300 ml) chicken stock
2 oz (50 g) softened butter	2 bay leaves
1 onion	1 tablespoon paprika pepper
2 carrots	Salt and freshly ground black pepper
2 sticks celery	¼ pint (5 fl oz 150 ml) double cream
1 small turnip	

Using a small, sharp, knife cut out the bones from the chicken thighs. Spread out the thighs between two sheets of greaseproof paper and beat them flat with a mallet. Cook the chicken livers in ½ oz (13 g) butter for 4 minutes. Remove the coarse stalks from the parsley. Peel and roughly chop the carrots and turnip. Roughly chop the celery. Peel the onion.

Double-bladed knife
Process the bread into crumbs and remove. Process the parsley until finely chopped and remove. Process the carrots, celery and turnip until finely chopped and remove.

Medium slicing disc
Slice the onion.

Double-bladed knife
Process the chicken livers and ham until finely chopped. Add the bread and parsley and season with salt and pepper. Process for just long enough to mix the ingredients.

Spread the chicken thighs with the stuffing and roll up neatly. Fasten with toothpicks.

Melt the remaining butter in a heavy casserole. Add the chicken thighs and brown them quickly on all sides. Remove the thighs with a slotted spoon. Stir the paprika into the juices in the pan then add the vegetables and cook over a low heat, stirring, until the vegetables are soft.

Pour over the sherry and stock, season with salt and pepper, add the bay leaves and place the chicken thighs on top of the vegetables. Cover tightly and cook in a moderate oven (350°F. 175°C. Reg. 4) for 30 minutes or until the juices from the thighs run clear when spiked with a skewer.

Remove the toothpicks from the chicken thighs and discard the bay leaves. Strain off the juices from the vegetables and arrange the vegetables and thighs on a serving plate – keep warm.

Put the liquid into a small saucepan and boil to reduce until thickened and shining. Stir in the cream. Pour the sauce over the thighs and garnish with some extra chopped parsley.

Chicken Pirri

A simple but pleasant chicken dish which goes down nicely on a summer evening when something "not too complicated" is required.

For four people

4 chicken joints
4 oz (100 g) butter
1 medium onion
2 carrots
Pinch thyme
½ pint (10 fl oz 300 ml) chicken stock
3 tablespoons cornflour

¼ pint (5 fl oz 150 ml) dry cider
3 tablespoons single cream
4 oz (100 g) Cheddar cheese
Salt and freshly ground black pepper
Pinch nutmeg
2 teaspoons French Dijon mustard

Peel and roughly chop the onion. Peel the carrots.

Coarse grating disc Process the cheese and remove.

Double-bladed knife Process the onion until fairly finely chopped and remove.

Chipper disc Process the carrots and remove.

Combine the onion and carrot with the stock, add the thyme, season with salt and pepper, bring to the boil and simmer until the vegetables are tender. Drain off and measure ¼ pint (5 fl oz 150 ml) stock. Place the vegetables on a serving dish and keep warm.

Melt the butter in a heavy frying pan, add the chicken joints and cook over a medium high heat, turning the joints frequently until they are cooked and tender (about 20 minutes). Place the chicken joints on top of the vegetables and keep warm.

Heat the ¼ pint (5 fl oz 150 ml) stock in a small saucepan, blend the cornflour with 1 tablespoon of the stock and mix until smooth. Add the cornflour to the stock and stir until the mixture comes to the boil and is thick and smooth. Add the cider and mustard and stir until boiling; remove from the heat and stir in the cream and half the cheese. Season with salt, pepper and nutmeg, pour the sauce over the chicken and vegetables, top with the remaining cheese and brown under a very hot grill until golden brown.

Gallina a la Mexicana

An unusual chicken stew that is traditionally served at the fiesta of Puebla in the Mexican mountains. It is rich and aromatic and for the Mexicans and Indians who come down from the mountains once a year for the fiesta it will probably be the only time they can afford to eat chicken during the year.

For six to eight people (depending on how the chicken is cut)

1 large chicken (a boiling fowl is perfect for this if you can get one)
2 bay leaves
Chicken stock (or water and stock cubes)
2 tablespoons oil
2 medium onions
4 cloves garlic
2 tins (15 oz 425 g) tomatoes
4 tablespoons tomato purée
8 oz (225 g) cooked ham
1 tablespoon ground almonds
2 tablespoons capers
12 stuffed green olives
4 oz (100 g) raisins
½ teaspoon dried thyme, oregano and marjoram
Salt and freshly ground black pepper
½ pint (10 fl oz 300 ml) medium sherry

Joint the chicken – if it is a large one divide the leg and thigh joints into two pieces each – the sauce for this dish is very substantial. Cover the chicken with stock, add two bay leaves, bring to the boil, cover and cook very slowly until just tender. Peel and roughly chop the onions and garlic. Roughly chop the ham. Cover the onions with hot water and leave to soak for five minutes.
Drain the onions.

Double-bladed knife Process the onions and garlic until finely chopped. Heat the oil in a large, heavy, fireproof casserole (I use one that is made from cast iron), add the onions and garlic and cook over a low heat until the onions are soft and transparent. Remove from the heat.

Double-bladed knife Process the ham until finely chopped.
Add the ham to the onions in the casserole.

Double-bladed knife Combine the capers and olives in the Magimix bowl with one tin of the tomatoes and process until the tomatoes are roughly chopped. Add the mixture to the onions and ham.

Process the second tin of tomatoes until chopped and add to the casserole with the almonds, raisins, herbs, sherry and tomato purée, and mix well. *Note* If using the Grande Famille you can process both tins of tomatoes together.

Drain the chicken joints and add to the ingredients in the casserole together with 8 fl oz (230 ml) chicken stock. Season with salt and pepper, mix well, cover tightly and simmer very slowly for 1 hour. Serve with rice and salad.

Herbed Chicken Patties

I had these at a cocktail party and found myself unable to stop eating them. They were served piping hot and were what can only be described as exquisite.

For four people

14 oz (400 g) frozen puff pastry, defrosted
6 oz (175 g) chicken breast
3 oz (75 g) belly pork
1 small onion or shallot
1 clove garlic
3 sprigs parsley
Small bunch chives
Stock
1 tablespoon dry vermouth
1 egg
Salt and freshly ground black pepper

Cut the meat into cubes. Peel and roughly chop the onion and garlic. Remove the stalks from the parsley. Combine the meat, onion, garlic, herbs and vermouth in a saucepan, add a little stock to moisten, season with salt and pepper and simmer gently for about 35 minutes or until the meat is cooked through. Strain off most of the excess liquid.

Double-bladed knife

Process the egg until well beaten and remove.

Process all the cooked ingredients until they are reduced to a coarse paste.

Roll out the pastry until it is about ¼ in. (0·75 cm) thick and cut into 2½ in. (6 cm) rounds. Mount the forcemeat on half the rounds and cover with the remaining rounds dampening the edges with water and pressing them firmly together with the back of a fork.

Brush the top of the pastry with beaten egg and bake in a hot oven (400°F. 200°C. Reg. 6) for about 10 minutes until puffed and golden brown.

Curried Chicken in Yoghurt

For four people

1 chicken, jointed
2 onions
2 cloves garlic
1 oz (25 g) blanched almonds
1 tablespoon ground coriander
1 tablespoon desiccated coconut
1 teaspoon ground turmeric

½ teaspoon ground cumin
½ teaspoon ground chilli
½ pint (10 fl oz 300 ml) natural yoghurt
2 fl oz (60 ml) sunflower oil
Salt
Juice ½ lemon

Peel and roughly chop the onions and garlic.

Double-bladed knife

Process the onions and garlic until they are fairly finely chopped and remove.

Process the almonds until finely ground add the coriander, coconut, turmeric, cumin, chilli, yoghurt and lemon juice, season with salt and process until well mixed.

Heat the oil in a large heavy frying pan, add the onions and garlic and cook over a low heat, stirring, until the onions are soft and golden. Add the chicken and pour over the yoghurt and spices. Mix well, cover and cook over a low heat for 30 minutes or until the chicken is tender. Serve with rice and some of the curry accompaniments on page 273.

Chicken Pie

This is made with the same pastry as a raised pie but its much more simple to shape since it is free formed rather than cooked in a tin. The filling is a delicious savoury mixture of pork and bacon forcemeat and chicken and the dish has the advantage of being as good cold as it is hot. Its a perfect summer picnic dish.

For six people	12 oz (350 g) hot water crust pastry (see page 243)
	Small bunch parsley
	1 small onion
	8 oz (225 g) fat streaky bacon rashers

8 oz (225 g) lean pork
2 breasts chicken
¼ teaspoon mixed herbs
Salt and freshly ground black pepper
1 egg

Remove any tough stalks from the parsley. Peel and roughly chop the onion. Remove the bacon rinds and roughly chop half of the rashers. Cut the pork and chicken into cubes.

Double-bladed knife Process the parsley until finely chopped and remove.

Process the onion until finely chopped, add the pork and roughly chopped bacon and process until the meat is reduced to a smooth paste. Add the chicken, parsley and herbs, season with salt and pepper and process until the chicken is finely chopped.

Roll out the pastry to a rectangle about 12 in. × 18 in. (30 cm × 45 cm). Remove the rinds from the remaining bacon rashers and place half of them along the centre of the pastry. Top with the chicken mixture making it into a neat loaf shape and then put the remaining rashers on top of the forcemeat. Fold over the longer edges of the pastry, damp the edges and press them firmly together. Turn the pie over onto a baking sheet so that the sealed edge is on the bottom and seal and trim the open edges of the pie. Decorate the top of the pie with a lattice of thin strips of pastry.

Double-bladed knife Process the egg with a little salt until it is smooth. Brush the top of the pie with egg wash, cut three vents in the pastry to allow the air to escape during the cooking time and bake in a hot oven (400°F. 200°C. Reg. 6) for 1 hour covering the pastry with greaseproof paper if it becomes too brown.

Serve hot or cold.

Note This is a basic recipe which can be elaborated on to become an even more sophisticated dish.

Add some sliced white truffle in a layer in the middle of the chicken forcemeat.

Add some chopped pistachio nuts to the chicken forcemeat.

Add some chopped pickled cucumber to the forcemeat.

Add some chopped ham or tongue to the forcemeat.

Creamy Chicken and Cider Pie

For six people	1 recipe special pastry dough (see page 238)
	12 oz (350 g) cooked chicken
	6 oz (175 g) streaky bacon rashers
	1 bunch parsley
	1 onion
	2 oz (50 g) butter
	3 tablespoons flour
	½ pint (10 fl oz 300 ml) milk

¼ pint (5 fl oz 150 ml) cider
4 bay leaves
Salt and freshly ground black pepper
2 oz (50 g) firm button mushrooms
1 small egg
1 tablespoon water
¼ pint (5 fl oz 150 ml) double cream
2 egg yolks

Double-bladed knife
Roughly chop the chicken and bacon having removed the rinds from the rashers. Remove any tough parsley stalks. Peel and roughly chop the onion. Process the parsley until finely chopped and remove. Process the chicken until coarsely chopped and remove. Process the onion and bacon together until coarsely chopped.

Heat the butter in a large saucepan, add the onion and bacon and cook over a low heat, stirring to prevent browning, until the onion is soft and transparent. Add the flour and mix well, gradually add the milk and cider stirring continually over a medium high heat until the sauce is thick and smooth. Mix in the parsley, season well with salt and pepper, bring to the boil, add the bay leaves and simmer for 10 minutes stirring every now and then to prevent sticking.

Medium slicing disc
Slice the mushrooms.

Remove the bay leaves from the sauce and mix in the mushrooms and chicken.

Double-bladed knife
Process the cream and egg yolks until smooth.

Add the egg yolks and cream to the chicken mixture and turn it into a pie dish with a pie funnel in the middle.

Roll out the pastry and cut a thin strip to press round the dampened edges of the pie dish. Cover with the remaining pastry pressing it firmly to the pastry strip which has been dampened on the top with a little water.

Process the whole egg until smooth with a little water and salt. Brush the egg glaze over the pastry and chill in a refrigerator for 30 minutes before baking in a hot oven (425°F. 220°C. Reg. 7) for 10 minutes. Lower the heat to moderate (350°F. 175°C. Reg. 4) and continue to bake for a further 25 minutes or until the pastry is golden brown.

Serve the hot pie.

Eugenie's Chicken Pie

A deliciously rich and creamy chicken pie that will please everyone in the family whatever their age.

For six to eight people

1 chicken (about 3½ lbs 1·5 kg)
1 inch (2·5 cm) piece of ginger root
2 green peppers
2 leeks
3 onions
8 oz (225 g) firm button mushrooms
2 carrots
2 sticks celery
2 tablespoons sunflower oil
3 oz (75 g) butter
4 tablespoons flour
½ pint (10 fl oz 300 ml) milk

½ pint (10 fl oz 300 ml) good chicken stock
6 tablespoons dry sherry
2 tablespoons finely chopped parsley
2 teaspoons dried tarragon
Salt and freshly ground black pepper
4 egg yolks
½ pint (10 fl oz 300 ml) double cream
8 oz (225 g) special pastry dough (see page 238)
1 small egg

Peel the ginger root. Peel the onions. Clean and trim the leeks. Remove the core and seeds from the green peppers. Peel the carrots. Trim the celery.

Thin slicing disc Slice one of the onions and the ginger root.

In a large saucepan, combine the sliced onion and ginger with enough cold water to cover the chicken. Add one teaspoon salt, bring to the boil and boil for five minutes. Add the chicken, return to the boil and cook for 35 minutes. Leave the chicken in the stock until cool enough to handle. Remove the chicken skin and cut the meat off the bones into bite sized pieces.

Thin slicing disc Slice the remaining two onions and the leeks and remove. Slice the mushrooms and remove. Slice the carrots and celery and remove.

Double-bladed knife Process the green peppers until fairly finely chopped and remove. Melt the butter in a saucepan. Add the flour and mix well. Gradually blend in the milk and chicken stock, stirring continually over a medium high heat until the sauce is thick and smooth. Add the sherry, season with salt and pepper and simmer for three minutes.

Double-bladed knife Process the egg yolks and cream until smooth.

Add the egg yolks and cream to the sauce, stirring over a low heat, without boiling, until the sauce is smooth and satiny. Mix in the parsley and tarragon.

Heat the oil in a frying pan. Add the onion and leeks and cook over a low heat until the onion and leeks are soft and transparent. Cover the carrots and celery with cold salted water, bring to the boil and cook for 15 minutes. Drain well. Blanch the mushrooms and peppers in boiling salted water for three minutes and drain well. Add the chicken and vegetables to the sauce and mix lightly. Turn into a pie dish with a funnel and cover with the pastry.

Double-bladed knife Process the egg until smooth.

Brush the pastry with the egg and bake in a hot oven (425°F. 220°C. Reg. 7) for 10 minutes then lower the heat to moderate (350°F. 175°C. Reg. 4) and continue to cook for a further 30 minutes.

Curried Chicken and Ham

You can serve this in a rice ring, in vol-au-vent cases or in a bread loaf case (cut the top off a sandwich loaf, pull out the bread from the inside of the loaf, brush the inside of the case with oil and bake in a hot oven until crisp and golden brown).

For four people

1 large onion	1 teaspoon curry powder
4 oz (100 g) mushrooms	1 tablespoon flour
4 oz (100 g) ham	½ pint (10 fl oz 300 ml) chicken stock
10 oz (275 g) cooked chicken	¼ pint (5 fl oz 150 ml) double cream
1 oz (25 g) butter	Salt and freshly ground black pepper

Peel the onion. Roughly chop the ham and chicken.

Double-bladed knife Process the chicken and ham until coarsely chopped and remove. Process the onion until fairly finely chopped and remove.

Medium slicing disc Process the mushrooms through the disc.

Heat the butter in a saucepan, add the onion and cook over a medium heat until the onion is soft. Add the mushrooms and cook for another minute. Add the curry powder and flour and mix well. Gradually mix in the stock, stirring continually over a medium high heat until the sauce is thick and smooth. Add the chicken and ham and season with salt and pepper. Simmer for five minutes and then stir in the cream, and heat through without boiling.

Maidenwell Rissoles

I do not know quite what decided me to put some cottage cheese into rissoles one evening or to use cooked rice in the place of the more common leftover mashed potatoes – whatever the inspiration the result was a triumph and the common or garden leftover rissole became a thing of excellence no longer relegated to family lunch but quite worthy of being served at a lunch or supper party. Make the rissoles from leftover ham or chicken, or a mixture of both (you could use turkey in the place of chicken) and accompany them with a home made tomato sauce, (see page 259).

For six people

10 oz (275 g) cooked rice
8 oz (225 g) cooked chicken or ham (or a mixture of both)
3 – 4 spring onions
1 egg

Salt and pepper
4 oz (100 g) cottage cheese
Coarse browned breadcrumbs made from granary bread

Double-bladed knife Roughly chop the ham and/or chicken and spring onions.

Combine the ham and/or chicken in the Magimix bowl with the spring onions and process until the ingredients are coarsely chopped. Add the rice and egg, season with salt and pepper and process until well mixed. Add the cottage cheese and switch on and off to mix ingredients. Turn into a bowl and chill in a refrigerator for an hour.

Shape the mixture into twelve flat, round, cakes, press the cakes into the breadcrumbs so that they are coated on both sides and fry in hot shallow oil (about ¼ in. (0·75 cm) in a large non-stick frying pan) until the rissoles are crisp and golden on both sides (about 4 minutes each side).

Chicken and Spinach Stuffed Pancakes

Keep a stack of pancakes in your freezer to make quickly prepared but excellent supper dishes like this one.

For four people	8 savoury pancakes (see page 245) 8 oz (225 g) cooked chicken 1 lb (450 g) spinach 8 oz (225 g) cottage cheese	2 oz (50 g) Cheddar cheese 6 tablespoons single cream Salt and freshly ground black pepper Ground nutmeg and a little paprika

Roughly chop the chicken. Cook the spinach in a little boiling salted water until just tender (about 6 minutes) and drain well.

Double-bladed knife   Process the chicken until coarsely chopped. Add the spinach and 4 oz cottage cheese, season with salt, pepper and nutmeg and process until the spinach is chopped and the ingredients are mixed. Fill the pancakes with the spinach mixture and arrange them in a buttered fireproof dish.

Course grating disc   Grate the Cheddar cheese.

Double-bladed knife   Combine the grated cheese, the remaining cottage cheese and the cream and process until smooth. Spread the topping over the pancakes with a spatula and sprinkle with a little paprika. Bake the dish in a hot oven (400°F. 200°C. Reg. 6) for about 20 minutes until the pancakes are hot through and the topping is golden.

Chicken and Mushroom Filling for Pancakes, Vol-au-vents, Bread Cases or Patties

Left over chicken can be put to good use as a filling ingredient. Bread cases are made from a stale white loaf with the crusts removed; cut the bread into 2 in. (5 cm) thick slices and cut through one side ½ in. (1·25 cm) from the edge and to within ¼ in. (0·56 cm) from the base. Remove the bread carefully from the centre of the case, brush the outside and inside of the case with oil and bake them in a moderate oven (325°F. 160°C. Reg. 3) for about 30 minutes until crisp and golden before filling with savoury ingredients in a sauce.

For four people	Small bunch parsley 12 oz (350 g) cooked chicken 1 medium onion 2 carrots 8 oz (225 g) firm button mushrooms 1 teaspoon of lemon juice 2 oz (50 g) butter	2 heaped tablespoons flour ¾ pint (15 fl oz 450 ml) chicken stock ¼ pint (5 fl oz 150 ml) dry white wine Salt, freshly ground black pepper, pinch cayenne 2 egg yolks 6 tablespoons double cream

Remove the stalks from the parsley. Roughly chop the chicken. Peel and roughly chop the onion. Peel the carrots.

Double-bladed knife   Process the parsley until finely chopped and remove.
Process the chicken until coarsely chopped and remove.
Process the onion until finely chopped and remove.

Chipper disc   Process the carrots through the chipper disc.

Medium slicing disc   Slice the mushrooms and remove. Cook the carrots in boiling salted water until just tender and drain well. Cook the mushrooms in boiling, salted water with the lemon juice until just tender and drain well. Heat the butter in a saucepan, add the onion and cook gently until the onion is soft, add the flour and mix well. Gradually blend in the stock and wine stirring continually over a medium high heat until the sauce comes to the boil and is thick and smooth. Season with salt and pepper and cayenne and simmer for 5 minutes.

Double-bladed knife   Process the egg yolks with the cream until smooth. Add the egg yolk mixture to the sauce and stir over a gentle heat (do not boil) until the sauce is thick and glossy. Add the chicken, carrots, mushrooms and parsley, check the seasoning and stir gently until the sauce is hot through.

Aromatic Casserole of Partridge with Red Cabbage

For four people

2 partridges (these can be older birds)
2 oz (50 g) pork fat
2 carrots
1 small onion
1 medium red cabbage
4 oz (100 g) streaky bacon
Bouquet garni

6 oz (175 g) garlic sausage
Salt and freshly ground black pepper
¼ pint (5 fl oz 150 ml) dry white wine
¼ pint (5 fl oz 150 ml) chicken or game
    stock
½ oz (13 g) butter
1½ tablespoons flour

Prepare the partridges for cooking but do not truss. Roughly chop the pork fat. Peel the carrots. Peel the onion. Remove the rinds from the bacon and the skin from the garlic sausage.

Double-bladed knife   Process the fat until coarsely chopped.

Place the fat in a large fireproof earthenware pot or casserole and cook over a medium heat until it has produced all the fat it will release (about 20 minutes). Remove any remaining fat with a slotted spoon. Add the partridges and brown them all over in the pork fat.

Remove the partridges with a slotted spoon.

Medium slicing disc   Slice the carrots and remove.

Slice the onion and remove.

Slice the cabbage and remove.

Slice the garlic sausage and remove.

Double-bladed knife   Process the bacon until coarsely chopped.

Add the onion and bacon to the juices in the casserole in which the partridges were browned and cook over a medium heat until the onion is soft and transparent. Add the cabbage and stir until the cabbage is transparent. Remove the vegetables with a slotted spoon leaving the juices in the bottom of the casserole.

Cover the bottom of the casserole with the carrots, place the birds on top and smother with the cabbage, onion and bacon. Add the bouquet garni, season with salt and pepper and add the wine and enough stock to cover the ingredients. Cover and cook in a slow oven (300°F. 150°C. Reg. 2) for 2 hours.

Add the garlic sausage and continue to cook for a further hour.

Double-bladed knife Combine the butter and flour and process until the mixture is reduced to a paste. Spoon off the liquid from the casserole with a ladle. Add the liquid to the flour and butter mixture in the Magimix and process until smooth. Turn into a small saucepan, bring to the boil, stirring all the time until smooth and thick.

Transfer the partridges to a serving dish, surround with the vegetables and serve the sauce separately.

A Whole Cabbage stuffed with a Partridge

There is no doubt that this is a fiddly job to do but the resulting tender partridge and its well flavoured stuffing make it one that is worth doing when you want to woo a lover or get a mink coat out of a husband.

For two people

1 partridge
4 thin slices back, fat bacon for larding
1 large cabbage
8 oz (225 g) belly of pork with the skin removed
3 onions
2 cloves garlic
2 oz (50 g) country style pâté (home made or bought)

Pinch mixed dried thyme
1 tablespoon finely chopped parsley
Salt and freshly ground black pepper
Pinch ground nutmeg and allspice
2 egg yolks
4 thin slices streaky bacon
1 tablespoon flour
½ pint (10 fl oz 300 ml) game stock
2 tablespoons brandy

Cover the partridge with the slices of back fat and brown in a very hot oven (450°F. 240°C. Reg. 8) for 15 minutes, basting every five minutes. Heat half the brandy, set it alight and pour it over the partridge. Leave the partridge to cool.

Cook the cabbage in boiling salted water for 10 minutes, drain well (upside down) and, when cool, separate the outside leaves and cut out enough out of the centre to make a space large enough to take the partridge.

Peel and roughly chop the onions. Peel and roughly chop the garlic. Cut the pork into cubes. Roughly chop the streaky bacon.

Double-bladed knife Process the onions until coarsely chopped and remove two thirds of the onions. Add the garlic to the onion in the bowl and process until the onion is finely chopped. Add the pork and process until the pork is finely chopped. Add the pâté, herbs and egg yolks and season with salt and pepper, nutmeg and allspice. Process to mix the ingredients.

Cook the streaky bacon without extra fat for five minutes over a medium high heat. Remove the bacon with a slotted spoon and add the reserved onions to the juices in the pan. Stir the onions over a medium heat until they are soft and transparent, add the flour, mix well and stir in the stock and brandy.

Put the cabbage into a buttered or oiled casserole.

Place the partridge in the centre of the cabbage. Using a spoon spread the pork stuffing in between the outside leaves folding them over the partridge as you do so until all the stuffing has been used up and the partridge is completely enclosed with the leaves. Spoon over the onion, bacon and stock.

Cover with buttered foil and bake in a slow oven (325°F. 150°C. Reg. 3) and cook for 3 hours.

To serve, halve the cabbage and the partridge and serve with mashed potatoes and, perhaps, stuffed tomatoes.

Fried Crumbs to serve with Roast Chicken or Game

2 slices white or brown bread with the crusts removed
2 oz (50 g) butter

Double-bladed knife Process the bread until reduced to fairly fine crumbs.

Melt the butter in a frying pan, add the crumbs and stir over a medium high heat until the crumbs are crisp. Drain well on kitchen paper.

Note: In place of the butter you can use two-three tablespoons sunflower oil for frying.

Pheasant Breasts Maidenwell

If you are fortunate enough to have access to your own pheasants or can buy them for a reasonable price I think one of the nicest ways of utilizing them is to serve the breasts at a dinner party and use the tougher legs and wings to make rich game soups or pâtés.

For four people
4 pheasant breasts
1 onion
1 carrot
2 sticks celery
2 tomatoes
4 juniper berries
4 thin rashers bacon
2 oz (50 g) butter

2 tablespoons sunflower oil
Salt and freshly ground black pepper
Pinch mixed herbs
Dry red wine
Juice of 1 orange
2 firm, tart eating apples (Granny Smiths are ideal for this)

Remove the skin from the pheasant breasts and wrap each breast in a slice of streaky bacon with the rinds removed.

Chinese Stir-Fry Vegetables (Page 169)

Peel the onion and the carrot. Trim the celery. Cover the tomatoes with boiling water for three minutes, drain and slide off the skins. Halve the tomatoes, scoop out the seeds and any tough cores and roughly chop the flesh.

Thin slicing disc Process the onion and the celery through the thin slicing disc and remove.

Chipper disc Process the tomatoes with the juniper berries through the chipper disc and remove.

Julienne disc Process the carrot through the julienne disc.

Heat the oil in a heavy, flame proof casserole. Add the onion and celery and cook until the onion is soft and transparent. Add the carrot and cook until softened. Add the tomatoes, season with salt and pepper and mix in the herbs. Place the bacon wrapped pheasant breasts on top of the vegetables, cover tightly and simmer gently for 15 minutes. Pour over the wine and orange juice and cook for a further 5 minutes. Strain off the cooking liquid remove the bacon from the pheasant breasts keep the pheasant breasts and vegetables warm. Boil the cooking liquid to reduce by half.

Double-bladed knife Peel and core the apples.

Process the bacon until finely chopped and remove.

Thick slicing disc Slice the apples and fry them in butter until just soft. Arrange the apple slices on top of the vegetables, top with the pheasant breasts and chopped bacon and pour over the reduced stock.

Serve at once with potatoes and a green vegetable.

Stuffed Pigeons with White Grapes

For four people

4 young pigeons, dressed	Pinch thyme and sage
1 small fillet pork	2 oz (50 g) butter
1 small onion	12 oz (350 g) seedless white grapes
1 egg	4 pastry shells (see page 242)
Salt and freshly ground black pepper	Watercress for garnish

Hold the pigeons and press firmly with the fingers on either side of the breast bone to soften it. Remove the bone with a small sharp knife (a fiddly job but quite easy to do). Remove any sinews from the pork fillet and roughly chop the meat. Roughly chop the pigeon livers and hearts if you have them.

Peel and roughly chop the onion. Remove grapes from their stalks.

Double-bladed knife Process the onion until finely chopped. Add the pork fillet, pigeon hearts and livers and process until the fillet is very finely chopped (ground). Add the egg, season with salt and pepper and add the herbs and process until the ingredients are well mixed.

Stuff the pigeons with the pork mixture and sew up the vents and truss the birds neatly.

Melt the butter in a flameproof casserole, add the pigeons and brown them all over, sprinkle with a little salt, cover tightly and cook over a low heat for 40 minutes. Add the grapes to the juices in the pan and continue to cook for a further 10 minutes or until the pigeons are tender.

A Salad Arrangement (Salads: Pages 183–192)

Remove the pigeons and cut them neatly in half with kitchen scissors, removing the sewing string.

Remove the grapes with a slotted spoon and arrange them in warmed pastry shells. Arrange the pigeons on a serving dish and pour over the strained juices from the pan, arrange the pastry shells around the pigeons and garnish with watercress.

Jugged Hare

A classic country style dish garnished with delicious forcemeat balls.

For six people

1 hare jointed
Flour
1 tablespoon oil or dripping
2 onions
2 carrots
2 sticks celery
Bouquet garni
1½ pints (900 ml) good brown stock

2 tablespoons port
Juice ½ orange
Salt and freshly ground black pepper
1 slice of white bread with the crusts
  removed
½ lb (225 g) sausage meat
½ teaspoon mixed herbs
Oil for frying

Reserve the blood from the hare if possible.

Peel the onions and carrots and trim the celery.

Medium slicing disc Slice the onions, carrots and celery through the slicing disc. Coat the joints of hare with seasoned flour. Heat the oil in a frying pan, add the hare joints and cook over a high heat until the joints are browned on all sides. Remove the hare with a slotted spoon to a casserole. Add the vegetables to the juices in the pan, cover and simmer them gently for 10 minutes. Add the vegetables, removed with a slotted spoon, to the hare. Stir the stock into the residue in the pan, stirring well to pick up all the flavours. Strain the stock over the hare and vegetables, add the bouquet garni and simmer in a moderate oven (350°F. 175°C. Reg. 4) or over a low heat for about 2 hours until the hare is tender. Strain off the stock.

Heat the stock in a saucepan with the hare blood, port and orange juice and season with salt and pepper. Pour the sauce over the hare and vegetables and keep warm.

Double-bladed knife Process the bread until reduced to very fine crumbs. Add the sausage meat and herbs and season with salt and pepper.

Form into small balls with dampened hands.

Fry the balls until crisp and golden in hot shallow oil, drain well on kitchen paper and serve piled on top of the jugged hare.

RICE & PASTA

Risotto a la Signora

I have never had this risotto in any of the many Italian restaurants I frequent and I am, in fact, not sure it wasn't the dream of an Italian family I stayed with as a child. Whatever its origins it remains one of our most popular family meals at home, loved for its country flavour and robust and satisfying nature.

Note: If possible get the proper Italian risotto rice called "Arborio"; if I can't get that I use a good quality pudding rice rather than long grain which doesn't soak up the liquid in the right way. Take care not to overcook the rice, it should have a slight crunch to it.

For six people	10 oz (275 g) Arborio rice
	3 medium aubergines
	7 oz (200 g) Mozzarella cheese
	4 – 6 oz (100 – 150 g) uncooked gammon (or use lean bacon)
	2 tablespoons olive or sunflower oil
	1 small onion
	2 cloves garlic
	2 tins (15 oz 425 g) tomatoes

2 tablespoons tomato purée
1½ pints (30 fl oz 900 ml) good chicken stock
1 teaspoon dried basil
2 oz (50 g) butter
2 oz (50 g) Parmesan cheese
Oil for frying
Salt and freshly ground black pepper

Parmesan grating disc   Process the Parmesan cheese and remove.

Medium slicing disc   Process the Mozzarella cheese and remove.

Peel the aubergines. Process the aubergines and remove to a colander, sprinkle with salt and leave to "sweat" for one hour. Wipe the slices dry on kitchen paper.

Fry the slices until soft in a little oil and drain well on kitchen paper.

Roughly chop the gammon. Peel and roughly chop the onion.

Double-bladed knife   Process the gammon until finely chopped and remove. Process the onion and garlic until finely chopped and remove.

Process the tomatoes (If using the standard Magimix you will have to do it one tin at a time) until smooth. Heat 2 tablespoons oil in a large saucepan, add the gammon and cook until the fat is transparent. Add the onion and garlic and stir until the onion is transparent. Add the tomatoes, season with salt and pepper, mix in the basil and bring to the boil. Stir in the tomato purée and cook over a high heat, stirring every now and then, for 30 minutes. Remove ⅔ of the sauce. Add the rice to the sauce in the pan and stir until the rice is transparent. Cook the rice over a low heat, adding some of the stock every now and then until the stock is absorbed and rice is just tender. Add the butter and two-thirds of the Parmesan cheese and mix well. Place a layer of the rice in the bottom of a baking dish, cover with the aubergine and half of the tomato sauce, place over the slices of Mozzarella cheese and top with the remaining rice. Pour over the remaining sauce and sprinkle with the remaining Parmesan cheese.

Bake the dish in a moderate oven (350°F. 175°C Reg. 4) for about 20 minutes until hot through.

Mushroom Risotto

A substantial first course (or vegetable dish) but a delicious one before roast or grilled meat or poultry, try serving with a salad.

For five to six people

12 oz (350 g) Arborio or pudding rice	1 large onion
Small bunch parsley	¼ pint (5 fl oz 150 ml) dry white wine
8 oz (225 g) firm button mushrooms	1½ pints (30 fl oz 900 ml) chicken stock
3 oz (75 g) butter	4 oz (100 g) Parmesan cheese
2 oz (50 g) olive or sunflower oil	Salt and freshly ground black pepper

Remove the coarse stems from the parsley. Peel and roughly chop the onion.

Double-bladed knife   Process the parsley until finely chopped and remove.

Parmesan disc   Grate the Parmesan and remove.

Medium slicing disc   Process the mushrooms through the slicing blade and remove.

Double-bladed knife   Process the onion until finely chopped.

Heat half the butter with the oil.

Add the onion and cook over a low heat, stirring to prevent browning, until the onion is soft and transparent. Add the rice and stir over a low heat until the rice becomes transparent (about three minutes). Add the wine and stir until the wine has evaporated. Add the mushrooms and parsley and two thirds of the hot stock, season with salt and pepper and simmer gently (adding more stock as the mixture dries out) for about twenty minutes until the rice is soft and the liquid has all been absorbed. Stir in the remaining butter and half the Parmesan. Check the seasoning. Serve hot with the remaining Parmesan on the side.

Tomato Rice

Serve with a plain dish such as roast chicken or pork or use as an accompaniment to a curry. The mixture can also be used as a stuffing for tomatoes that are being served as a vegetable.

For four people

12 oz (350 g) long grain rice
1½ lbs (675 g) ripe tomatoes
4 cloves garlic
2 medium onions
Small bunch coriander or parsley
½ stick cinnamon
3 tablespoons sunflower oil

8 fl oz (240 ml) chicken stock
Salt and freshly ground black pepper
1 teaspoon salt
3 teaspoons sugar
½ teaspoon ground cumin or coriander

Soak the rice in cold water for thirty minutes and leave to drain well in a sieve. Cover the tomatoes with boiling water, leave to stand for three minutes and then slide off the skins. Discard the seeds and tough cores of the tomatoes. Peel and roughly chop the garlic and onions.

Double-bladed knife
Process the coriander or parsley until finely chopped and remove.
Combine the garlic and onions and process until the onions are fairly finely chopped.
Add the tomatoes and process until they are coarsely chopped. Heat the oil in a heavy, deep frying pan. Add the garlic, onions and tomatoes, the cinnamon and a generous grinding of black pepper. Cook over a high heat stirring occasionally, for ten minutes. Add the stock bring to the boil and cook for fifteen minutes over a moderate heat. Remove the cinnamon.

Double-bladed knife
Process the onion and tomato mixture until reduced to a purée. Place the rice in a saucepan, pour over the tomato purée and mix in the salt, sugar, cumin or coriander. Bring to the boil, stir well, lower the heat and simmer gently (if the mixture gets too dry add a little extra stock or water) for about 20 minutes until the rice is tender. Stir well, cover and leave to stand for 10 minutes before serving, sprinkle the top with coriander or parsley.

Classic Fried Rice

A wonderful mixture of rice and savoury ingredients finely chopped, dressed with sherry and soy sauce. Serve with other Chinese dishes or as a supper dish in its own right.

For four people

½ lb (225 g) cooked rice
2 spring onions
1 piece fresh ginger root (about ¾ in.
   2 cm long)
6 oz (175 g) cooked chicken
4 oz (100 g) cooked ham
2 oz (50 g) mushrooms
1 stick celery

4 water chestnuts (can be bought in tins)
½ green pepper
2 eggs
Salt and freshly ground black pepper
4 tablespoons sunflower oil
1½ tablespoons soy sauce
2 teaspoons dry sherry

Trim and roughly chop the spring onions.
Peel and roughly chop the ginger. Roughly chop the chicken and ham. Trim the celery stick.

Double-bladed knife

Process the ginger until very finely chopped. Add the spring onions and process until they are finely chopped. Add the celery and pepper, process until those are finely chopped and remove the ingredients.

Thin slicing disc

Process the mushrooms and water chestnuts through the slicing disc and remove.

Double-bladed knife

Process the chicken and ham until fairly finely chopped and remove.
Process the eggs until well mixed.
In a wok or a large heavy frying pan, heat 3 tablespoons of the oil until smoking. Add the ginger, onion, celery and pepper and stir over a high heat for 1 minute. Add the mushrooms and water chestnuts and stir for 30 seconds. Then add the rice and stir over a high heat for another minute. Add the sherry and soy sauce, season with salt and pepper and mix in the ham and chicken. Stir over a high heat for two minutes.
Heat the remaining oil in a non stick frying pan. When it is really hot, add the eggs, swirling them around the pan until they form a thin skin over the surface. Cook over a high heat until the eggs are set. Turn on to a board, roll up tightly and cut through the roll into thin strips.
Turn the fried rice on to a serving dish and scatter over the pieces of omelette. Serve at once.

MAGIMIX PASTA

Making your own pasta is as satisfactory as making home made bread and it isn't as difficult as you might think. It does take time though and if you plan to make a fair amount of your own pasta it is worth while investing in a pasta cutting machine (there is one available as an accessory to the Magimix) which both rolls out the dough and cuts it into even strips of varying thicknesses. Once you have perfected the basic pasta recipe you can then experiment with adding flavour and colour to the dough with other ingredients; the most usual variation is the green pasta 'verdi' made by adding spinach and herbs to the dough but you can also produce red pasta with a tomato colouring, yellow with saffron, orange with carrots and even ruby red with beetroot. Use 'strong' flour for your dough as it gives a better texture and flavour. The pasta can be dusted with polenta flour (available from Italian Delicatessens) and kept in an airtight container once it has dried out. It will keep for about two to three weeks. The elasticity of your pasta will vary according to the temperature of your kitchen and the general humidity. If it goes sticky while you work the dough then use more flour.

Basic pasta dough

12 oz (350 g) strong flour	3 eggs
Pinch salt	Water if necessary

Double-bladed knife Combine the flour, salt and eggs and process until the dough forms a smooth ball around the knife (add a little water if the dough is too dry but the dough needs to be stiff in order to work it properly). Turn on to a lightly floured board and knead for a few minutes until the dough is elastic. Wrap in polythene and leave to stand in a cool place for 1 hour.

If using the Magimix accessory follow the instructions that come with it.

Rolling by hand Take a little of the dough at a time, roll it out on a well floured board until it is almost transparently thin and cut into strips of the required thickness. Hang the finished dough over the backs of chairs and leave until dry to the touch before cooking.

Rolling by machine Feed the 'rested' dough through the rollers set at their thickest opening three times until it is absolutely smooth. Take a little dough at a time and roll it through the rollers set at their thinnest setting. Always flour the rollers before rolling. Adjust the machine to the thickness of pasta you require and roll through the flat sheets of prepared pasta. Hang the finished pasta over the backs of chairs to dry out completely before cooking or storing.

Cannelloni: Thin pasta cut into rectangles about 9 in. x 6 in. (22 x 15 cm) cooked filled with a savoury stuffing and reheated with a sauce.

Tagliatelle or fettucine: Thin ribbons of pasta which can be as thin as matchsticks.

Ravioli: Thin, flat sheets of pasta made into small square envelopes which are filled with a savoury filling.

Lasagne: Wide strips of pasta cooked and then formed into layers with a savoury filling sauce.

Tagliatelle verde

8 oz (225 g) spinach	Pinch salt and nutmeg
14 oz (400 g) strong flour	2 eggs

Wash over the spinach and cook it in a little boiling water, salted, until it is soft. Drain well, press out the excess water through a sieve and then squeeze out the remaining water by pressing the spinach in a clean dry cloth (it is important to get rid of all possible moisture).

Double-bladed knife   Process the spinach until reduced to a smooth purée, remove and leave to cool.

Double-bladed knife and a clean, dry bowl   Combine the flour, eggs and spinach and season with a little salt and ground nutmeg. Process the dough until it forms a smooth ball around the knife. Turn on to a lightly floured board and knead for a few minutes until the dough is elastic. Wrap in polythene and leave to stand in a cold place for one hour before rolling out as above.

Cooking pasta Bring a large pan of salted water to a brisk, rolling boil. Add the pasta and stir well to make sure none of the strands stick to each other. Boil over a high heat for about 8 minutes and taste by testing a strand of the pasta – it should be soft and tender but still firm and biteable.

Pasta with Spinach and Cheese Sauce

This dish requires pasta with a hole in it like short macaroni or penne so that the sauce goes into the pasta when it is tossed.

For six people

1 lb (450 g) pasta	2 tablespoons single cream
1 lb (450 g) spinach	2 tablespoons grated Parmesan cheese
8 oz (225 g) ricotta or cottage cheese	Salt and freshly ground black pepper
1 egg	Ground nutmeg

Wash the spinach and cook it in a small amount of boiling water salted, until the spinach is just tender (about 5 minutes). Drain well.

Double-bladed knife   Combine the spinach, ricotta or cottage cheese and Parmesan. Season with salt, pepper and a little ground nutmeg, add the egg and process until the spinach is finely chopped and the ingredients are well mixed. Turn into a basin and cook over hot water, stirring for five minutes. Cook the pasta in plenty of boiling salted water for about 10 minutes until it is just tender and drain well. Put the drained pasta into a clean saucepan, add the cream and mix well, pour over the sauce and toss over a moderate heat until the pasta is coated with the sauce. Serve at once.

Pasta with Carbonara Sauce

One of the classic pasta sauces which makes an excellent and delicious beginning to a meal. Choose a fairly robust pasta like a thick tagliatelle, bucatini, penne or elbow macaroni.

For six people

1 lb (450 g) pasta
5 oz (50 g) Parmesan cheese
3 tablespoons olive or sunflower oil
8 oz (225 g) fat streaky bacon with the rinds removed.

4 large eggs
5 oz (150 g) butter
6 tablespoons double cream
Salt and freshly ground black pepper

Parmesan disc
Double-bladed knife

Roughly chop the bacon rashers. Process the Parmesan cheese and remove. Process the bacon until finely chopped and remove. Combine the eggs, butter and cream in the Magimix bowl and process until the eggs are completely broken up and the ingredients are well mixed. Season with salt and pepper and switch on and off to mix in the seasoning. Cook the pasta in plenty of boiling salted water for about 8 minutes or until just tender and drain well. Heat the oil in the frying pan, add the bacon and stir over a medium high heat until the bacon is crisp. Put the cooked pasta into a large clean saucepan. Add the bacon and half the cheese and toss over a moderate heat until the ingredients are well mixed. Season with plenty of freshly ground black pepper. Add the egg mixture and continue to toss until the eggs begin to thicken and the pasta is lightly coated with the sauce – do not overcook, the eggs should still be a little runny. Turn on to a serving dish and serve at once with the remaining cheese on the side.

Variations Add 6 oz (175 g) cooked or tinned asparagus tips to the pasta when you add the egg sauce.
Use a finely chopped Parma ham instead of bacon. Don't cook the ham but instead add it to the pasta with the oil before adding the egg sauce.

Tagliatelle Verde with Tomatoes, Olives and Basil

Illustrated on page 126

One of those marvellously simple and rustic Italian first courses which puts you in a good mood for the whole of the rest of the meal.

For six people

1 lb (450 g) tagliatelle verde (see page 156)
Small bunch fresh basil (or use 1 teaspoon dried basil softened in a little warm lemon juice.)

1 ½ lb (675 g) firm, ripe tomatoes
24 black olives
2 tablespoons olive or sunflower oil
2 oz (50 g) butter
Salt and freshly ground black pepper

Cover the tomatoes with boiling water, leave to stand for three minutes and then slide off the skins. Remove the coarse cores and seeds.

Cut the olives off their stones. Remove any coarse stems from the basil.

Double-bladed knife   Process the basil until finely chopped. Add the tomatoes and olives and process until the olives are finely chopped. Add the oil, season with salt and pepper and process to mix. Cook the tagliatelle verde with plenty of boiling salted water for about 8 minutes and drain well. Put the tagliatelle into a warm bowl, add the sauce and the butter cut into small pieces and toss until the ingredients are well mixed. Serve at once.

Baked Tagliatelle with Sauce

An aromatic dish similar to the Turkish dish of Moussaka but with the aubergines being replaced by tagliatelle. Make your own tagliatelle with your Magimix or buy the Italian commercial varieties.

For eight people

10 oz (275 g) white tagliatelle (see page 155)
10 oz (275 g) green tagliatelle made with spinach (see page 156)
1 large onion
2 cloves garlic
3 oz (75 g) bacon rashers
2 tablespoons sunflower oil
1 lb (450 g) leg of lamb

1 tin (15 fl oz 425 g) tomatoes
¼ pint (5 fl oz 150 ml) white wine
Salt and freshly ground black pepper
½ teaspoon oregano
4 eggs
¼ pint (5 fl oz 150 ml) cream
2 oz (50 g) Cheddar cheese
1 oz (25 g) grated Parmesan cheese
Pinch ground nutmeg

Cook the tagliatelle in boiling salted water until just tender and drain well. Peel and roughly chop the onion and garlic. Remove the rind from the bacon rashers. Cut the meat into cubes.

Fine grating disc   Grate the Cheddar cheese and remove.

Double-bladed knife   Process the onion and garlic until finely chopped. Heat the oil in a saucepan, add the onion and garlic and cook over a low heat until the onion is soft and transparent.

Process the bacon until finely chopped.

Add the bacon to the onion and continue to cook for three minutes.

Process the meat until finely ground.

Add the meat to the onion and bacon and brown over a high heat. Add the tomatoes, wine and oregano, season with salt and pepper and bring to the boil. Cook over a medium high heat, stirring every now and then, without a cover for 30 minutes.

Double-bladed knife and a clean bowl   Combine the Cheddar, Parmesan, cream and eggs and process until smooth. Season with salt, pepper and nutmeg. Mix the meat sauce with the cooked tagliatelle and transfer the ingredients to a deep, lightly buttered, baking dish. Pour over the custard mixture and bake in a moderate oven (350°F. 175°C Reg. 4) for 30 minutes until the custard is set and lightly browned.

Baked Macaroni with Chicken and Cheese

Such a simple dish and yet one that is both subtle and sophisticated. Serve it with a green or mixed salad.

For four people

1 lb (450 g) macaroni
4 oz (100 g) cooked chicken
3 oz (75 g) cottage cheese
2 oz (50 g) cream cheese

3 oz (75 g) Gruyère cheese
Salt and freshly ground black pepper
Pinch ground nutmeg
2 oz (50 g) butter

Double-bladed knife

Process the chicken until coarsely chopped and remove.

Coarse grating disc

Grate the Gruyère cheese.

Double-bladed knife

Process the cottage cheese until smooth. Add the cream cheese and Gruyère, season with salt and freshly ground black pepper and a pinch of nutmeg, process to mix. Cook the macaroni in plenty of fast boiling salted water until just tender and drain well. Add the mixed cheeses to the drained pasta and toss until well mixed. Add the chicken and mix well. Turn the pasta into a greased baking dish, dot with butter and bake in a hot oven (400°F. 200°C Reg. 6) for 10 minutes.

Pasta with Chicken Livers and Tomatoes

Pasta with a rich, savoury, sauce. Use spaghetti, macaroni, tagliatelle or tagliatelle verde.

For four to six people

1 lb (450 g) pasta
1 small onion
8 oz (225 g) chicken livers
1 lb (450 g) tomatoes
4 tablespoons olive or sunflower oil

3 fl oz (90 ml) strong chicken stock
3 oz (75 g) Parmesan cheese
Pinch rosemary and oregano
Salt and freshly ground black pepper

Peel and roughly chop the onion. Trim the chicken livers, removing any fibres or yellow flesh. Cover the tomatoes with boiling water for three minutes and then drain, slide off the skins and remove the core and seeds.

Parmesan grating disc

Process the Parmesan and remove.

Double-bladed knife

Process the onion until finely chopped and remove. Process the chicken livers until fairly finely chopped and remove. Process the tomatoes until puréed. Heat the oil in a small saucepan, add the onion and cook over a medium heat until the onion is lightly browned. Add the chicken livers and brown quickly over a high heat. Add the tomato purée and chicken stock, mix in the herbs and season with salt and plenty of freshly ground black pepper. Cook over a medium heat, stirring, for about five minutes until the sauce is thick and rich.

Cook the pasta in plenty of boiling salted water until it is just tender and drain it well. Add the Parmesan to the pasta and mix well. Add the sauce and toss the pasta to mix well. Serve at once.

Ravioli Milanese

Ravioli is a bit fiddly to make but your own will be infinitely superior to a commercial brand, and worth the effort. You can buy special ravioli tins from good kitchen shops which makes the job easier.

For four people	
Home made pasta (see page 155)	**Sauce**
8 oz (225 g) chuck steak	4 oz (100 g) chuck steak
1 onion	1 large onion
6 oz (175 g) fresh or frozen spinach	1 clove garlic
2 oz (50 g) Parmesan cheese	4 oz (100 g) Parmesan cheese
1 tablespoon tomato purée	2 tablespoons olive or sunflower oil
1 egg	3 tablespoons tomato purée
2 tablespoons olive oil	8 fl oz (240 ml) chicken or beef stock
Salt and freshly ground black pepper	

First make the filling for the ravioli. Cut the meat into cubes. Peel and roughly chop the onion. Cook the spinach in a little boiling, salted water until just tender and drain well, pressing out all the excess water.

Parmesan disc
Double-bladed knife
Process the Parmesan and remove.
Process the onion until finely chopped and remove. Process the spinach until puréed and remove. Process the meat until finely chopped (ground) and remove. Process the egg with the tomato purée until smooth.

Heat the oil in a saucepan, add the onion and cook over a medium high heat until the onion is lightly browned. Raise the heat, add the meat and brown quickly. Add the spinach and Parmesan and mix well. Mix in the tomato purée and egg, season with salt and pepper and cook over a high heat until the filling is thick.

Make the sauce. Cut the meat into cubes. Peel and roughly chop the onion and garlic.

Parmesan disc
Double-bladed knife
Process the Parmesan and remove.
Process the onion and garlic until finely chopped and remove. Process the meat until finely chopped (ground). Heat the oil in a saucepan, add the onion, garlic and meat and brown over a high heat. Add half the cheese and the tomato purée and mix well. Mix in the stock, season with salt and pepper and simmer for 15 minutes.

Roll out the pasta, very thinly, into two equal sized rectangles. Place teaspoonfuls of the filling at 1 in. (2·5 cm) intervals on one sheet of the pasta. Moisten the pasta in between the spoonfuls of filling with a little water and cover with the second layer of pasta. Press firmly in between the filling with the fingertips to seal the ravioli and then cut into squares with a pastry wheel.

Cook the ravioli in boiling salted water for 15 minutes, remove with a slotted spoon from the water and drain on kitchen paper.

Arrange the ravioli in layers in an oiled baking dish with a layer of sauce and some of the remaining Parmesan cheese in between each layer. Finish with a layer of sauce and Parmesan and bake in a hot oven (400°F. 200°C Reg. 6) for 15 minutes.

Spaghetti or Tagliatelle with Tuna and Parsley Sauce

For six people

1 lb (450 g) spaghetti or tagliatelle
1 large bunch parsley
1 6/7 oz (175/200 g) tin tuna
2 cloves garlic

2 anchovy fillets
8 fl oz (240 ml) olive or sunflower oil
Salt and freshly ground black pepper

Double-bladed knife

Remove the tough stalks from the parsley.

Process the parsley until finely chopped. Add the tuna and the oil from the tin and process until the tuna is reduced to a paste. Add the garlic and anchovies and continue to process until a smooth paste is formed. With the motor still running add the olive or sunflower oil at little at a time, to make a thick, smooth paste like a mayonnaise. Add salt and pepper to taste and process to mix.

Cook the pasta in plenty of boiling salted water for 10–12 minutes until just tender and drain well. Put into a clean pan with the sauce and toss lightly with two forks to incorporate the sauce into the pasta. Serve at once.

Tagliatelle with Tomatoes, Mozzarella and Oregano

For six people

1 lb (450 g) tagliatelle
Salt and freshly ground black pepper
6 small, firm, ripe tomatoes

2 teaspoons dried oregano
8 oz (225 g) Mozzarella cheese
7 fl oz (210 ml) olive or sunflower oil

Double-bladed knife Roughly chop the Mozzarella cheese.
Process the Mozzarella cheese until finely chopped, and remove.

Chipper disc Process the tomatoes through the chipper disc without putting any pressure on the pusher.
Cook the tagliatelle in plenty of salted boiling water for about 8 minutes and drain well. Put into a clean saucepan with the oil and oregano, season with salt and pepper and mix well. Add the tomatoes and cheese and toss lightly over a medium heat. Serve at once.

Scallopped Macaroni with Chicken Sauce

For four people

6 oz (175 g) short macaroni
Salt and freshly ground black pepper
1½ slices of white bread with the crusts removed
6 oz (175 g) cooked chicken
1 oz (25 g) Parmesan cheese
2 oz (50 g) Gruyère cheese

1 large onion
4 rashers streaky bacon with the rinds removed
6 oz (175 g) firm button mushrooms
3 tablespoons of sunflower oil
7 fl oz (210 ml) double cream
A pinch nutmeg

Double-bladed knife Process the bread until reduced to fine crumbs and remove.
Process the chicken until finely chopped and remove.
Parmesan disc Process the Parmesan and remove.
Fine grating disc Process the Gruyère cheese and remove.
Peel and roughly chop the onion. Roughly chop the bacon.
Double-bladed knife Process the onion and bacon together until both are finely chopped.

Medium slicing disc Slice the mushrooms.
Cook the macaroni in plenty of boiling salted water with 1 tablespoon oil for about 10 minutes until tender. Drain well.
Heat the remaining oil in a saucepan. Add the onion and bacon and cook until the onion is soft and transparent. Add the mushrooms and cook for a further 3 minutes. Add the cream, chicken and pasta and season with salt, freshly ground black pepper and a pinch of nutmeg.
Butter 4 ramekin dishes or scallop shells, fill them with the pasta mixture, sprinkle with the breadcrumbs and mixed Parmesan and Gruyère cheese and brown under a moderately hot grill. Serve as a first course or a supper dish with baked potatoes and a salad on the side.

Pasta with Tuscan Chicken Sauce

Some things in the way of food are so simple and yet so utterly, utterly delicious you almost cannot believe it is possible. This is just such a sauce – I had something like it in Tuscany, in a small wayside trattoria; I was unable to get the exact recipe at the time but I experimented and came up with my own version, which if not 100% authentic, is very similar and very, very, good. Serve it with home made tagliatelle.

For six people

1 lb (450 g) home made tagliatelle verde (see page 156)
6 oz (175 g) raw chicken
1 bunch parsley
4 oz (100 g) streaky bacon
1 onion

1 clove garlic
1 green pepper
2 tablespoons olive oil
1 tin beef consommé
¼ pint (5 fl oz 150 ml) double cream
Salt and freshly ground black pepper

Cut the chicken into cubes. Remove the coarse stalks from the parsley. Remove the rinds from the bacon and roughly chop the rashers. Peel and roughly chop the onion and the garlic. Remove the core and seeds from the green pepper and roughly chop the flesh. Bring the consommé to the boil in a small saucepan and boil over the highest possible heat until it is reduced by half. Add the cream, mix well and continue to boil until the liquid is again reduced by half. Season with salt and pepper.

Double-bladed knife

Process the parsley until finely chopped and remove. Process the onions and garlic with the bacon until they are all finely chopped and remove. Process the green pepper until it is finely chopped and remove. Process the chicken until coarsely chopped.

Heat the oil in a frying pan. Add the bacon, onion and garlic, cook over a low heat until the onion is soft and transparent. Add the chicken and green pepper and continue to cook over a medium heat until the chicken is tender. Season with salt and pepper.

Cook the tagliatelle verde in plenty of fast boiling, salted water until it is just tender and drain well. Put the tagliatelle into a warmed serving bowl, add the chicken mixture and toss well. Add the hot consommé sauce and parsley and toss with two forks to mix the sauce into the other ingredients.

Serve at once.

Pasta with a Sauce from the Lipari Islands

This is one of the best pasta sauces I know. It makes pasta into a good, hearty and inexpensive main course and should be followed by a crisp, mixed salad. I discovered this recipe on a sailing trip around the coast of Italy and have been serving it successfully ever since. In the original recipe raw chuck steak is used but I have also made the sauce with great success with cooked salt brisket or silverside of beef.

For six people

1 oz (25 g) Parmesan cheese
10 oz (275 g) chuck steak
1 medium aubergine
1 onion
2 tablespoons olive or sunflower oil
2 tablespoons tomato purée

¼ pint (5 fl oz 150 ml) red wine
Pinch dried oregano
Salt and freshly ground black pepper
1 lb fat macaroni or penne pasta
2 eggs
2 oz (50 g) butter

Parmesan disc — Grate the Parmesan cheese and remove. Roughly chop the steak. Halve the aubergine. Peel and roughly chop the onion.

Double-bladed knife — Process the onion until fairly finely chopped and remove. Process the meat until coarsely chopped and remove.

Chipper disc — Process the aubergine through the chipper disc. Heat the oil in a medium saucepan, add the onion and cook over a low heat until the onion is soft and transparent. Raise the heat and add the meat, cook the meat over a high flame until browned on all sides. Lower the heat again, add the aubergine and mix well until the oil has been absorbed. Add the wine, tomato purée and oregano, season with salt and pepper and cook over a low heat, stirring every now and then to prevent sticking, for about 45 minutes until most of the liquid has been absorbed and the meat is fork tender.

Double-bladed knife and a clean bowl — Process the eggs until well mixed.
Cook the pasta in plenty of fast boiling, salted water until it is just tender and drain well. Return the pasta to a clean pan. Add the butter, eggs and a light seasoning of salt and pepper and mix in the meat sauce. Toss lightly over a medium heat and serve at once with the Parmesan cheese on the side.

Chilli Meat Sauce for Pasta

For six people

1 large onion
1 clove garlic
1 lb (450 g) chuck steak
1 large green pepper
4 tablespoons sunflower oil
2 teaspoons chilli powder

Salt and freshly ground black pepper
1 tin (15 oz 425 g) tomatoes
1 chicken stock cube
Pinch mixed herbs
4 tablespoons red wine

Peel and roughly chop the onion and garlic. Cut the meat into cubes. Remove the core and seeds from the green pepper.

Double-bladed knife   Process the onion and garlic until fairly finely chopped, and remove. Process the pepper until finely chopped and remove. Process the meat until fairly finely chopped (ground) and remove.

Heat the oil in a frying pan, add the onion and garlic and cook over a low heat, stirring every now and then until the onion is soft and transparent.

Raise the heat to high, add the meat and cook, stirring, until the meat is well browned. Add the green pepper, tomatoes, chicken stock cube, chilli powder, seasoning, herbs and red wine. Mix with a fork to break up the tomatoes, bring to the boil and cook, uncovered for about 30 minutes or until the meat is absolutely tender.

Serve with hot, buttered, pasta.

Smoked Salmon Sauce for Pasta

Buy end cut pieces of smoked salmon from a good fishmonger for this dish and serve the sauce with spaghetti, noodles or short cut pasta.

For five to six people

1 oz (25 g) Parmesan cheese
4 oz (100 g) smoked salmon or smoked salmon pieces
½ pint (10 fl oz 300 ml) double cream
¼ pint (5 fl oz 150 ml) whisky

Salt and freshly ground black pepper
Pinch cayenne
1 lb (450 g) spaghetti, tagliolini or other pasta
½ oz (13 g) butter

Parmesan Grating disc
Double-bladed knife

Process the Parmesan cheese and remove.

Process the smoked salmon until coarsely chopped. Add the cream, whisky, and season with salt, pepper and cayenne. Process until smoked salmon is fairly finely chopped and the ingredients are well mixed.

Bring a pot with plenty of salted water to the boil, drop in the pasta and boil for about 12 minutes, or until just tender. Drain well. In a large saucepan, melt the butter, add the pasta and toss well. Add the smoked salmon sauce and toss over a medium heat until the pasta is warmed through. Serve at once with the grated Parmesan on the side.

VEGETABLES

Courgettes Flan

In France a 'flan' does not always, necessarily, mean incorporating pastry into the ingredients. This typical 'flan' from the South of France is merely layers of courgettes cooked with a cheesy egg custard. You can serve it as a first course, as a vegetable dish or, if you add some chopped ham, as a main course.

For four people

1 lb (450 g) small courgettes
2 oz (50 g) Cheddar cheese
4 eggs

½ pint (10 fl oz 300 ml) milk
Salt and freshly ground black pepper
Pinch nutmeg and cayenne

Cut off the stalks from the courgettes.

Medium slicing disc
Slice the courgettes. Place them in a colander, sprinkle the slices with salt and place a plate with a weight on top. Leave to stand for 1 hour and then rinse them in cold water and blanche the slices in boiling salted water for 3 minutes. Drain really well.

Medium grating disc
Grate the cheese, and remove.

Double-bladed knife
Combine the eggs and milk, season with salt, pepper, nutmeg and cayenne and process until smooth.

Arrange the courgette slices in a buttered baking dish, sprinkle over the cheese and pour over the custard. Bake in a hot oven (400°F. 200°C Reg. 6) for 35 minutes or until the custard is set and the dish is puffed and golden brown. Serve at once.

Variation. To use a main course dish sprinkle the courgettes with 6 oz (175 g) ham, chopped with the double-bladed knife, before adding the custard.

Mixed Vegetable Casserole

A useful way of letting vegetables cook by themselves to serve as a side dish to a main course or even by themselves as a supper dish with a baked potato on the side.

For four people	8 oz (225 g) firm small tomatoes	2 sticks celery
	8 oz (225 g) courgettes	2 oz (50 g) firm button mushrooms
	1 medium onion	2 oz (50 g) Cheddar cheese
	1 clove garlic	¼ pint (5 fl oz 150 ml) chicken stock
	1 large carrot	Salt and freshly ground black pepper

Fine grating disc Grate the Cheddar cheese and remove. Remove the stalks from the tomatoes and wash if necessary. Peel and halve the onion. Peel the garlic. Peel the carrot. Trim the celery sticks.

Chipper disc Process the tomatoes and remove.

Thin slicing disc Slice the onion and garlic and remove. Slice the mushrooms and remove. Slice the celery stalks and remove. Slice the carrot and remove.

Medium or thick slicing disc Slice the courgettes and remove.

Layer the vegetables in a buttered baking dish in the following order. Onion and garlic, carrot, celery, mushrooms, courgettes and tomatoes, seasoning the layers with salt and pepper. Pour over the stock, cover with foil and bake in a hot oven (400°F. 200°C Reg. 6) for 45 minutes. Remove the foil, cover with the cheese and bake for a further 15 minutes or until the vegetables are tender.

Ratatouille

Ratatouille is one of those excellent dishes that you can make how you will with no firm rules, and only the taste at the end to tell whether this particular dish has been more of a triumph than usual. Ratatouille is versatile in every way; you can serve it hot as a vegetable; cold as a salad or first course or even make what is left of it (if any) into a first rate soup. The basic ingredients are aubergines, onion, tomatoes, peppers and courgettes – you can do without the peppers and courgettes but the aubergines, tomatoes and onions are essential.

For six people	2 onions	1 tin (15 oz 425 g) tomatoes
	2 cloves garlic	2 tablespoons olive or sunflower oil
	1 large aubergine	4 tablespoons red wine
	1 green pepper	1 tablespoon tomato purée
	1 red pepper	Salt and freshly ground black pepper
	8 oz (225 g) courgettes	½ teaspoon dried oregano

Peel the onions and garlic and chop them roughly. Remove the core and seeds from the peppers.

Double-bladed knife Process the onions and garlic until fairly finely chopped and remove. Process the tomatoes until roughly chopped and remove.

Chipper disc Process the aubergine through the disc.

Medium slicing disc Process the peppers and remove.

Process the courgettes.

Heat the oil in a large heavy frying pan or flameproof casserole. Add the onions and garlic and cook over a medium heat, stirring every now and then, until the onion is soft and transparent. Add the aubergine and peppers and continue to stir over a medium heat for four minutes. Add the courgettes and cook for a further minute. Add the tomatoes, red wine, tomato purée and oregano, season with salt and pepper, mix well, bring to the boil and cook, without covering, for about 30 minutes until the aubergine is soft and all the flavours have amalgamated. If there is too much juice, raise the heat for the last five minutes or so to reduce it. Check seasoning before serving.

To serve as an *hors d' oeuvres* chill the ratatouille and garnish it with finely chopped parsley, black olives and fillets of anchovy.

Provençal Vegetable Casserole

The combination of these vegetables is so good that I can highly recommend this dish as a light supper, first or main course, although it is also a delight to serve with a plain main course.

For four people

1 tablespoon juniper berries	2 oz (50 g) clarified butter (better still
1 lb (450 g) potatoes	use chicken, duck or goose fat)
1 lb (450 g) tomatoes	3 tablespoons stock
2 large onions	Salt and freshly ground black pepper

Peel the potatoes. Peel and halve the onions.

Crush the juniper berries with a knife on a chopping board.

Medium slicing disc Slice the potatoes and remove. Slice the onions and remove (if the potatoes are to stand for any time they should be covered with cold water at this point and then drained well).

Chipper disc Process the tomatoes through the chipper disc.

Butter or grease a baking dish with some of the butter or fat. Arrange a third of the potatoes in the bottom, cover with half the onions and tomatoes, dot with butter or fat, season with salt and pepper and sprinkle over half the juniper berries. Fill the dish with the remaining vegetables in the same way finishing with a layer of potatoes. Dot the top with butter or fat, season with salt and pepper and pour over the stock. Cover tightly with foil and bake in a moderately hot oven (375°F. 190°C Reg. 5) for 1 hour.

Stuffed Aubergines

Serve this as a vegetable or a substantial main course. I like it cold too, cut into thick slices, with a spread of salads.

For four people

2 medium to large aubergines
Oil
1 onion
2 cloves garlic
4 courgettes
4 tomatoes

Salt and freshly ground black pepper
¼ teaspoon oregano
1 tablespoon tomato purée
6 oz (175 g) cooked long grain rice
2 oz (50 g) Gruyère cheese
A pinch of cayenne

Halve the aubergines lengthwise. Using a sharp pointed knife score around the sides of the cut aubergine about ¼ in. (·6 cm) from the skin and then score across the cut surface without piercing the skin.

Brush with oil and bake in a hot oven (425°F. 220°C Reg. 7) cut side up for about 25 minutes until the flesh of the aubergine is tender.

Leave to cool, then scoop out the flesh.

Peel and roughly chop the onion and garlic. Roughly chop the courgettes. Cover the tomatoes with boiling water, leave them to stand for three minutes and then slide off the skins. Halve the tomatoes and scoop out the seeds and any coarse cores.

Double-bladed knife   Process the onion and garlic until finely chopped and remove. Process the courgettes and aubergine flesh until finely chopped and remove.

Process the tomatoes until finely chopped and remove.

Heat two tablespoons oil in a frying pan. Add the onion and garlic and cook over a low heat, stirring, until the onion is soft and transparent. Add the courgettes, aubergines and tomatoes, season with oregano, salt and freshly ground black pepper and mix in the tomato purée. Simmer for 15 minutes and mix in the rice. Pile the aubergine skins with the vegetable and rice mixture.

Coarse grating disc   Grate the Gruyère cheese and spread it on top of the aubergines. Dribble a little oil over the top, sprinkle with a little cayenne and bake in a moderate oven (350°F. 175°C Reg. 4) for about 30 minutes until hot through and golden brown.

Chinese Stir-Fry Mixed Vegetables

Illustrated on page 147

For eight people

1 clove garlic
1 walnut-sized piece of fresh ginger root
3 firm small tomatoes
2 courgettes
1 small onion
1 small green pepper

1 stalk celery
4 oz (100 g) fresh or frozen peas
3 tablespoons vegetable oil
2 tablespoons soy sauce
Salt and freshly ground black pepper

Double-bladed knife Peel and roughly chop the garlic and ginger. Peel and halve the onion. Remove the seeds and core from the green pepper. Trim the celery.

Double-bladed knife Process the garlic and ginger until finely chopped and remove.
Process the onion until coarsely chopped and remove.

Medium slicing disc Slice the pepper and remove.
Slice the celery and remove.

Chipper disc Process the courgettes and remove.
Process the tomatoes and remove.
Heat the oil in a large frying pan or 'wok' until a haze rises from the oil. Add the garlic and ginger and stir over a high heat for 30 seconds.
Add the onion and stir for 30 seconds.
Add the celery and stir for 30 seconds.
Add the courgettes and pepper and stir for 2 minutes.
Add the tomatoes and peas and cook for a further 3 minutes, stirring all the time.
Add the soy sauce, season with salt and pepper and serve as soon as possible.

Purée of Red Peppers and Rice

Another example of the new vegetable dishes which are emerging with the new cuisines of the 1980s. An extremely tasty dish to serve with plain meat, fish and poultry dishes.

For four people

3 large red peppers
1 large onion
4 oz (100 g) butter
8 oz (225 g) cooked rice

3 fl oz (90 ml) chicken stock
¼ pint (5 fl oz 150 ml) double cream
Salt and freshly ground black pepper

Pierce the peppers with a fork and turn them under a grill or over a gas flame until the skins are blackened and will peel off easily. Cool the peppers and slide off the skin. Remove the core and seeds from the peppers and roughly chop the flesh. Peel and roughly chop the onion.

Double-bladed knife Process the pepper and onion until finely chopped.
Heat half the butter in a frying pan. Add the onion and pepper and cook over a medium heat until the vegetables are soft and tender.

Double-bladed knife Process the cooked onion and pepper until reduced to a purée. Return the purée to a clean pan. Add the rice and stock and cook until the liquid is absorbed into the rice and vegetables, season with salt and pepper and stir in the remaining butter and cream.
Heat through without boiling.

Purée of Beetroot

The excitements of 'Cuisine Minceur' and 'Nouvelle Cuisine' have introduced us to the delights of puréed vegetables. This unusual way of serving beetroot makes an otherwise rather mundane vegetable into a delicious accompaniment to pork and game dishes.

For four people

1 lb (450 g) cooked beetroot
1 medium onion
1 clove garlic
1 tablespoon sunflower oil
2 tomatoes

3 tablespoons red wine vinegar
Salt and freshly ground black pepper
4 tablespoons double cream
4 tablespoons chicken stock

Peel the beetroot if necessary. Peel and roughly chop the onion and garlic. Cover the tomatoes with boiling water, leave them to stand for 3 minutes and slide off the skins. Scoop out the seeds and any tough core with a teaspoon and roughly chop the tomato flesh.

Coarse grating disc

Grate the beetroot and remove.

Double-bladed knife

Process the onion and the garlic until finely chopped and remove.
Process the tomato until finely chopped.
Heat the oil in a heavy frying pan or saucepan. Add the onion and garlic and cook over a low heat, stirring to prevent sticking, until the onion is soft and transparent. Add the vinegar and boil until the vinegar has evaporated. Mix in the beetroot and tomato purée, season with salt and pepper, mix well, cover and simmer for 30 minutes.

Double-bladed knife

Process the vegetables until smooth. Add the cream and stock, check seasoning and process to mix the ingredients. Garnish the purée with some finely chopped parsley.

Other good Vegetable Purées

Cauliflower Purée: Purée cooked cauliflower with a little butter, cream, salt, pepper and nutmeg.

Carrot Purée: Cook the carrots with some finely chopped onion and purée with a little cooked potato to make a rich orange purée. Garnish the purée with finely chopped parsley.

Purée of Peas: Purée cooked peas with some finely chopped onion softened in butter and some cream and season with salt, pepper and a pinch of ground nutmeg. The purée can be garnished with finely chopped mint.

Purée of Celeriac: One of the best of all purées; serve it by itself or use it to fill some halved scooped out skinned tomatoes. Purée cooked celeriac with a little lemon juice, some cooked potato, a little cream and seasoning.

Purée of Broad Beans: Purée young broad beans with some butter and cream and season with salt, pepper and a little freshly chopped or dried savory.

French Beans with Tomato and Black Olive Sauce

For four people   1 lb (450 g) French beans
2 cloves garlic
1½ tablespoons olive or sunflower oil
6 small, firm, ripe tomatoes

Pinch mixed herbs or oregano
Salt and freshly ground black pepper
6 black olives

Top and tail the beans and cook them in a little boiling salted water for 4 minutes. Drain well and refresh in cold water; drain well again.
Peel the garlic cloves and roughly chop.
Double-bladed knife   Process the stoned olives until coarsely chopped and remove.
Chipper disc   Process the tomatoes through the chipper blade.
Heat the oil in a frying pan. Add the garlic and tomatoes and cook over a low heat, stirring, until the sauce is thick. Season with salt, pepper and herbs. Add the beans and olives and stir gently over a medium high heat until the beans are hot through.

Broccoli with Bacon, Onion and Hermes Sauce

This recipe can also be used with florettes of cauliflower, calabrese or with cabbage.

For four people   1½ lbs (675 g) purple sprouting broccoli
Salt
4 oz (100 g) bacon

1 large onion
1½ tablespoons sunflower oil
Hermes sauce (see page 256)

Blanch the broccoli in boiling salted water for five minutes and drain well.
Remove the rinds from the bacon and roughly chop the rashers. Peel and roughly chop the onion.
Double-bladed knife   Process the onion until finely chopped and remove.
Process the bacon until finely chopped and remove.
Heat the oil in a frying pan. Add the bacon and cook over a medium heat, stirring for three minutes, add the onion and cook until it is soft and transparent. Add the blanched broccoli and toss over a medium heat for three minutes or until the broccoli is just tender but still crisp. Turn into a serving dish and pour over the Hermes Sauce.
Note: This is such a good vegetable dish that I sometimes serve it as a first course in its own right.

Buttered Courgettes and Mushrooms

For four people

Small bunch parsley
8 oz (225 g) courgettes
8 oz (225 g) button mushrooms

1½ oz (40 g) butter
1 teaspoon lemon juice
Salt and freshly ground black pepper

Double-bladed knife

Remove any coarse stalks from the parsley.
Process the parsley until finely chopped and remove.

Medium slicing disc

Process the courgettes and the mushrooms.
Melt the butter in a frying pan. Add the courgettes and mushrooms and cook over a medium heat, shaking the pan, for about 4 minutes. Sprinkle over the lemon juice and season with salt and pepper. Turn onto a serving dish and sprinkle over the parsley.

Courgettes with Tomatoes, Mushrooms and Bacon

Even in the winter when courgettes are expensive they go a long way if you slice them thinly and always provide an attractive vegetable dish to go with almost any main course. This dish can also be served, with a vinaigrette dressing, as a first course. Flavour it with some garlic squeezed through a garlic press and some finely chopped parsley chopped in your Magimix and serve it hot or cold.

For four to six people

8 oz (225 g) courgettes
6 oz (175 g) tomatoes
3 oz (75 g) firm button mushrooms
2 oz (50 g) streaky bacon rashers with the rinds removed

Salt and freshly ground black pepper
2 tablespoons oil

Double-bladed knife

Trim off the ends from the courgettes. Roughly chop the bacon.
Process the bacon until finely chopped and remove.
Process the tomatoes until coarsely chopped and remove.

Medium slicing disc

Slice the courgettes and mushrooms.
Heat the oil in a frying pan. Add the bacon, stirring it around the pan to prevent sticking and to separate the pieces and cook until the bacon is crisp. Remove the bacon on to a piece of kitchen paper with a slotted spoon. Add the courgettes and mushrooms to the fat in the pan and cook over a medium high heat, tossing the ingredients or stirring them lightly with a spoon. After two minutes add the tomatoes and continue to cook for a further two minutes until the vegetables are tender but still crisp and firm. Season with salt and pepper. Turn into a serving dish and sprinkle over the bacon pieces.

Leeks with Cream and Cheese Sauce

For six people

2 lbs (900 g) leeks
Salt
Small bunch parsley
2 rashers streaky bacon
1½ oz (40 g) butter
3 oz (75 g) Cheddar cheese

1 oz (25 g) Gruyère cheese
2 tablespoons flour
7 fl oz (210 ml) milk
Freshly ground black pepper
Ground nutmeg and cayenne

Double-bladed knife
Fine grating disc
Medium or Thick slicing disc

Trim and wash the leeks and drain them well. Remove any tough stalks from the parsley. Remove the rinds from the bacon.
Process the parsley until finely chopped and remove.
Process the bacon until coarsely chopped and remove.
Grate the Cheddar and Gruyère cheeses and remove.
Slice the leeks.
Cook the leeks in boiling salted water until just tender and drain well.
Melt the butter in a saucepan, add the bacon and cook over a low heat without browning for four minutes, stirring to prevent sticking. Add the flour and mix well. Gradually blend in the milk stirring continually over a medium high heat until the sauce comes to the boil and is thick and smooth. Add the parsley and threequarters of the cheese and season with salt, pepper, cayenne and nutmeg and cook, stirring, for two minutes. Add the leeks to the sauce and mix lightly. Turn into a serving dish, scatter over the remaining cheese and a little cayenne and bake in a hot oven (400°F. 200°C Reg. 6) for 10 minutes.

Cauliflower Cheese with Bacon

Cauliflower cheese by itself always makes a good vegetable but add some finely chopped bacon, flavour the cheese sauce with a little mustard and give it a lift with a touch of white wine and you have something extra special.

For six people

1 medium cauliflower
Bicarbonate of soda
1 oz (25 g) butter
2 tablespoons flour
½ pint (10 fl oz 300 ml) milk
¼ pint (5 fl oz 150 ml) dry white wine
4 oz (100g) Cheddar cheese

1 oz (25 g) Parmesan cheese
1 egg
2 rashers streaky bacon
Salt, freshly ground black pepper, ground nutmeg and paprika
1 slice white bread

Remove most of the outside leaves of the cauliflower and score through the stalk. Cook the cauliflower upright in a little boiling water to which a touch of bicarbonate of soda has been added, for about 20 minutes, until just tender. Drain, cool and divide into florettes. Place the florettes in a buttered baking dish.

Remove the bacon rinds.

Double-bladed knife — Process the bread and 1 oz Cheddar cheese with a pinch of paprika into fairly fine breadcrumbs, remove.

Parmesan disc — Process the Parmesan cheese and remove.

Fine grating disc — Process the remaining Cheddar cheese and remove.

Double-bladed knife — Process the bacon until finely chopped and remove. Cook the bacon over a moderate heat for 5 minutes, stirring. Drain the bacon and reserve fat. Melt the butter with 1 tablespoon fat. Add the flour and mix well. Gradually add the milk and wine, stirring continually over a medium high heat until the sauce comes to the boil and is thick and smooth.

Double-bladed knife — Transfer the sauce to the Magimix and add the Parmesan and the grated Cheddar cheese. Process until smooth. With the machine switched on, add the egg through the feed tube and process until the sauce is smooth. Season with salt, pepper, and a touch of ground nutmeg, add the bacon and switch on and off to mix.

Pour the sauce over the cauliflower, lifting it a little with a fork, top with the breadcrumbs and cheese mixture and bake in a hot oven (400°F, 200°C Reg. 6) for about 15 minutes until the dish is hot through and the top is bubbling and golden.

Variations. Chopped ham and some tomatoes put through the chipper disc can be added to the cauliflower making a quick and inexpensive supper dish.

Some chopped, blanched, red pepper can be added to the cooked cauliflower to provide colour.

Creamy Brussel Sprouts

For two people

2 lbs (900 g) brussel sprouts
¼ pint (5 fl oz 150 ml) double cream
1 oz (25 g) butter

Salt and freshly ground black pepper
Pinch ground nutmeg

Trim the brussel sprouts, cut a cross in the bottom and cook them in a little boiling, salted water until just tender (they should still retain some texture and not be allowed to become mushy). Drain really well.

Double-bladed knife — Process the brussel sprouts until reduced to a coarse purée. Add the cream and butter and season with salt, pepper and nutmeg. Process to mix well.

Julienne of Carrots Vichy

I made this one weekend when I had an old and delightfully greedy friend staying. She thought they were so fantastic she ate them all before dinner was ready. Serve the carrots with cauliflower purée (see page 171) the contrast of orange and white is a marvellous one.

For six people	Leaves of a head of celery 1½ lbs (675 g) carrots	4 oz (100 g) butter Salt, white pepper and ground nutmeg

Double-bladed
knife
Julienne Blade

Process the celery leaves until finely chopped and remove.
Peel the carrots and cut them into lengths to fit sideways into the feed tube.
Process the carrots.
Melt ½ oz (13 g) butter in a heavy saucepan. Add the carrots and season with salt, pepper and nutmeg. Cover the carrots with a double layer of well buttered paper pressed down firmly on top of them and cook over a *low* heat for about 20 minutes or until the carrots are just tender. Add the remaining butter stirring lightly and mix in the celery leaves.
Note: Finely chopped parsley can be used in the place of celery leaves.

Pickled Red Cabbage on Apple Slices

A spectacular vegetable dish to serve with roast pork, boiled bacon or game.

For six people	1¾ lbs (825 g) red cabbage 2 eating apples ½ pint (10 fl oz 300 ml) red wine Juice 1 orange Juice ½ lemon Salt and freshly ground black pepper	1 teaspoon caraway seeds 3 oz (75 g) butter 2 oz (50 g) sugar 1 medium onion 2 cooking apples Chicken stock or consommé

Peel, core and quarter the eating apples.

Thin slicing disc
Medium slicing
disc

Slice the red cabbage through the thin slicing disc and remove.
Process the apples.
Combine the cabbage and apple in a bowl and pour over the red wine, orange and lemon juices. Season with salt and pepper, add the caraway seeds, mix well and leave to marinate for three hours.
Peel and halve the onion.

Thin slicing disc

Process the onion.
Heat the sugar in a heavy saucepan until melted and golden brown, add 2 oz butter and add the onion and cook until soft and transparent. Then add the marinated ingredients, bring to the boil and simmer slowly until the cabbage is tender and the liquid has been absorbed (if the liquid is absorbed before the cabbage is cooked add a little stock or consommé). Remove cabbage from heat and keep warm.
Peel and core the cooking apples and cut into three thick slices from the centre part of the apple, discarding the end pieces of the apple. Heat the remaining butter in a frying pan, add the apple rings and cook over a low heat for 1 minute on each side. Add enough stock to cover and gently simmer the apple rings for about four minutes until they are tender but still firm. Remove the apple rings to a warm serving dish with a slotted spoon and pile the cabbage on top of the rings.

Layered Parsnips

A dish made with thinly sliced parsnips which is similar to the famous potato dish, Pommes Anna. I have added a topping of finely chopped bacon and I blanch the parsnip slices with a little lemon juice before layering them.
A good dinner party dish to go with roast meat, poultry or game.

For four people

4 medium parsnips
1 medium onion
1 teaspoon lemon juice
1½ oz (40 g) butter

¼ pint (5 fl oz 150 ml) cream
Salt, freshly ground black pepper and a
  pinch of nutmeg
2 rashers streaky bacon

Thin slicing disc

Double-bladed knife

Peel the parsnips. Peel and halve the onion. Remove the rinds from the bacon. Slice the parsnips and onion through the disc. Blanch the parsnips and onion in boiling, slightly salted water, to which the lemon juice has been added, for three minutes and drain well.
Very finely chop the bacon.
Spread the parsnips and onion in a well buttered, shallow baking dish. Melt the butter, pour it over the vegetables, season them with salt, pepper and nutmeg, give them a good stir and flatten them in the dish. Pour over the cream and sprinkle the bacon over the top.
Bake in a moderate oven (350°F. 180°C. Reg. 4) for 45 minutes.

Game Chips

For four to six people

1 lb (450 g) potatoes
Deep oil for frying

Salt

Ripple cut or thin slicing disc

Peel the potatoes and cut them to fit the feed tube.
Process the potatoes.
Cover them with cold water, leave to stand for 30 minutes, drain, rinse in cold water, drain and dry well on a tea towel.
Heat the oil until a haze rises from it.
Fry the chips (not too many at a time) until pale gold and drain well on kitchen paper. When all the chips have been fried, drop them into the hot oil for a second time (you can fry quite a lot together in this second frying) and fry until crisp and golden brown. Drain well on kitchen paper and sprinkle with salt.
Note: You can store the cold, well drained, chips in an airtight tin for a few days.

French Fried Potatoes

Using the chipper disc of your Magimix you can get delicious small French fries. Cooking the potatoes twice ensures they are really crisp.

For four people   6 medium potatoes   Salt
                     Deep oil for frying

Chipper disc   Peel the potatoes and wipe dry on kitchen paper.
                  Process the potatoes through the disc, soak them in cold water for 30 minutes, drain and dry well in a kitchen towel.
                  Heat the oil until a cube of bread rises immediately to the surface and is golden brown. Cook small batches of the potatoes in the hot oil until a light golden, drain well and then leave to drain on kitchen paper. When all the potatoes have been fried make sure the oil is really hot and return the potatoes to the oil in larger batches frying until crisp and golden brown.
                  Drain well, put onto clean kitchen paper, sprinkle with salt, remove the paper and serve.

Potato Pancakes

Delicious crisp and golden pancakes made from grated potatoes which go well with almost any main course or which can be served as a satisfactory snack with fried eggs and bacon. I have also made these pancakes in mini size and served them with drinks most successfully.

For eight people   2 lbs (900 g) potatoes   3 eggs
                      4 cloves garlic   Salt and freshly ground black pepper
                      6 oz (175 g) plain flour   Pinch marjoram
                      3 fl oz (90 ml) milk   Oil for frying

Coleslaw disc   Peel the potatoes.
                   Process the potatoes, remove and cover them with cold water while making the batter.
                   Peel and roughly chop the garlic.

Double-bladed   Process the garlic until finely chopped. Add the flour, milk, eggs and marjoram,
knife and a   season with salt and pepper and process until smooth.
clean bowl   Drain the potatoes and pat them dry on a clean cloth. Put the potatoes in a bowl, add the batter and mix well. Heat about ¼ in. (0·6 cm) oil in a large, preferably non-stick, frying pan until a film of heat rises from the oil. Drop the batter in from a dessert spoon and cook until golden brown on both sides. Drain on kitchen paper and keep warm.

West Country Potatoes

A delicious combination of potatoes, leeks and cheese moistened with stock. Add a little chopped, lightly cooked bacon or some ham to the ingredients and you have an excellent supper dish.

For four people

4 medium potatoes, peeled
1 large leek
2 tablespoons sunflower or cooking oil
Salt and freshly ground black pepper

Pinch ground nutmeg
1½ oz (40 g) Cheddar cheese
4 tablespoons good stock

Fine grating disc
Thick slicing disc

Trim and clean the leek.
Grate the cheese and remove.
Parboil the potatoes for 20 minutes and drain and dry well. Process the potatoes through the slicing disc and remove. Process the leek and remove.
Heat the oil in a frying pan. Add the leeks and cook over a low heat, stirring to prevent sticking until the leeks are soft. Arrange a layer of potatoes at the bottom of a buttered baking dish, cover with a layer of leeks and then finish with the rest of the potatoes. Add the stock season with salt, pepper and a pinch of nutmeg, sprinkle over the cheese and bake in a moderate oven (350°F. 175°C Reg. 4) for about 20 minutes until the top is golden brown and the potatoes are quite tender.

New Potatoes with Paprika Sauce

In Germany small new potatoes are often served in a creamy cheese sauce; the result is delicious. You can add cream, finely chopped chives, a little crushed garlic and some finely chopped parsley to the cream cheese. In this version the cream cheese is mixed with tomato and paprika pepper and these potatoes go very well indeed with roast meat, poultry or game or with simple fish dishes.

For four people

1½ lbs (675 g) new potatoes
1 teaspoon caraway seeds
1 oz (25 g) butter
4 oz (100 g) cream cheese
1 small onion

Salt
Pinch cayenne pepper
1 teaspoon paprika pepper
1 tablespoon tomato ketchup

Double-bladed knife

Scrape the potatoes and boil them until just tender with the caraway seeds.
Peel and roughly chop the onion.
Process the onion until finely chopped. Add the cream cheese, season with salt, cayenne and paprika, add the tomato ketchup and process until the ingredients are well mixed. Melt the butter in a saucepan. Add the cooked potatoes and toss them over a high heat until the potatoes are coated with the butter. Add the cream cheese mixture and toss over the heat until the ingredients are hot through.

Potato Gnocchi

This free hand version on the Gnocchi theme takes only a short time to make and the resulting dish makes a delicious vegetable to serve with roast or leftover dishes; combine it with homemade tomato sauce and you have a cheap and substantial supper dish.

For four to six people

1 lb (450 g) peeled potatoes
8 oz (225 g) plain flour
4 rashers streaky bacon
1 egg

4 oz (100 g) Gruyère cheese
¼ pint (5 fl oz 150 ml) single cream
Salt and freshly ground black pepper
2 stock cubes

Coarse grating disc

Grate the potatoes, put them immediately into a sieve and run cold water through them to remove excess starch. Drain the potatoes well and pat them dry with kitchen paper.

Double-bladed knife

Combine the flour with the egg and process until well mixed. Add the potatoes, season with salt and pepper and process, scraping down the sides of the bowl every now and then, until the ingredients are well mixed. Bring a large saucepan of water, flavoured with stock cubes, to a gentle boil and drop in tablespoons of the potato mixture. Simmer the gnocchi for about 5 minutes until the potatoes are tender – do not overcrowd the pan – remove them with a slotted spoon. Put the cooked gnocchi in a well buttered baking dish.

Double-bladed knife

Roughly chop the bacon rashers and fry the pieces without extra fat, until they are lightly crisped. Arrange the bacon over the gnocchi.

Coarse grating disc

Grate the Gruyère cheese and sprinkle it over the gnocchi. Season the cream with salt and pepper, pour it over the gnocchi and bake the dish in a moderate oven (350°F. 175°C Reg. 4) until hot through and golden brown.

Potato Sambal

For six people

2 lbs (900 g) cooked new potatoes
2 green chilli peppers
1 small onion or shallot
½ teaspoon curry powder

Salt and freshly ground black pepper
4 tablespoons olive or sunflower oil
1 tablespoon lemon juice

Thick slicing disc

Slice the potatoes and remove.
Remove the seeds from the chilli peppers (wash your hands after you have done this) and roughly chop the flesh. Peel and roughly chop the onion or shallot.

Double-bladed knife

Process the chillies until very finely chopped. Add the onion or shallot and process until finely chopped. Season with curry powder, salt and pepper, add the oil and lemon juice and process to mix the ingredients. Pour the dressing over the potatoes and chill in a refrigerator for at least an hour before serving.

Janson's Temptation

This is one of my favourite vegetable recipes and one that I am continually changing the ingredients of by additions and variations. While Janson's Temptation (a Swedish dish) goes well with veal, chicken, fish and even pork recipes it also stands up as a simple supper dish by itself with perhaps a green vegetable or some simple stuffed tomatoes as an accompaniment. This is a new version for this book.

For four people

2 slices of white bread with the crusts removed.
Small bunch parsley
2 lbs (900 g) potatoes
8 anchovy fillets
2 oz (50 g) butter

2 onions
2 cloves garlic
Freshly ground black pepper
½ pint (10 fl oz 300 ml) whipping or single cream

Remove any coarse stalks from the parsley. Peel the potatoes. Peel and roughly chop the onions and garlic cloves.

Thin or medium slicing disc
Process the potatoes and remove to a bowl of cold water.

Double-bladed knife
Process the bread until reduced to fine breadcrumbs, and remove. Process the parsley until finely chopped and remove.
Process the onion and the garlic until finely chopped and remove.

Double-bladed knife
Process the butter and anchovies until reduced to purée and gradually add the cream processing until the mixture is smooth. Drain the potatoes and pat them dry then layer a third of them with half the onion and half the parsley in a shallow, well buttered baking dish. Spread over a third of the anchovy, butter and cream mixture and season with plenty of ground black pepper. Cover with a third of the potatoes and the remaining parsley and onion and spread with half the remaining anchovy and butter and cream mixture. Season again with pepper and top with the final potatoes and a spreading of the rest of the anchovy, butter and cream mixture. Sprinkle with the breadcrumbs, bake the dish in a hot oven (400°F. 200°C Reg. 6) for about 40 minutes until the potatoes are tender and the topping is golden brown.

Pommes Anna

An old standby. I have added sliced onions to this recipe but you can leave them out if you want a more simple potato dish.

For four people

2 lbs (900 g) potatoes
1 large onion
2 oz (50 g) butter

¼ pint (5 fl oz 150 ml) single cream
Salt and freshly ground black pepper

Thin or medium slicing disc

Peel the potatoes and cut them into cylindrical shapes to fit the feed tube. Peel and halve the onion.

Process the potatoes through the slicing disc and remove. Slice the onions through the slicing disc. Layer the potato and onion in a buttered baking dish finishing with a layer of potatoes. Dot each layer with small dabs of butter, season with salt and pepper and pour over the cream. Bake in a hot oven (400°F. 200°C Reg. 6) for about 40 minutes until the potatoes are tender and the top is golden brown.

Rice and Spinach Ring

This is the most attractive vegetable dish and one that is very easy to make. Serve it with curries, roast meat or with fish.

12 oz (350 g) long grain or Basmarti rice
Salt and freshly ground black pepper
1 lb (450g) fresh spinach (or 8oz (225g) frozen spinach)
1 small bunch parsley
1 large onion
1 green chilli pepper (or use ¼ teaspoon dried chilli pepper flakes)

2 cloves garlic
2 tablespoons oil
½ teaspoon ground cumin
½ teaspoon ground coriander
1 teaspoon garam masala
2 oz (50 g) butter

Cover the rice with enough cold water to come ¾ in. (2 cm) over the top of the rice, add ½ teaspoon salt, stir well, bring slowly to the boil, cover and simmer gently for 20 minutes. Stir well, to beat air into the grains, return the cover and simmer gently for 10 minutes by which time the rice should be tender and fluffy and all the water should have been absorbed.

Remove any tough stalks from the parsley.

Peel and roughly chop the onion and garlic.

Remove the seeds from the chilli pepper.

Cook the spinach until just tender and drain well.

Double-bladed knife

Process the parsley until finely chopped and remove. Process the onion, garlic and chilli untl finely chopped. Heat the oil in a frying pan, add the onion, garlic and chilli and cook over a medium heat until the onion is soft and transparent. Add the cumin, coriander and garam masala and cook, stirring, over a medium heat for four minutes.

Double-bladed knife

Process the spinach until puréed, add the butter and process for long enough to melt the butter.

Add the onion and garlic mixture, the spinach and parsley to the rice and season with salt and pepper. Press the rice into an oiled ring mould, cover tightly with foil and bake in a moderate oven (350°F. 170°C Reg. 4) for 45 minutes. Turn out onto a serving dish.

Note: The centre of the ring can be filled with a savoury mixture of leftovers.

SALADS

Tomato, Basil and Onion Salad

One of the most delicious and simple salads ever – grow basil on your windowsill throughout the summer. This salad smells of a Mediterranean summer and goes well with poultry or fish. As a first course for a summer lunch party, slice some Mozzarella cheese through the thin slicing disc and spread the salad on top of the sliced cheese. Garnish with watercress and black olives and, if you like, with some anchovy fillets as well.

| *For four people* | 6 small, firm, tomatoes | Vinaigrette dressing (see page 246) |
| | Small bunch basil | 1 small onion |

Double-bladed knife	Process the basil until finely chopped and remove.
Chipper disc	Process the tomatoes and remove.
Thin slicing disc	Process the onion and divide into rings. Lightly toss the tomatoes and basil in vinaigrette dressing. Transfer to a serving dish and top with the onion rings. Serve chilled.

Provençal Salad

Bread fried with garlic and chopped fried walnuts make this green salad something else. If possible use walnut oil for the dressing but if you cannot get that (it is available – at a price – from good delicatessen shops) use top quality olive oil.

For four people

1½ slices thick cut white bread with the crusts removed
2 oz (50 g) walnuts, shelled
1 small Batavian or Webbs lettuce
2 cloves garlic

6 tablespoons walnut oil
1½ tablespoons vinegar
½ teaspoon mixed dried salad herbs
Salt and freshly ground black pepper

Double-bladed knife

Process the garlic until finely chopped. Add the bread and process the bread until coarsely chopped and remove. Process the walnuts until coarsely chopped and remove. Combine 4 tablespoons of the oil with the vinegar and herbs, season with salt and pepper and process until well mixed. Roughly shred the lettuce with your hands.

Heat the remaining two tablespoons of oil. Add the bread and cook until the bread is a pale golden colour. Add the walnuts and stir over a medium high heat until the bread is golden brown and crisp and the walnuts are crisp. Drain on kitchen paper and leave to cool.

Combine the shredded lettuce, bread, walnuts and dressing in a bowl and toss lightly until all the ingredients are coated with the dressing.

September Salad

This is a strongly flavoured robust salad. It makes a good dish for a buffet or an ideal partner for a platter of cold meat or poultry.

For six people

12 oz (350 g) radishes
1 small cucumber
Juice of ½ lemon
2 tablespoons olive oil
1 medium onion
2 tomatoes

1 clove garlic
2 tablespoons tomato ketchup
Small bunch dill
Salt and freshly ground black pepper
Pinch sugar

Chipper blade

Peel the cucumber, cut in half lengthwise and remove the seeds. Trim the radishes. Process the radishes and cucumber through the chipper blade using a firm pressure on the pusher. Remove the radishes and cucumber to a bowl and pour over the oil and lemon juice and sprinkle with a little sugar. Leave the radishes and cucumber to marinate for 30 minutes.

Peel and roughly chop the onion and garlic. Cover the tomatoes with boiling water for 3 minutes then drain and slide off the skins. Quarter the tomatoes and remove the core and seeds.

Double-bladed knife

Process the onion and garlic until finely chopped. Add the tomatoes, tomato ketchup and dill, season with salt and pepper and process until the tomatoes are finely chopped. Pour this dressing over the cucumbers and radishes and chill well before serving.

Marinated Sliced Mushrooms

Serve these with crusty French bread as a first course or as a side salad dish. I usually have them as part of a cold summer buffet.

For six to eight people

1 lb (450 g) button mushrooms
2 medium onions (mild ones – the red are particularly good – if possible)
2 cloves garlic
6 fl oz (180 ml) white wine vinegar
3 fl oz (90 ml) olive or sunflower oil
6 fl oz (180 ml) water

1 tablespoon brandy (optional)
Pinch sugar
Pinch salt
Bouquet garni with 2 bay leaves
5 white and 5 black peppercorns
1½ tablespoons finely chopped parsley

Thick slicing disc

Slice the mushrooms and place them in a shallow, non metal, dish.

Thin slicing disc

Slice the onions and garlic and place them on top of the mushrooms.
Combine all the other ingredients except for the parsley in a saucepan, bring to the boil and simmer, uncovered, very gently for 8 minutes. Cool for five minutes and then pour the hot marinade over the mushrooms and onions. Leave to cool and then chill in the refrigerator for 24 hours.
Remove the bouquet garni and garlic cloves and strain off the marinade. Arrange the mushrooms and onions in a serving dish, pour over a little of the marinade and garnish with finely chopped parsley.

Mushrooms with a Salad Sauce

For four people

8 oz (225 g) large, firm button mushrooms
4 shallots or small onions
2 sticks celery
2 lettuce hearts
2 firm ripe tomatoes
1 tablespoon tomato purée

¼ pint (5 fl oz 150 ml) dry white wine
Sprig of thyme
Pinch of oregano
½ teaspoon coriander seeds
7 fl oz (210 ml) olive or sunflower oil
Salt and freshly ground black pepper
2 teaspoons lemon juice

Remove the stalks from the mushrooms.

Medium slicing blade

Slice the mushroom stalks.
Heat half the oil in a large frying pan, add the mushrooms and mushroom stalks and cook over a medium heat until the mushrooms are soft. Remove the mushrooms with a slotted spoon.
Peel and roughly chop the onions.
Cover the tomatoes with boiling water. Leave them to stand for three minutes and then drain them well and slide off the skins. Halve the tomatoes, scoop out the seeds

and any tough cores from the tomatoes and roughly chop the flesh. Trim the celery stalks and roughly chop the flesh.

Thin slicing disc Slice the celery and lettuce through the thin slicing disc and remove.

Double-bladed knife Process the onions or shallots until finely chopped. Add the tomatoes and tomato purée and process until the tomatoes are reduced to a coarse pulp.

Add the remaining oil to the juices in which the mushrooms were cooked. Add the celery, lettuce, onions and tomato pulp, stir in the white wine, lemon juice, herbs and seasoning and cook over a medium high heat for 20 minutes until quite thick.

Double-bladed knife Process the sauce until reduced to a purée, pour it over the mushrooms and chill in a refrigerator until cold.

Serve as a first course or as a salad dish.

Spinach, Mushroom and Bacon Salad

One of my favourites and a salad I go mad about when the first tender leaves of spinach or chard appear in my garden. Serve as a first course or side salad.

For four people

1 lb (450 g) spinach or chard leaves	1 tablespoon French Dijon mustard
4 rashers streaky bacon with rinds removed	1 clove garlic
2 oz (50 g) firm button mushrooms	1 teaspoon sugar
3 tablespoons olive or sunflower oil	Salt and freshly ground black pepper
1 tablespoon white wine vinegar	1 tablespoon sesame seeds

Remove the stalks from the spinach (these can be finely chopped and added to vegetable soups). Coarsely shred the leaves into a bowl.

Double-bladed knife Process the bacon until fairly finely chopped.

Fry the bacon without extra fat until crisp and drain well on kitchen paper.

Thin or medium slicing disc Process the mushrooms, remove and add to the spinach together with the bacon.

Double-bladed knife Process the peeled garlic until finely chopped. Add the oil, vinegar, sugar, salt, pepper and mustard and process to mix well.

Roast the sesame seeds until golden in a hot oven and leave to cool. Add the sesame seeds and dressing to the spinach and toss lightly to coat the leaves and other ingredients with the dressing. Serve at once.

Carrot Salad with Mint and Yoghurt

For four people

Small bunch mint
4 large carrots
1 carton (5 fl oz 150 ml) natural yoghurt
1 teaspoon sugar

1 teaspoon lemon juice
Pinch cumin
Salt and freshly ground black pepper

Double-bladed knife
Course grating disc or the Julienne disc

Remove the stalks from the mint and peel the carrots.
Process the mint until finely chopped. Add yoghurt, sugar, lemon juice and cumin, season with salt and freshly ground black pepper and process to mix.
Process the carrots.

Toss the carrots with the dressing and serve chilled.

Chinese Cabbage Salad

Chinese cabbage is on sale during most of the winter and makes a good alternative to lettuce. It is usually sold by the pound.

For four people

1 lb (450 g) Chinese cabbage
2 crisp red apples
1 small onion
1 tablespoon sultanas
3 tablespoons sunflower or olive oil
1 tablespoon white wine vinegar

½ teaspoon dried mustard
1 teaspoon sugar
3 tablespoons yoghurt
Salt and freshly ground black pepper
1 teaspoon caraway seeds

Thick slicing disc
Thin slicing disc
Double-bladed knife

Cut the cabbage into four, lengthwise, to fit into the feed tube. Halve and core the apples without peeling them. Peel the onion.
Slice the cabbage and apples.
Combine the cabbage and apples in a bowl with the sultanas.
Process the onion and divide into rings. Add to the cabbage.

Combine the oil, vinegar, mustard, sugar and yoghurt in the Magimix bowl, season with salt and pepper and process to mix well. Add the caraway seeds and switch on and off to mix.
Add the dressing to the cabbage and other ingredients and toss lightly to mix. Turn onto a serving dish and serve within one hour.

Savoury Rice Salad

Use to fill pepper cups or large, scooped out, tomatoes or serve in a big bowl and garnish with chopped chives and black olives. Serve with cold meat, fish or poultry.

For six people

8 oz (225 g) long grain rice
1 green pepper
½ red pepper
1 stick celery
¼ cucumber
3 small ripe tomatoes
2 rashers streaky bacon
1 medium onion

1 clove garlic
4 tablespoons olive or sunflower oil
1 tablespoon white wine vinegar
Pinch ground cumin and coriander
½ teaspoon made English mustard
Salt and freshly ground black pepper
6 black olives
Finely chopped parsley or chives

Wash the rice in cold water, place it in a saucepan add enough water to come ¾ in. (2 cm) above the rice, stir well, bring slowly to the boil, stir again with a fork to separate the grains, cover tightly and cook over the lowest possible heat for 20 minutes. Stir again with a fork to beat in air, cover and remove from the heat. Peel and roughly chop the onion and garlic.

Double-bladed knife
Process the onion and garlic until finely chopped. Add the oil, vinegar, spices and mustard and season with salt and pepper. Process to mix well and then pour over the still warm rice. Mix well into the rice, cover again and leave to cool.

Remove the core and seeds from the green and red pepper. Roughly chop the celery. Peel the cucumber.

Double-bladed knife
Process the bacon until finely chopped. Fry the bacon without extra fat until crisp and drain on kitchen paper. Process the peppers and celery stick until finely chopped and add them to the rice.

Chipper disc
Process the tomatoes and cucumber without putting any pressure on the pusher. Add the tomatoes and cucumber to the rice, together with the bacon. Mix the rice, taste for seasoning (you may find you need a little more vinegar and salt as rice tends to absorb these flavours) and garnish the salad with chopped parsley or chives and slices of black olives.

Avocado Salad with Stilton Dressing

For four people

2 medium sized avocados
1 teaspoon lemon juice
¼ pint (5 fl oz 150 ml) vinaigrette
    dressing (see page 246)

1½ oz (40 g) Stilton cheese
1 tablespoon finely chopped spring
    onion tops
1 medium carrot

Halve the avocados and remove the skins and stones. Cut each half avocado in thin slices, arrange the slices on four small plates and brush the avocados with lemon juice.

Double-bladed knife Very roughly crumble the Stilton cheese. Peel the carrot. Combine the vinaigrette dressing and the cheese in the bowl and switch the machine on and off to process the cheese until it is finely chopped (the dressing should have a slightly rough texture and not be smooth). Pour the dressing over the pears.

Julienne slicing disc Process the carrot, and top each salad with a small mound of the julienned carrot and sprinkle with the spring onion tops.
Chill for half an hour before serving.

Curried Chicken and Ham Salad

A quick salad to make from leftovers. You can use cooked turkey instead of the chicken.

For six people

12 oz (350 g) cooked chicken or turkey
12 oz (350 g) cooked ham
2 stalks celery
6 oz (175 g) French beans
1 green pepper
1 small onion
1 clove garlic
1 tablespoon sunflower oil

1 tablespoon curry powder
1 teaspoon tomato purée
1 tablespoon mango chutney
½ pint (10 fl oz 300 ml) mayonnaise (see page 250)
4 tablespoons double cream
6 large crisp (iceburg) lettuce leaves
Salt and freshly ground black pepper

Roughly chop the chicken and ham. Peel and roughly chop the onion and garlic. Remove the seeds and core from the pepper and roughly chop the flesh.

Double-bladed knife Process the chicken and ham until coarsely chopped and remove. Process the pepper and celery until finely chopped and mix them with the chicken and ham.

Thick slicing disc Slice the French beans, blanch them in boiling salted water for five minutes, refresh in cold water, drain well and add them to the chicken and ham mixture.

Double-bladed knife Process the onion and garlic until finely chopped.
Heat the oil in a small saucepan, add the onion and garlic and cook over a low heat, stirring continually until the onion is soft and transparent and slightly browned. Add the curry powder and mix well, stirring for 2 minutes. Leave to cool.

Double-bladed knife Combine the onion and curry mixture, tomato purée and chutney and process until reduced to a purée. Add the mayonnaise and cream, season with salt, and pepper and process to mix well. Add the sauce to the other ingredients and toss lightly. Place a large, crisp lettuce leaf on each plate and fill it with the salad. Serve chilled.

Meat and Vegetables in Aspic

You can use your own home made aspic for dishes of this sort or you can resort to powdered aspic. One alternative I use quite often is to add a little softened gelatine to tinned consommé with a light flavouring of a little lemon juice and sherry and I find this quite acceptable as an alternative to the real thing.

For four people

1 pint (600 ml) aspic jelly (or substitute, see above)
10 oz (275 g) undercooked roast beef
2 carrots
2 gherkins
1 red pepper
Salt and pepper as necessary
½ crisp (iceberg) lettuce

Remove any fat and gristle from the meat and roughly chop the meat. Peel the carrots. Roughly chop the gherkins. Remove the core and seeds from the pepper and roughly chop the flesh.

Medium slicing disc
Slice the carrots. Cook the carrots in boiling salted water until just tender, drain well and leave to cool.

Double-bladed knife
Process the gherkins and red pepper together until finely chopped and remove. Process the meat until finely chopped.

Coat a mould with some of the aspic jelly, and set in a refrigerator swirling the jelly around the sides of the mould as it sets until the sides are coated.

Press slices of carrot into the sides and bottom of the mould and brush with a little more of the liquid aspic to set the carrot slices. Chill until set firm.

Fill the mould with alternate layers of meat, gherkins and pepper and any remaining carrot slices pour over the remaining jelly and chill in a refrigerator until set firm.

Medium or thick slicing disc
Slice the lettuce.

Arrange the sliced lettuce on a serving dish, turn out the mould and place it on top of the lettuce. Serve with Cumberland sauce (see page 268) and horseradish sauce.

Jambon Persille de Bourgogne

A delicious combination of ham and parsley in jellied stock. You can use the stock which the ham was cooked in (providing it is not too salty) with some chicken stock to make the jelly.

For four to five people

1 large bunch parsley with the stalks removed
1 lb (450 g) cooked ham
4 tablespoons dry white wine
¾ pint (15 fl oz 450 ml) well flavoured chicken or chicken and ham stock
Freshly ground black pepper
Pinch ground nutmeg
1 tablespoon white wine vinegar
¼ teaspoon dried tarragon
1 tablespoon (1 packet 13 g) gelatine powder

Double-bladed knife Process the parsley until very finely chopped and remove.
Roughly cube the ham and process until coarsely chopped.
Bring the stock to the boil, add the white wine, season with pepper and nutmeg and add the tarragon and vinegar. Bring to the boil, simmer for five minutes and add the ham. Simmer for five minutes and drain the ham reserving the stock.
Soften the gelatine in 4 tablespoons of the stock. Add the gelatine mixture to the remaining stock. Dampen a pudding basin or glass bowl and coat the sides with some of the finely chopped parsley.
Combine the ham with the rest of the parsley and fill the mould with the meat. Pour over the cooled stock, cover with foil and refrigerate for at least three hours or until set firm.
Dip the mould into boiling water and turn out to serve.

Variations Substitute half the ham for chopped tongue or chicken.
Serve the mould with a French dressing with herbs (see page 247).

Ham Brawn

This can be served as a main course but I prefer it with hot French bread as a first course. If you like you can serve a tomato coulis (see page 260) or Cumberland sauce (see page 268) on the side.

For six people

1 pint (600 ml) well setting aspic jelly (use a packet or a tin of consommé in which you have added some gelatine powder).
Salt and freshly ground black pepper
Pinch ground nutmeg, ground mace and ground cloves

1 tablespoon sherry
8 oz (225 g) carrots
8 oz (225 g) ham
1 bunch parsley
1 bunch watercress
Chicken stock

Add the sherry to the aspic jelly and season the jelly with salt and pepper, ground nutmeg, mace and cloves. Put about ⅓ of the jelly into a two pint pudding basin and leave it to set in the refrigerator swirling it round every now and then as it sets so that it coats the sides of the bowl. Roughly chop the ham removing any fat or rind. Remove any tough stalks from the parsley and watercress.

Medium slicing disc Peel the carrots and slice them. Cook the carrots until just tender in chicken stock, drain well and leave to cool.

Double-bladed knife Process the parsley until finely chopped and remove. Process the watercress until finely chopped and remove. Process the ham until finely chopped. Arrange a thin layer of parsley in the bottom of the bowl, cover with a layer of ham, then a layer of watercress and then one of carrots. Layer all the ingredients, pour over the remaining aspic and chill in a refrigerator until absolutely set firm.
Dip the mould bowl quickly into very hot water, turn out the brawn and serve chilled, cut into slices like a cake.

Potted Tongue and Ham

If you put this in a small loaf tin it will set like a meat loaf and be easy to cut into slices for a summer picnic or buffet party. The success of all potted dishes depends on the seasoning which, since the dish is to be served cold, should be more pronounced than if the dish were a hot one.

For six to eight people

6 oz (175 g) cooked tongue
4 oz (100 g) cooked ham
8 oz (225 g) unsalted butter
Salt and freshly ground black pepper

Pinch mixed herbs
1 tablespoon brandy
Pinch ground mace and allspice

Double-bladed knife

Roughly chop the ham and tongue.
Melt the butter in a small saucepan, bring to the boil and when it is foaming (but before it turns brown), strain it through a fine sieve or through muslin.
Process the tongue and ham until finely chopped, season with salt, pepper, add the brandy and herbs and a pinch of mace and allspice. Add the clarified butter and process to mix the ingredients – do not over-process the ingredients. Turn the mixture into a small terrine or loaf tin and chill in the refrigerator until set. Turn out and serve chilled cut into thin slices.

DESSERTS

Cream and Brandy Snap Filled Oranges

Use your Magimix citrus fruit juice extractor to produce neat cups in which to serve the cream.

For four people

4 medium oranges
Grated rind of 1 orange
6 brandy snaps

¾ pint (15 fl oz 450 ml) double cream
2 tablespoons caster sugar

Citrus fruit juice extractor
Double-bladed knife and a clean dry bowl
Plastic blade

Cut a slice off the top of the oranges.
Process the oranges, one by one, until all the juice is extracted and the orange "cups" are nice and neat inside.
Process the brandy snaps until coarsely chopped, and remove.

Process the cream until thick. Add the grated orange rind and process until well mixed. With the machine switched on add ¼ pint (5 fl oz 150 ml) of the orange juice through the feed tube. Add the crushed brandy snaps and sugar and process for just long enough to mix the ingredients.
Spoon the cream into the orange cases and freeze for at least two hours before serving.
Note: Extra brandy snaps can be served with the pudding which looks attractive if a brandy snap is poked into the top of each filled orange.

Orange Suprémes

Exciting orange cases filled with sliced strawberries and topped with crunchy praline. You will find there will almost certainly be some praline left over from this recipe for four servings – store it in a screw topped jar and use it as a garnish for iced soufflés, ice creams or mousses.

For four people

4 medium oranges
Sugar
12 oz (375 g) firm strawberries

6 oz (175 g) granulated sugar
Grated rind of ½ orange
2 oz (50 g) blanched almonds

Citrus fruit juice extractor
Thick slicing disc

Cut the top third off the oranges and process leaving a neat shell. Sprinkle with a little sugar around the inside of the orange shells. Hull the strawberries. Slice the strawberries.

Fill the orange shells with the sliced strawberries pressing them down gently in the shells. Pour about 1½ teaspoons orange juice over the strawberries and chill in a refrigerator. Put the granulated sugar into a small heavy saucepan and heat gently over a low heat until the sugar has melted and it is golden brown. Add the orange rind and almonds and stir over a low heat for about 5 minutes until the almonds are crisp and golden brown. Pour on to an oiled marble slab or baking sheet and leave until set firm. Break up the praline.

Double-bladed knife

Process the praline until coarsely chopped. Pile praline on top of the strawberries just before serving.

Variations. Whip ¼ pint (5 fl oz 150 ml) cream until thick using the plastic blade, fold in two tablespoons praline and pile this on top of the oranges. If the dish is for grown ups only you can sprinkle the strawberries with Kirsch or Poire William liqueur instead of the orange juice.

Pear Mousse with Ginger

A simply made but elegant pudding to serve after a rich main course.

For four people

3 ripe eating pears
Juice ½ lemon
3 pieces preserved ginger, in syrup
2 tablespoons ginger syrup

8 fl oz (240 ml) whipping or double
    cream
3 tablespoons water
1 packet (½ oz) (13 g) gelatine powder

Peel, core and roughly chop the pears.

Double-bladed knife

Process the pears with the lemon juice until reduced to a coarse purée. Add the ginger syrup and ginger and process until the ginger is coarsely chopped.

Melt the gelatine in the hot water over a low heat until the gelatine is dissolved. Add

Plastic blade the gelatine to the pear mixture and process for just long enough to mix the ingredients. Remove to a bowl and refrigerate until just beginning to set. Process the cream until just thick. Add the pear mixture and process for just long enough to mix the ingredients. Turn into a glass bowl or glass goblets.

Alternative toppings Top the pear mousse with thickly sliced strawberries and small sprigs of mint or with golden brown, roasted, chopped almonds.

Avocado Mousse

In Latin America it is as common to find avocados served as a dessert as it is to find them used as a first course – and why not for they are after all a fruit? This is a rich, smooth and creamy pudding with a pretty colour and a light flavour.

For four people

2 large ripe avocados	3 fl oz (90 ml) milk
1 tablespoon lime or lemon juice	¼ pint (5 fl oz 150 ml) double cream
6 oz (175 g) caster sugar	

Double-bladed knife Peel the avocados, remove the stones and cover them with the milk and lime or lemon juice. Leave to stand for five minutes. Process the avocados with the milk and lime or lemon juice until smooth. Add the sugar and cream and process until the ingredients are well mixed. Pile into glass goblets and chill before serving.

Banana and Lemon Mousse

A gorgeous nursery pud. that is so simple to make and yet so good to eat. A topping of browned nuts and sugar gives a little sophisticated touch but really this is straight "kids'" food.

For six people

3 bananas	4 eggs, separated
Juice of 1½ lemons	½ pint (10 fl oz 300 ml) double cream
1 tablespoon (1 packet 13 g) gelatine powder	2 oz (50 g) mixed nuts
6 oz (175 g) granulated sugar	1 oz (25 g) caster sugar

Double-bladed knife Soften the gelatine in the lemon juice over a low heat until it has melted. Process the sugar until it is reduced to a coarse powder. With the machine running add the egg yolks one at a time processing until each egg has been absorbed into the sugar (scrape down the sides if necessary). When all the egg yolks have been added continue to process for about 2 minutes until the mixture is pale in colour. Add the lemon juice and gelatine mixture, and then add the bananas, roughly chopped, and process until the mixture is almost smooth. Add the cream and process until well mixed.

Transfer to a mixing bowl and chill in the refrigerator until the mixture begins to set.

Beat the egg whites until stiff and fold them into the banana mixture. Transfer to a soufflé dish or serving dish and chill for one hour before serving.

Double-bladed knife and a clean bowl   Process the nuts until coarsely chopped. Place the nuts on a baking sheet and bake in a moderate oven (350°F. 175°C Reg. 4) for about 10 minutes until golden brown. Mix with 1 oz (25 g) sugar and sprinkle over the pudding before serving.

Raspberry & Banana Fool

For six people   ½ lb (225 g) raspberries   4 oz (100 g) sugar
3 large ripe bananas   ½ pint (10 fl oz 300 ml) double cream
Juice ½ lemon and ½ orange

Double-bladed knife   Peel and roughly chop the bananas.
Process the bananas until reduced to purée. Add the raspberries, lemon and orange juice and sugar and process to a smooth purée. Whip the cream until thick and gradually mix in the fruit purée, check for sweetness adding more sugar if necessary and turn into six glass goblets. Chill well before serving.

Raspberry Highland Flings

An exotic mixture of fresh fruit and a whisky topping.

For four people   12 oz (375 g) raspberries   ½ pint (10 fl oz 300 ml) whipping or
2 oz (50 g) blanched almonds   double cream
2 tablespoons porridge oats   1 tablespoon whisky
2 tablespoons strawberry jam

Double-bladed knife   Process the almonds until finely chopped. Roast the almonds and oatmeal in a hot oven (400°F. 200°C Reg. 6) until crisp and golden brown and leave to cool. Reserve half the almonds and oatmeal for the topping.

Double-bladed knife   Combine the strawberry jam and cream and process until the mixture is thick. Add the whisky and half the nuts and oatmeal and process to mix the ingredients. Arrange raspberries in four glass goblets, spoon over the cream topping and scatter over the reserved nuts and oatmeal. Chill in a refrigerator before serving.

Eton Mess

One of the ultimately most simple sweets and as much loved by scruffy school boys as it is by grown ups.

For four people

1 lb (450 g) strawberries
3 tablespoons caster sugar

¾ pint (15 fl oz 450 ml) double cream

Double-bladed knife

Hull the strawberries.
Reserve about 12 strawberries for garnish. Process the strawberries until reduced to a coarse pulp. Add the cream and sugar and process until the mixture is thick. Transfer to four glass goblets and serve chilled with a few whole strawberries on top of each serving.

Orange Cheesecake

A rich, dreamy cheesecake. Prepare this in a china flan case which can be brought to the table.

For six to eight people

10 in. (25 cm) flan lined with ginger
   biscuit pie crust
   (see page 243)
Grated rind and juice of 2 oranges
8 oz (225 g) cream cheese and
4 oz (100 g) creme fraîche (available
   from good delicatessens and
   supermarkets) (or use 12 oz (350 g)
   cream cheese)

1 packet gelatine powder (½ oz)
4 oz (100 g) caster sugar
½ pint (225 g) double cream

Double-bladed knife

Sprinkle the gelatine over the orange juice and heat gently, stirring, until the gelatine has completely dissolved.
Process the cream cheese with the creme fraîche until smooth. Add the sugar and the orange rind and process to mix well. With the machine running, add the orange juice and gelatine mixture and process until the ingredients are well incorporated. Turn in to a bowl.

Plastic disc

Process the cream until stiff. Fold the cream into the cheese mixture. Turn the mixture into a prepared ginger biscuit pie crust and chill in a refrigerator until set.

Old Fashioned Cheese Cake

For six to eight people

Ginger biscuit pastry case (see page 243).
½ lb (225 g) cream cheese
¼ pint (5 fl oz 150 ml) fromage fraîche (available from good supermarkets or delicatessens)
¼ pint (5 fl oz 150 ml) double cream

3 oz (75 g) caster sugar
Grated rind of 1 lemon
Juice ½ lemon
1½ oz (40 g) cornflour
2 eggs
3 tablespoons seedless raisins

Double-bladed knife

Process the cream cheese and fromage fraîche until smooth. Add the cream, sugar, lemon rind, lemon juice and cornflour and process until smooth. Add the eggs and process until smooth. Sprinkle the raisins over the bottom of a 10 in. (25 cm) lined ginger biscuit case. Pour the mixture into the prepared flan case and bake in a moderate oven (350°F. 175°C Reg. 4) for 35 minutes, turn off the oven and leave the cheesecake to stand in the oven for a further 20 minutes. Remove and leave to cool.

Suggested toppings This cheesecake which is of the substantial variety is delicious in its own right but if you want to make it something extra special top it with a raspberry or blackcurrant topping.

Raspberry topping

6 oz (175 g) fresh or frozen raspberries   4 oz (100 g) sugar

Combine the raspberries and sugar, bring to the boil for 20 minutes. Rub through a sieve to remove the pips and leave to cool. Pour the cool raspberry sauce over the cheesecake and chill before serving.

Blackcurrant topping

6 oz (175 g) blackcurrants   6 oz (175 g) sugar

Combine the blackcurrants and sugar in a saucepan, bring to the boil and boil over a high heat for 20 minutes. Sieve through a fairly fine sieve to remove the blackcurrant pips and leave to cool. Spread the cooled blackcurrant sauce over the cheesecake and chill before serving.

Blackcurrant Charlotte

For six people

1 lb (450 g) blackcurrants
  (fresh or frozen)
½ pint (10 fl oz 300 ml) water
5 oz (125 g) sugar
1 tablespoon (1 packet. 13 g) gelatine
  powder

4 tablespoons Cassis
¼ pint (5 fl oz 150 ml) double cream
1 packet sponge fingers
2 oz (50 g) blanched almonds
2 oz (50 g) caster sugar
Few drops vanilla essence

Combine the picked over blackcurrants with the water and sugar, bring to the boil and cook until the sugar has all dissolved. Rub the blackcurrants through a sieve to remove the pips.

Double-bladed knife
Put the blackcurrants into the Magimix bowl, sprinkle over the gelatine and process until the gelatine has melted. Chill the mixture until just beginning to set. Line the bottom and sides of an 8 in. (20 cm) cake tin with a removable base with non-stick paper and line with sliced sponge fingers. Sprinkle the sponge cakes with the Cassis.

Pour half the setting purée into the prepared tin. Cover with a thin layer of sponge and refrigerate until set. Leave the remaining mixture at room temperature while the cake is setting to prevent it becoming too firm.

Plastic blade
Process half the cream until thick. Add the remaining purée and process for just long enough to mix the ingredients. Spread the mixture over the other ingredients, cover with greaseproof paper and refrigerate until set firm.

Double-bladed knife
Process the almonds until coarsely chopped. Roast the almonds in a hot oven on a baking tin for three minutes until golden and leave to cool.

Plastic blade
Process the remaining cream until thick. Add the sugar and vanilla and switch the machine on and off to mix – be careful about over processing. Unmould the charlotte and cover it with the sweetened cream. Sprinkle with almonds and serve well chilled.

Chocolate Mousse

A quick stand-by, but one that is always voted tops by both grown-ups and children.

For four to six people

8 oz (225 g) plain chocolate
5 oz (150 g) caster sugar
5 eggs

1 tablespoon rum (optional) or
1 tablespoon strong black coffee

Melt the broken-up chocolate and rum or coffee in a bowl placed over a saucepan of boiling water.

Double-bladed knife Place the melted chocolate, the sugar and the egg yolks in the bowl and process for about a minute or until very well mixed. Beat the egg whites until stiff. Transfer the chocolate mixture to a large bowl, add the beaten egg whites and fold gently to mix. Pour into a serving dish and refrigerate for several hours. Serve with whipped cream.

Chocolate and Walnut Refrigerator Cake

For eight to ten people

2½ packets sponge fingers
6 oz (175 g) caster sugar
2 tablespoons cornflour
¾ pint (15 fl oz 450 ml) milk
¼ pint (5 fl oz 150 ml) double cream
2 oz (50 g) plain chocolate

2 teaspoons instant coffee powder
2 egg yolks
1½ oz (40 g) unsalted butter
1 tablespoon (1 packet 13 g) gelatine
3 oz (75 g) walnuts
1 tablespoon brandy

Line a 3½ pint (2 l) loaf tin with non stick paper. Cover the base and sides of the tin with sponge fingers cutting them to size if necessary. Blend the cornflour to a paste with the sugar and some of the milk. Put the mixture into a saucepan and gradually add the remaining milk and cream stirring continually over a medium heat until the mixture comes to the boil. Boil, stirring for three minutes until thickened and smooth. Add the chocolate broken into pieces and the coffee powder and stir until the chocolate has melted.

Double-bladed knife Process the egg yolks until smooth. With the machine running gradually add the hot mixture in a slow stream. Return to the saucepan and stir over a low heat for three minutes. Add the butter and stir until the butter has melted. Sprinkle the gelatine over 1 tablespoon of water and heat gently until the gelatine has dissolved.

Double-bladed knife Combine the custard, walnuts and gelatine, add the brandy and process for just long enough to mix the ingredients. Leave to cool until just beginning to set. Spoon half the mixture over the fingers, press a layer of more sponge fingers on top and then finish with the remaining mixture and sponge fingers. Cover with greaseproof paper and leave to set overnight in the refrigerator. Turn out the set cake and decorate, if you like, with whipped cream and some halves of walnuts.

Pear Sorbet

A really delicate and delicious sorbet which can be served with a fresh raspberry sauce to make a spectacular dessert.

For six people

1½ lb (675 g) ripe but not bruised pears
6 oz (175 g) sugar

Juice of 2 lemons
Water

Peel, halve and core the pears and put them into a saucepan with the sugar and lemon juice and enough cold water to cover the pears. Bring gently to the boil and simmer for 15 minutes to tenderize the pears. Remove the pears from the syrup and boil the syrup until reduced by about ½ and until the liquid has thickened.

Double-bladed knife   Process the pears with a little of the syrup until puréed. Mix the purée with the remaining syrup and turn the mixture into a metal container or freezing tray. Freeze for one hour. Break up the sorbet with a fork.

Double-bladed knife   Process the sorbet until smooth and return to the metal tray. Freeze for a further hour and then repeat the breaking up and processing twice more at the end of the second and third hours. Remove the sorbet from the freezer twenty minutes before required and serve in scoops in glass goblets.

Fresh Raspberry sauce

8 oz (225 g) raspberries   1 teaspoon lemon juice
3 oz (75 g) sugar

Double-bladed knife   Combine raspberries, sugar and lemon juice and process until the raspberries are reduced to a purée. Rub the sauce through a sieve to remove the pips.

Apricot Sorbet

Photographs – 294-295

For four people   1 tin apricots (14 oz 400 g)   Juice 1 lemon

Drain off and reserve the juice from the apricots.

Double-bladed knife   Process the apricots until smooth. With the motor running slowly add the apricot syrup and the lemon juice. Turn into a freezing tray and freeze in the freezer for 1 hour or until beginning to crystalize around the edges.

Double-bladed knife   Process the half frozen apricot sorbet until smooth, return to the freezing tray and freeze for a further three hours.

Serve in scoops with raspberry sauce (see above).

Prune Sorbet

For four to six people
1 lb (450 g) prunes   ¼ pint (5 fl oz 150 ml) red wine
China tea   5 oz (125 g) sugar
Grated rind and juice of 1 lemon

Cover the prunes with hot tea and leave to soak overnight. Drain off excess liquid and remove the prune stones. Combine the prunes with the lemon rind and juice,

Double-bladed knife   the red wine and the sugar and stir over a medium heat until the sugar has melted. Process the prunes until reduced to a purée. Turn into a metal tin or ice tray and freeze for 1 hour. Break up the sorbet with a fork.

Process the sorbet until smooth and return it to the metal container. Freeze again for 1 hour and then repeat the breaking up and processing twice more at the end of the second and third hour.

Remove from the freezer twenty minutes before required and serve in scoops in glass goblets.

Prune Ice Cream

I rate this as rather an unusual ice cream in the same class as that delicious brown bread ice cream. Try serving it on top of sliced strawberries – the taste is sensational.

For four to six people

8 oz (225 g) prunes	Juice 1 lemon
2 fl oz (60 ml) water	3 tablespoons brandy
2 oz (50 g) sugar	½ pint (10 fl oz 300 ml) double cream
3 egg yolks	Few drops vanilla essence

Sprinkle the prunes with the brandy and lemon juice and leave them to stand over night. Stew them gently, with the liquid and a little extra water if needed until they are soft. Leave until cool and then remove the stones.

Combine the sugar and water in a small saucepan, bring to the boil and boil for 5 minutes.

Double-bladed knife   Process the prunes until reduced to a purée and remove. Process the egg yolks until pale and fluffy. With the machine switched on add the sugar syrup in a slow steady stream and process until the mixture is creamy and mousse like. Leave to cool. Add the prunes to the yolk mixture with the cream and vanilla essence and process until well mixed. Turn into a freezing tray and freeze until beginning to crystalize around the edges.

Double-bladed knife   Break up the ice cream into the bowl and process until smooth. Return to the freezing tray and freeze for at least three hours until solid. Remove from the freezer for twenty minutes before scooping into balls and serving.

This method of making ice cream can be used equally well with fresh fruit such as peaches, raspberries, gooseberries. With fresh fruit there is no need to cook the fruit, but you may want to sieve out the pips.

Raspberry and Yoghurt Ice Cream

A deliciously sharp and refreshing ice cream to serve at the end of a substantial meal. Use either fresh or frozen raspberries.

For six people

12 oz (350 g) raspberries
¼ pint (5 fl oz 150 ml) water
6 oz (175 g) sugar

Juice ½ lemon
2 eggs separated
½ pint (10 fl oz 300 ml) plain yoghurt

Combine the raspberries, water, sugar and lemon juice in a saucepan and stir over a medium heat until the sugar has melted. Rub through a sieve to remove the pips and return to the pan. Bring to the boil and boil for 5 minutes.

Plastic blade Process the egg yolks until pale and frothy. With the motor running add the boiling fruit syrup in a slow and steady stream through the feed tube. Leave to cool, add the yoghurt and process until well mixed.

Turn the mixture into a freezing tray and freeze until the mixture is fairly well crystalized (about 1½ hours). Break up the ice cream with a fork. Whip the egg whites until stiff.

Double-bladed knife Process the ice cream until smooth. Add the egg whites and switch the machine on and off a few times for just long enough to incorporate the egg whites into the ice cream. Return to the freezing tray and freeze until firm. Remove the ice cream from the freezer twenty minutes before you require it to enable the ice cream to soften and 'mature'.

Rum Baba

When we tried out this recipe in our kitchen we just couldn't believe how easy this highly sophisticated pudding is to make in the Magimix. Surprise your guests with rum baba when you have a dinner party – serve it with sweetened whipped cream and some fresh fruit salad.

8 oz (225 ml) plain flour
1 tablespoon (½ oz 13 g) dried yeast
5 tablespoons warm milk
2 small eggs
1 teaspoon sugar
2½ oz (65 g) unsalted butter

For the syrup
12 oz (350 g) caster sugar
½ pint (10 fl oz 300 ml) water
¼ pint (5 fl oz 150 ml) rum

Cream the yeast with the warm milk and sugar and leave to stand in a warm place until foaming.

Double-bladed knife Place the flour in the Magimix bowl. Break in the eggs, add the yeast mixture and process until the ingredients are well mixed and form a moist, sticky, dough. Turn into a bowl, cover and leave to stand in a warm place until the dough is doubled in bulk.

Return the dough to the Magimix bowl and add the butter cut into small pieces. Process until the butter is incorporated into the dough.

Half fill a well buttered circular mould with the dough and leave to rise in a warm place for ½ an hour. Place in a hot oven (400°F 200°C Reg. 6) and cook until the baba is golden brown. Reduce the heat to moderately hot (350°F. 175°C Reg. 4) and continue to cook for about 20 minutes or until a needle plunged into the cake will come out clean. Leave to cool in the mould and then turn out.

Combine the sugar for the syrup with the water, bring to the boil and boil for five minutes.

Add the rum and spoon the hot syrup over the cake until all the syrup has been absorbed into the cake. Serve chilled.

Apple and Treacle Tart

A delicious mixture of traditional apple and classic treacle tarts.

For six people

1 x 12 in. (30 cm) flan case lined with pâte sucrée (see page 241)
3 oz (75 g) white bread with the crusts removed

1½ oz (40 g) butter
3 cooking apples
10 tablespoons golden syrup

Double-bladed knife

Process the bread until reduced to fairly fine crumbs. Melt the butter in a frying pan, add the bread and cook over a medium heat, stirring, until the breadcrumbs are crisp and golden.

Heat the syrup until runny.

Peel and core the apples.

Thick slicing disc

Process the apples.

Arrange the apples in the bottom of the flan, sprinkle over the breadcrumbs and pour over the syrup. Bake in a hot oven (425°F. 225°C. Reg. 7) for 10 minutes and then lower the heat to moderate (350°F. 175°C. Reg. 4) and continue to cook for a further 20 minutes or until the pastry is golden brown and the apples are soft. Serve hot, warm or cold with cream.

Apple and Apricot Flan

For six people

8 oz (225 g) shortcrust pastry
  (see page 239)
10 oz (275 g) dried apricots

10 oz (275 g) granulated sugar
2 tablespoons water
1 lb (450 g) cooking apples

Cover the apricots with boiling water and leave them to stand overnight.

Line a 8 in. (20 cm) flan case with the rolled out pastry. Line the pastry with foil, fill with dried beans and chill in the refrigerator for 30 minutes. Bake the case 'blind' in a moderately hot oven (400°F. 200°C. Reg. 6) for 10 minutes. Remove the beans and foil and continue to cook for a further 10 minutes until crisp and golden brown. Add 4 oz (100 g) sugar to the soaked apricots and cook them (in the liquid they were steeping in) for about 30 minutes or until the apricots are tender, drain the apricots. Peel and core the apples.

Medium slicing disc

Slice the apples.

Double-bladed knife

Purée the apricots.

Put the sliced apples, water and the remaining sugar in heavy frying pan and heat it over a moderate heat until the apple slices are transparent.

Spread half the apricot mixture over the bottom of the flan case. Remove the apple slices from the syrup with a slotted spoon and arrange the slices on top of the apricots. Spread over remaining apricots, pour over the syrup and chill in a refrigerator until set and serve chilled with cream.

Apple and Mincemeat Flan

For six to eight people

1 x 12 in. (30 cm) flan case lined with
  pâte sucrée (see page 241)
2 cooking apples
4 oz (100 g) sugar

Juice ½ large lemon
8 oz (225 g) mincemeat (see page 277)
1 egg

Peel and core the apples.

Thick slicing disc

Process the apples and remove.

Double-bladed knife

Combine the mincemeat, egg and lemon juice and process until the egg is well mixed with the other ingredients.

Spread the apples over the bottom of the flan case, sprinkle over the sugar and spread over the mincemeat mixture. Bake in a hot oven (425°F. 225°C. Reg. 7) for 10 minutes and then lower the heat to moderate (350°F. 175°C. Reg. 4) and continue to bake for a further 20 minutes until the pastry is golden brown. Serve hot or warm with cream.

Bakewell Tart

For six to eight people

1 x 12 in. (30 cm) flan case lined with
    pâte sucrée (see page 241)
6 oz (175 g) blanched almonds
2 oz (50 g) butter

2 oz (50 g) sugar
2 eggs
Juice and rind of ½ large lemon
4 tablespoons raspberry jam

Double-bladed knife

Roughly chop the butter.
Process the almonds until reduced to a coarse paste. Add the butter and sugar and process until the ingredients are well mixed. Add the eggs and juice and rind of the lemon and process until all the ingredients have become a smooth paste.
Spread a layer of jam over the bottom of the flan case and then spread over the almond mixture. Bake the tart in a hot oven (425°F. 225°C. Reg. 7) for 10 minutes and then reduce to a moderate heat (350°F. 175°C. Reg. 4) and continue to cook for a further 20 minutes until the tart is golden and the pastry crisp. Serve hot or warm with cream.

Almond Pie

For six people

1 x 10 or 12 in. (25 or 30 cm) flan case
    lined with almond pastry
    (see page 242)
10 oz (275 g) blanched almonds
4 oz (100 g) butter

4 tablespoons double cream
1 tablespoon brandy
4 tablespoons runny honey
2 egg yolks
2 eggs

Double-bladed knife

Process 8 oz (225 g) of the almonds until they are finely ground. Add remaining almonds and process until they are coarsely chopped. Add the butter and process until the butter is well mixed with the almonds. Add the other ingredients and process until well mixed. (The second addition of almonds should by now be fairly finely chopped). Transfer the mixture to the pastry shell and bake in a hot oven (425°F. 225°C. Reg. 7) for 10 minutes, lower the heat to moderate (350°F. 175°C. Reg. 4) and continue to bake for a further 20 minutes until the pastry and filling are golden brown. Eat hot or cold with cream on the side.

Rhubarb Tart

For four people

6 oz (175 g) plain flour
Pinch salt
¼ teaspoon ground ginger
1 tablespoon sugar
3 oz (75 g) butter
1 – 2 tablespoons cold water
1 lb (450 g) rhubarb

6 oz (175 g) sugar
1 oz (25 g) plain flour
1 egg
Finely grated rind of 1 orange
2 tablespoons orange juice
3 fl oz (90 ml) milk
Water

Roughly chop the butter.

Double-bladed knife
Combine 6 oz (175 g) of flour with the salt, ginger and 1 tablespoon sugar and process to mix. Add the butter and continue to process until the mixture resembles fine breadcrumbs. With the motor running add the water through the feed tube and process until the pastry forms a ball around the knife. Roll out the pastry on a well floured board and use to line an 8 in. (20 cm) flan case. Reserve the pastry trimming and chill the case in the refrigerator while making the filling.

Medium or thick slicing disc
Slice the rhubarb and remove.

Double-bladed knife
Combine 1 oz flour with the egg, orange rind and 6 oz (175 g) sugar and process to mix well.

Combine the orange juice with enough water to make ¼ pint (5 fl oz 150 ml) in a saucepan and bring to the boil. With the motor running add the liquid through the feed tube and process until well mixed.

Return the ingredients to the saucepan, mix in the milk and stir until the mixture boils.

Spread the rhubarb in the pie case and pour over the filling. Decorate with lattice strips of pastry. Bake in a hot oven (425°F. 220°C. Reg. 7) for 30 minutes. Serve hot or cold with cream.

Pitcairn Banana Pie

I like the idea of eating food from all around the world, especially when I am sitting in my home in Cornwall surrounded by winter rain and mists. This is a pie made for me by a visiting guest, Glynn Christian, who had just been on an expedition to trace his ancestor Fletcher Christian and it brought a wonderful touch of the sun to an otherwise miserable March day.

For six people

Short crust pastry (see page 239)
6 large firm bananas
Juice of 1 orange
2 tablespoons muscovado sugar (soft dark brown sugar)

2 tablespoons cornflour
3 oz (75 g) desiccated coconut
6 fl oz (180 ml) boiling water

Double-bladed knife

Thick slicing disc

Double-bladed knife

Pour the boiling water over the coconut and leave to stand for 45 minutes. Combine the cornflour and sugar and process until all the sugar lumps are broken up.

Slice the bananas, put them into a bowl, sprinkle over the sugar and cornflour, pour over the orange juice and toss lightly to coat the banana slices. Leave to stand for 40 minutes.

Process the desiccated coconut with the water for 20 seconds to press the milk from the coconut. Drain the coconut and press out the liquid by rubbing the coconut in a sieve with the back of a wooden spoon. Roll out the pastry and line a 10 in. (25 cm), fairly deep flan case.

Arrange the bananas in the case and pour over the coconut liquid. Sprinkle the desiccated coconut over the top of the flan and bake in a moderately hot oven (375°F. 190°C. Reg. 5) for about 40 minutes until the pastry and the topping are golden brown and most of the liquid has been absorbed by the bananas. Serve warm or cold with cream.

Top Hat

For six people

12 oz (350 g) self-raising flour
6 oz (175 g) shredded suet
Pinch salt
1½ lb (675 g) cooking apples
2 oz (50 g) raisins

3 oz (75 g) sugar
Pinch cinnamon
Pinch ground ginger
Grated peel and juice of 1 orange

Double-bladed knife

Combine the flour and suet with a pinch of salt and process to mix well. With the machine running, add enough water to form a firm dough around the blade. Turn onto a floured board, roll out to about ⅛ in. (0·5 cm) thickness and use ⅔ of the dough to line a generously buttered 1½ pint (900 ml) pudding basin.
Peel, quarter and core the apples.

Thick slicing disc

Process the apples.

Place the apple slices in the basin with the raisins, sprinkle over the sugar, spices and orange peel and pour over the orange juice.

Roll out remaining pastry, cover the pie, wetting the edges of the pastry and pressing them well together. Trim off excess pastry and crimp the edges together with the back of a fork.

Cover the top of the pie with a sheet of well buttered greaseproof paper with a fold in it, wrap the basin lightly in two layers of foil and stand in a large pan with water coming one third of the way up the sides of the basin. Steam for 2 hours and serve hot with cream.

Note: for special occasions the basin should be wrapped in a white damask napkin to serve.

Profiterolles (Page 244)

Normandy Apple Cake

A moist rich pudding which should be served warm with cream.

1½ lb (675 g) cooking apples	6 oz (175 g) butter or margarine
2 oz (50 g) blanched almonds	3 large eggs
1 oz (25 g) plain flour	8 oz (225 g) self-raising flour
2 oz (50 g) soft brown sugar	¼ teaspoon baking powder
1 teaspoon cinnamon	1 teaspoon mixed spice
5 oz (150 g) caster sugar	3 fl oz (90 ml) cider

Double-bladed knife Process the almonds until fairly finely chopped. Add the plain flour, soft brown sugar, cinnamon and 1 oz butter and process until the mixture resembles coarse breadcrumbs. Remove the mixture.
Peel and core the apples.

Medium slicing disc Slice the apples, cover them with cold water and drain when required.

Double-bladed knife Combine the remaining butter with the sugar and process until just mixed. With the machine running add the eggs, one at a time through the feed tube processing after each addition until the mixture is smooth and light.
Add half the self-raising flour, the mixed spice and baking powder and switch the machine on and off for just long enough to mix the ingredients lightly. Add the cider and process to mix well. Add the remaining flour, and switch the machine on and off to mix the ingredients lightly – do not over process. Turn into a well oiled 8 in. (20 cm) cake tin with a removable bottom, lined with non stick paper. Arrange the apples over the top of the cake and sprinkle over the almond topping. Bake the cake in a moderate oven (350°F. 175°C. Reg. 4) for 1½ hours or until the sides of the cake are coming away from the tin. Leave to cool in the tin before turning out. Serve warm as a dessert or as cold cake.

Apple Upside Down Cake

I made this with my own brandied nectarines the first time I tried it but the dish was just as good with apples and the effect of turning the pudding upside down is really sensational.

3 cooking apples	4 oz (100 g) plain flour
5 fl oz (150 ml) cider	2 oz (50 g) butter
2 oz (50 g) caster sugar	1 oz (25 g) icing sugar
Soft brown sugar	1 egg yolk
1 oz (25 g) glacé cherries	4 fl oz (120 ml) cider

A Picnic Tea (Breads, Cakes and Biscuits: Pages 218–237)

Peel and core the apples.

Thick slicing disc   Process the apples.
Combine the apples, caster sugar and 5 fl oz cider and cook until the apples are soft and liquid has been absorbed. Boil 4 fl oz cider until reduced by half, and leave to cool.

Double-bladed knife   Process the glacé cherries until chopped and remove. Place the flour and butter in the Magimix bowl and process until the mixture is reduced to fine breadcrumbs. Add the egg yolk, icing sugar and reduced cider and process until a stiff dough is formed around the Magimix blade. Wrap in cling film and chill for 20 minutes. Line the base of an 8 in. (20 cm) diameter tin with greaseproof paper, well buttered. Sprinkle with a thin layer of brown sugar and sprinkle over the cherries. Spread the apple over this mixture. Roll out the dough, place it on top of the apple mixture and bake in a moderate oven (350°F. 175°C. Reg. 4) for about 40 minutes until the pastry is risen and golden brown. Invert the pudding onto a serving plate, peel off the greaseproof paper and serve with cream.

Apple Inside Out

For six people   4 oz (100 g) plain flour   2 oz (50 g) raisins
½ pint (10 fl oz 300 ml) milk   1½ oz (40 g) butter
2 small eggs   3 tablespoons soft brown sugar
3 cooking apples   1½ oz (40 g) lard

Double-bladed knife   Combine the flour, milk and eggs and process into a smooth batter. Pour into a jug and leave to stand for 20 minutes. Peel and core the apples.
Thick slicing disc   Process the apples.
Melt the butter in a heavy frying pan. Add the apples, sprinkle over the sugar and cook over a low heat, with the pan covered, shaking every now and then to prevent sticking, for about 10 minutes or until the apples are transparent but not broken up. Heat the lard in a baking dish until smoking. Add the apples, sprinkle over the raisins and pour over the batter. Cook in a hot oven (425°F. 225°C. Reg. 7) for 10 minutes then reduce the heat to moderate (350°F. 175°C. Reg. 4) and continue to bake for a further 20 minutes until firm and golden brown.

Apricot Clafouti

Traditionally this is a dish made with slightly sour cherries but, since these are hard to get hold of, I make it with apples or dried apricots finding it a useful dish to serve during the winter.

For six to eight people	12 oz (350 g) dried apricots	2 eggs
	6 oz (175 g) granulated sugar	½ pint (10 fl oz 300 ml) milk
	4 oz (100 g) self-raising flour	Few drops vanilla essence
	4 oz (100 g) caster sugar	2 tablespoons sunflower oil

Cover the apricots with water, add the granulated sugar and leave them to soak overnight.

Stew the apricots with the liquid they were soaked in for about 20 minutes or until soft.

Double-bladed knife   Combine the flour, caster sugar, eggs and milk and process until a smooth batter is formed. Add a few drops of vanilla essence and process until well mixed.

Heat the oil in a small roasting tin until very hot in a hot oven (425°F. 225°C. Reg. 7) add the drained apricots and then pour in the batter. Lower the heat to moderately hot (375°F. 190°C. Reg. 5) and bake for about 35 minutes until risen and golden brown. Serve at once with cream.

Rhubarb Crisp

For six people	2 lb (900 g) rhubarb	6 oz (175 g) granulated sugar
	3 tablespoons of water	2 oz (50 g) butter
	4 slices of white bread with the crusts removed	2½ oz (65 g) mixed candied peel
		¼ pint (5 fl oz 150 ml) whipping cream

Trim the rhubarb and roughly chop the stems. Combine the rhubarb with the water and sugar in a saucepan, bring to the boil and simmer until the rhubarb is soft and the sugar has all dissolved. Drain off the syrup and leave to cool.

Double-bladed knife   Process the bread until reduced to fairly fine breadcrumbs. Heat the butter in a frying pan add the breadcrumbs and cook over a medium heat stirring, until the butter has all been absorbed and the crumbs are crisp. Add the syrup from the rhubarb and the mixed peel and stir to mix. Leave the crumbs to cool.

Plastic blade   Process the cream until thick. Add the rhubarb and process to mix well. Spread half of the rhubarb in a glass bowl (or use individual glass goblets), cover with half the crumbs and then finish with the remaining rhubarb and crumbs. Serve well chilled with cream.

Steamed Banana Puddings

For six people	2 bananas	5 oz (150 g) margarine
	1 teaspoon lemon juice	5 oz (150 g) caster sugar
	2 eggs	5 oz (150 g) self-raising flour

Double-bladed knife   Process the bananas with the lemon juice until smooth, remove.

Double-bladed knife and a clean bowl   Process the margarine until light. With the machine switched on add the sugar through the feed tube in a slow stream. Add the eggs, one at a time, through the feed tube with the machine switched on and process until the mixture is light. Add the bananas and process to mix. Add the flour and switch on and off to mix the flour into the other ingredients – do not overprocess.

Pour the mixture into six well oiled muffin tins, cover each one tightly with a layer of foil and stand in a saucepan with enough water to come half way up the sides of the tins. Steam the puddings for about 20 minutes turn out and serve at once with custard.

Sweet Crêpes

Makes 20 thin crêpes

6 oz (175 g) plain flour
1 tablespoon caster sugar
3 eggs
½ pint (10 fl oz 300 ml) milk

¼ pint (5 fl oz 150 ml) water
1 oz (25 g) melted butter
2 tablespoons brandy
1 teaspoon grated orange rind

Double-bladed knife   Combine all the ingredients and process until smooth. Put into a jug and leave to stand for 30 minutes.

Rub an omelette or pancake pan with a thin smear of oil. Heat until a haze rises from the pan. Pour about two tablespoons of batter into the hot pan swirling it around the pan until the batter forms a thin film over the bottom of the pan. Cook over a moderate heat until the pancake is set firm. Turn over and cook the remaining side until it is pale golden. Stack the pancakes as you cook them with pieces of greaseproof paper in between the pancakes.

Crêpes Suzette

For four to six people

12 crêpes as recipe
2 oz (50 g) softened, unsalted butter
4 oz (100 g) icing sugar
2 oz (50 g) candied peel

Juice and rind of 1½ oranges and 1 lemon
4 tablespoons brandy

Double-bladed knife   Process the butter and sugar until light and fluffy. Add the peel and process until the peel is finely chopped. Add the orange rind and the orange and lemon juice and two tablespoons of the brandy and process to mix. Spread some of the filling on each pancake and fold them in half and then in half again to form a triangle. Place the filled pancakes in a large frying pan, side by side. Spoon over any remaining filling and heat over a high heat, shaking the pan now and then until any sauce in the pan has become boiling hot and syrupy. Pour over two tablespoons brandy, bring to the boil, set the sauce alight and bring immediately to the table.

Crêpes Normande

For six people

12 crêpes as recipe
1½ lb (675 g) cooking apples
3 tablespoons water
6 oz (175 g) sugar

Juice and rind of 1 lemon
4 tablespoons Calvados
2 oz (50 g) unsalted butter

Double-bladed knife

Peel and core the apples and combine them in a saucepan with the water, sugar and lemon juice and rind. Cook over a medium heat until the apples are soft. Process the apples with the butter until a smooth purée is formed. Add two tablespoons Calvados and process to mix. Spread the filling over the pancakes, roll them up neatly and arrange them in a buttered baking dish. Heat through in a hot oven (400°F. 200°C. Reg. 6) for 15 minutes. Heat the remaining Calvados, set it alight with a match and pour the flaming liqueur over the pancakes. Serve at once.

Crêpes Parisien

For six people

12 crêpes as recipe

Filling
3 oz (75 g) blanched almonds
6 peaches
Juice 1 lemon
4 oz (100 g) sugar

Topping
1½ oz (40 g) unsalted butter
2 oz (50 g) sugar
¼ pint (5 fl oz 150 ml) double cream
2 oz (50 g) blanched almonds

Double-bladed knife

To make the filling:— Process the almonds until coarsely chopped. Roast the almonds in a hot oven (400°F. 200°C Reg. 6) until golden and leave to cool. Peel the peaches with a stainless steel or silver knife and remove the stones.

Double-bladed knife

Combine the peaches, sugar, and lemon juice and process until reduced to a smooth purée. Add the toasted almonds and process to mix.

Double-bladed knife **To make the topping:—** Combine the butter and sugar and process until light and fluffy. Add the almonds and process until the almonds are coarsely chopped. With the machine switched on add the cream through the feed tube, processing to mix the ingredients.

Spread the peach filling over the crêpes, roll them up neatly and arrange them in a shallow baking dish. Spoon over the topping and put under a high grill until the topping is bubbling and golden brown. Serve at once.

Orange Flavoured Pancakes

Although this dish is similar to crêpes suzette it is less expensive and less elaborate to prepare.

For six people

For the pancakes
2 eggs
2½ oz (65 g) plain flour
¼ pint (5 fl oz 150 ml) single cream
4 fl oz (120 ml) water
1 oz (25 g) melted butter
1 tablespoon dry Vermouth
Oil for frying

For the filling
1 oz (25 g) butter
2 tablespoons icing sugar
Rind and juice of 1 orange
3 tablespoons Dry Vermouth
2 tablespoons brandy to flame

Double-bladed knife **To make the pancakes:—** Combine the eggs, flour, cream, water, butter and Vermouth in the Magimix bowl and process until the mixture becomes a smooth batter.

Heat an omelette pan (or crêpe pan), rub the surface with a piece of kitchen paper soaked in oil and when a haze of heat rises from the surface add a tablespoon or more of batter, swirling it around the pan until the bottom becomes thinly and evenly coated. Cook over a medium heat until the batter is set and then turn the pancake over and cook until the bottom is golden. Remove to a plate and continue to cook the remaining pancakes.

Note: Don't worry if the first pancake is a disaster – it often is!

Double-bladed knife and a clean bowl **To make the filling:—** Combine the butter and icing sugar in the Magimix bowl and process until creamed. Add the orange juice, orange rind and vermouth and process until well mixed. (Do not worry if the mixture looks curdled). Spoon a little of the mixture onto each pancake and fold them in half and then in half again. Arrange the pancakes in a large frying pan with the rounded edges facing out and heat over a high flame for about 4 – 5 minutes until the pancakes and sauce are hot through. Pour over the brandy and set it alight as soon as it has bubbled. Serve the pancakes from the pan.

Brandy Butter

One of the essentials for Christmas day. You can make it a few days before and store it, covered in the bottom of the refrigerator.

4 oz (100 g) unsalted butter 3 – 4 tablespoons brandy
4 oz (100 g) icing sugar

Double-bladed knife Put the butter in 1 in. (2·5 cm) cubes into the bowl with the sugar and process until light and creamy. Slowly add the brandy through the feed tube and continue processing until it is amalgamated.

Christmas Pudding

1 dessert apple ½ teaspoon ground cinnamon
1 tablespoon black treacle pinch salt
3 eggs 4 oz (100 g) shredded suet
¼ pint (5 fl oz 150 ml) dark ale 4 oz (100 g) soft brown sugar
1 tablespoon brandy or rum 4 oz (100 g) seedless raisins
grated rind of a lemon 4 oz (100 g) sultanas
4 slices white bread 4 oz (100 g) currants
4 oz (100 g) self-raising flour 2 oz (50 g) flaked almonds
½ teaspoon mixed spice 2 oz (50 g) chopped mixed peel

Grating disc Peel and core the apple, grate through the disc and remove. Heat the treacle until warm and runny and then mix with the eggs, ale, brandy or rum and the lemon rind.
Double-bladed knife Remove the crusts from the bread and then process the bread into fine breadcrumbs. Add the sieved flour, salt, spices, suet and sugar and process to mix. With the motor running add the treacle and egg mixture through the feed tube. If using the Grande Famille add the fruit and nuts and process briefly to mix. If using the standard Magimix transfer the pudding mixture to a large bowl and add the fruit. Stir (while wishing) to mix.

Put the mixture into a well greased 2 pint (1 l) pudding bowl and cover with a double thickness of buttered greaseproof paper (fold a pleat in the middle to allow the pudding to rise). Tie the paper on securely and steam gently for four or five hours. The pudding will keep better if a little more brandy or rum is sprinkled over before storage. On Christmas day cover with a new piece of greased paper and steam for two to three hours.

BREAD, CAKES & BISCUITS

Basic White Bread

photographs – pages 286-287

Makes 2 small loaves or 1 large loaf

2 level teaspoons ¼ oz (6 g) dried yeast
½ pint (10 fl oz 300 ml) warm water
1 teaspoon sugar

1 lb (450 g) strong plain flour
2 teaspoons salt
½ oz (13 g) lard

Combine the warm water with the sugar, mix until the sugar has dissolved and whisk in the dried yeast. Leave to stand for 10 minutes in a warm place or until spongy. Cut the lard into pieces.

Dough blade or Double-bladed knife

Combine the flour, salt and lard in the bowl and process for a short time to cut the lard into the flour. With the machine switched on, add the yeast liquid through the feed tube, process for long enough for the dough to form a ball around the knife and then process for a further 20 seconds. Remove the dough, dust with flour, place in a lightly oiled polythene bag, leaving enough space for rising, and leave to rise in a warm place for about 1 hour or until doubled in bulk.

Remove the dough from the bag, knock down with the knuckles of both hands to knock out the air bubbles and return dough to the bowl. Process for 10 seconds to knead the dough and then remove from the bowl. Shape the dough into an oblong, or for two smaller loaves cut in half and shape twice. Fold in three and place in a well greased loaf tin with the seam underneath. Place the tin back in the oiled polythene bag and leave to rise in a warm place for 40 minutes.

Brush the top of the loaf with 1 tablespoon salt dissolved in 3 tablespoons water and bake in a very hot oven (450°F. 240°C. Reg. 8) for 30 minutes covering the top of the loaf with a sheet of greaseproof paper if it gets too brown.

Turn out onto a wire rack and leave to cool.

Brown Breakfast Rolls

These are light, pale brown rolls which are excellent breakfast fare. I like to eat them piping hot with plenty of butter and local honey.

Makes 12 rolls

8 oz (225 g) wholemeal flour
8 oz (225 g) strong white flour
1½ teaspoons salt
1 oz (25 g) butter

4 fl oz (120 ml) milk
¼ pint (5 fl oz 150 ml) water
3 level teaspoons dried yeast
1 teaspoon sugar

Dough blade or Double-bladed knife

Warm the milk and water to blood heat. Mix in the sugar and when dissolved whisk in the dried yeast. Leave to stand in a warm place for 10 minutes or until spongy. Warm the flour and the salt in a bowl and then put them into the Magimix bowl. Add the butter to the flour and process until the butter is well cut into the flour. With the machine running gradually add the yeast mixture. When the dough forms a ball around the knife continue processing for a further thirty seconds to knead. Turn on to a floured board and knead briefly to make smooth. Put into an oiled bowl, cover with a damp cloth and leave in a warm place to rise for 60 minutes. Punch the dough down with the knuckles, press into an oblong about ½ in. (1·25 cm) thick and divide into twelve pieces with a sharp knife. Place onto a baking sheet, cover with a damp cloth and leave to rise in a warm place for 30 minutes. Brush with salted water and bake in a pre-heated hot oven (400°F. 200°C. Reg. 6) for about 20 minutes until firm and golden brown.
Note: To make cumin and poppy rolls to go with soup: Add 1 teaspoon cumin seeds to the flour and sprinkle the top of the rolls with poppy seeds after brushing them with salted water.

Hot Cross Buns

I like the idea of hanging one of these buns in your kitchen to ward off evil from one Easter tide to another – I have tried it and it seems to work. Crosses made by cutting a cross with a knife on the top of the buns may not be as tidy as making a cross from a strip of pastry but to me it seems far more authentic.

2 level teaspoons (¼ oz 6 g) dried yeast
¼ pint (5 fl oz 150 ml) milk
1½ oz (40 g) caster sugar
12 oz (350 g) plain flour
Pinch salt
Pinch cinnamon, nutmeg and mixed
  spice
1½ oz (40 g) butter

1 egg
2 oz (50 g) currants
1 oz (25 g) chopped peel

For glazing
1 small egg
4 tablespoons milk
1 oz (25 g) caster sugar

In a warm bowl dissolve half the sugar in the milk and whisk in the yeast. Leave in a warm place until it is frothing.

Dough blade or Double-bladed knife

Combine the flour, salt and spices with the remainder of the sugar. Add the butter cut into small pieces and the yeast mixture and process until well mixed. With the machine running add the egg processing until the dough is smooth. Add the currants and peel and process until the dough forms a ball around the knife. Turn onto a floured board. Knead lightly, place in a bowl, cover with a cloth and leave to rise in a warm place for 1 hour. Knock down the dough, knead lightly and leave to rise for a further 30 minutes. Cut the dough into eight pieces and form into balls by rolling on a floured board with the palms of your hands. Place the buns on a baking sheet and leave to rise in a warm place for 15 minutes.

Dough blade or Double-bladed knife

Combine the egg, milk and sugar for the topping and process until smooth. Brush the buns with the glaze and lightly cut a cross in the top of each bun. Bake in a hot oven (425°F. 220°C. Reg. 7) for 15 minutes.

Brioches

Makes 12 brioches

1 tablespoon caster sugar
1½ tablespoons warm water
2 level teaspoons (¼ fl oz 6 g) dried
   yeast

2 oz (50 g) butter
3 eggs
8 oz (225 g) plain flour
½ teaspoon salt

Dissolve ½ teaspoon sugar in the warm water, sprinkle the dried yeast on top, whisk lightly and leave until spongy (about 10 minutes). Melt the butter and leave to cool.

Dough blade or Double-bladed knife

Place 2 eggs in the bowl and process until smooth. Add the flour, salt, remaining sugar and melted butter. Switch on the machine and pour the yeast mixture in through the feed tube, processing for long enough for the dough to form a ball around the knife. Continue to process for 1 minute then turn the dough onto a floured board and knead lightly with the fingertips for 1 minute. Place it in a lightly oiled polythene bag and leave to rise in a warm place for 2 hours or until doubled in bulk.

Grease twelve brioche or castle pudding tins. Turn the risen dough onto a floured board and divide into twelve pieces. Knead each piece lightly and form three-quarters of it into a ball. Place the balls in the tins and press a finger firmly into the centre. Roll the remaining dough into twelve small balls and place them on top of the dough in the tins. Place the tins in an oiled polythene bag and leave to rise in a warm place for 1 hour or until well risen.

Place the remaining egg in the Magimix bowl and add a teaspoon water. Process until smooth. Brush the risen brioches with the egg glaze and bake them in a very hot oven (450°F. 240°C. Reg. 8) for 10 minutes or until golden brown. Serve the brioches as soon as possible.

Variation: This dough can also be used to make a covering for a skinned savoury sausage or for a pâté. After the first rise, roll and dough out into an oblong. Fill with the chosen filling. Roll up neatly and leave to rise for 40 minutes in a warm place. Brush with an egg glaze and then bake in a hot oven until well risen and golden brown. Serve cut into slices.

Croissants

Fresh croissants are always one of the joys of a holiday in France and its not that difficult to make them yourself.

8 fl oz (250 ml) lukewarm water and milk, mixed	1 oz (25 g) butter
1 teaspoon sugar	1 teaspoon salt
1 tablespoon dried yeast	8 oz (225 g) butter
12 oz (350 g) strong white flour	1 egg beaten with 2 tablespoons milk

Dough blade or Double-bladed knife

Dissolve the sugar in the water and milk mixture, then sprinkle over the yeast and leave in a warm place for about ten minutes, or until foamy. Place the flour, salt and 1 oz (25 g) butter in the bowl and process until well mixed, then with the motor running pour in the yeast mixture through the feed tube. Process, to knead the dough, for a further minute. Turn the dough onto a floured board and knead lightly before transferring to a greased plastic bag. Chill in the refrigerator for at least an hour. Roll the chilled dough out into a rectangle. Dot the top two thirds with a third of the remaining butter, then fold up the bottom third of the rectangle, and fold the top third on top of it. Press down the sides with a rolling pin to seal. Return the dough to the plastic bag and chill for another half an hour. Repeat the process twice more, then chill for several hours or preferably overnight. Divide the dough into two and roll each half into a neat rectangle of approximately 6 in. x 18 in. (15cm x 45 cm). Cut each rectangle into three squares and then cut across each square to make two triangles. Brush the dough with the beaten egg mixture, then roll up starting with the base. Place onto a greased tray and curve in the ends to form the 'crescents'. Place the trays in a plastic bag (or cover with cling film) and leave to rise for about an hour, or until doubled in size. Brush the tops with the remaining beaten egg mixture and bake for 20 minutes in a hot oven (425°F. 210°C. Reg. 7) or until they are crisp and brown.

Quick Scones with or without Currants

12 oz (350 g) self-raising flour
Pinch salt
2 oz (50 g) butter
2 oz (50 g) lard

4 oz (100 g) caster sugar
3 oz (75 g) currants (optional)
Milk

Double-bladed knife Combine the flour, salt and butter, lard (cut into pieces) and sugar and process until the mixture is reduced to coarse breadcrumbs.
With the machine running, add just enough milk through the feed tube to make a stiff dough which forms in a ball around the knife. (Add the currants and process for just long enough to mix in the currants). Stop the machine at once, turn onto a floured board and knead lightly for about 30 seconds.
Roll out the dough to ¾ in. (2 cm) thickness and cut into 2 in. (5 cm) scones with a pastry cutter. Place on a greased baking tray. Brush the tops with milk and bake in a hot oven (400°F. 200°C. Reg. 6) for about 15 minutes until well risen and golden. Serve hot, split in half with butter or cold with clotted cream and home made strawberry jam.

Fruit Scone Wedges

A richer scone mixture, cut into triangles and delicious split into half and filled with clotted cream and strawberry jam.

8 oz (225 g) self-raising flour
2 tablespoons caster sugar
2 oz (50 g) raisins
1 large egg

2 tablespoons milk
1 oz (25 g) chopped candied peel
3 oz (75 g) butter

Double-bladed knife Roughly chop the butter.
Combine the flour, sugar and butter and process until the mixture resembles coarse breadcrumbs.
Add the egg and milk and process until the mixture is smooth and well mixed. Add the raisins and dried peel and process until the ingredients are mixed. Turn the dough on to a well floured board and knead lightly. Roll out to an oblong ½ in. (1·25 cm) thick, cut into six squares and then into halves to make triangles. Put the triangles on to an oiled baking sheet, dust lightly with flour and bake in a hot oven (425°F. 220°C. Reg. 7) for 15 minutes until well risen and golden brown. Serve hot, split into half and spread with butter or cool with clotted cream and strawberry jam.

Drop Scones

Light mouth-melting scones which have to be served as soon as they are ready although the batter can be made in advance.

4 oz (100 g) self-raising flour	1 large egg
Pinch salt	4 tablespoons milk
1 oz (25 g) caster sugar	Butter, for frying

Double-bladed knife Combine all the ingredients in the Magimix bowl and process until smooth. Rub a hot griddle or very hot, heavy frying pan with a piece of kitchen paper to make sure it is absolutely clean and then rub it with a little butter to make a shiny surface. Drop the batter from a dessertspoon and cook the scones for two minutes on each side until golden brown. Serve hot, straight from the pan, with butter and jam or honey.

Savoury Drop Scones
These can be served with eggs and bacon for a Sunday brunch or in the place of potatoes as a vegetable.
1. Omit the sugar and add 1 tablespoon mixed, finely chopped parsley and chives to the batter and season with salt, pepper and a pinch of paprika or cayenne.
2. Omit the sugar, add ½ teaspoon dried mixed herbs to the batter and season as above.
3. Omit the sugar and add 1 rasher of bacon, very finely chopped, lightly cooked and drained, to the batter and season as above.

Magimix Griddle Cakes

Wonderful light griddle cakes which melt in the mouth. Serve them warm with melted butter.

12 oz (350 g) plain flour	3 oz (75 g) mixed raisins, currants and
Scant teaspoon baking powder	dried peel
1 teaspoon salt	1 medium egg
3 oz (75 g) butter	A little milk for mixing
3 oz (75 g) Outline low fat spread	

Roughly chop the butter.
Double-bladed knife Combine the flour, salt and baking powder and process to mix. Add the butter and Outline and process until the mixture resembles coarse breadcrumbs. Add the dried fruit and egg and process to mix. With the machine running add just enough milk to form a dough around the knife.

Roll out the dough thinly on a well floured board and cut into 6 in. (15 cm) diameter circles around a saucer. Grease a heavy frying pan or griddle with a little oil and fry the cakes over a medium heat for about 3 minutes on each side or until golden and cooked through. Serve warm with butter.

Langue de Chat Biscuits

Make these elegant biscuits to serve with ice creams or other creamy puddings – they add tremendous class to the end of a dinner party.

2 oz (50 g) butter	1 large egg white
2 oz (50 g) caster sugar	2 oz (50 g) plain flour
Few drops of vanilla essence	

Double-bladed knife

Roughly chop the butter. Combine the butter, sugar, and vanilla essence and process until the mixture is light and creamy. Add the egg whites and process until the mixture, is well mixed and smooth. Add the flour and process for just long enough to mix the flour into the other ingredients. Pipe the mixture through a ¼ in. (0·75 cm) plain nozzle on to a well buttered and floured baking sheet leaving plenty of room between the biscuits and bake in a very hot oven (425°F. 225°C. Reg. 7) for 6–8 minutes until the biscuits are firm and beginning to go golden brown around the edges. Leave to cool for two minutes then remove with a spatula on to a wire rack and leave to get completely cold.
Store the biscuits in an airtight tin.

Chocolate Buttles

These, to my mind, are one of the most delicious form of cakes or cookies in the world. They *really* melt as you eat them and the only trouble is not to get through the whole batch in one sitting.
Do not expect your buttles to look the tidiest morsels in the world and make sure you refrigerate the mixture before trying to cut it into fingers. The results will enchant anyone who samples them.

6 oz (150 g) plain chocolate	1 teaspoon vanilla essence
3 oz (75 g) butter	12 oz (350 g) caster sugar
4 eggs	5 oz (150 g) plain flour
Pinch salt	4 oz (100 g) mixed shelled nuts

Break up the chocolate and combine it with the vanilla essence and butter in the top of a double boiler over hot, not boiling water. Heat stirring every now and then until the butter and chocolate have melted.

Double-bladed knife Combine the eggs with the salt and process until the eggs are light and fluffy. With the machine switched on add the sugar in a slow stream through the feed tube followed by the melted chocolate mixture. Add the flour and nuts and switch on and off a few times to mix the ingredients and roughly chop the nuts – do not over process.

Turn the mixture into an oiled 9 in. x 18 in. (22 x 45 cm) Swiss roll tin and bake in a moderate oven (350°F. 175°C. Reg. 4) for about 30 minutes until firm. Cool, refrigerate until chilled and then cut into fingers with a sharp knife.

If these are not devoured on the day they are made (and this doesn't happen often) I wrap them in cling film, in layers, and keep them in the refrigerator.

Chocolate and Fruit Cookies

Mouth-melting biscuits with chips of chocolate and mixed peel giving them a flavour both children and adults love.

4 oz (100 g) butter	Pinch salt
4 oz (100 g) soft brown sugar	½ teaspoon baking powder
4 oz (100 g) white sugar	2 oz (50 g) chopped, mixed, nuts
1 large egg	2 oz (50 g) plain chocolate
Few drops vanilla essence	1 oz (25 g) mixed peel
6 oz (150 g) plain flour	

Double-bladed knife Break up the chocolate, put it into the Magimix bowl and process until reduced to small pieces. Remove the chocolate.

Plastic blade Combine the sugars and butter in the Magimix bowl and process until the mixture is light and creamy. Add the egg and vanilla essence and process until the mixture is smooth. Add the flour, salt and baking powder and process until well mixed into the other ingredients. Add the nuts, chocolate and peel and process to mix. Drop the batter from a teaspoon (leave quite large spaces between the mounds) onto an oiled baking sheet and bake in a moderate oven (350°F. 175°C. Reg. 4) for about 10 minutes until firm and golden brown. Cool on a rack.

Rich Almond Biscuits

3 oz (75 g) blanched almonds	2½ oz (65 g) caster sugar
5 oz (150 g) butter (softened)	Grated rind of ½ orange
3½ oz (90 g) plain flour	Few drops of vanilla essence

Double-bladed knife Process the almonds until finely chopped. Add the remaining ingredients and process until a smooth dough forms around the knife. Dust with flour and wrap in polythene. Refrigerate for 1 hour. Roll out the dough on a well floured board to ¼ in. (0·75 cm) thickness and cut into 2 in. (5 cm) rounds with a pastry cutter. Bake on a baking sheet in a moderate oven (325°F. 150°C. Reg. 3) for 10 minutes, or until crisp and golden. Remove with a spatula onto a wire rack and leave to cool.
Note: For special occasions sandwich the biscuits together with apricot jam and cover the tops with plain chocolate which has been melted over hot water.

Swedish Christmas Biscuits

Although these are traditionally served in Sweden at Christmas time they are so good I make them all year round.

9 oz (250 g) plain flour	2 teaspoons brandy
1½ teaspoons ground cardamon	1 large egg
4½ oz (115 g) butter	Deep fat for frying
2½ oz (65 g) granulated sugar	Icing sugar
2 tablespoons double cream	

Roughly cut up the butter.
Double-bladed knife Combine the flour and cardamon. Add the butter and process until the mixture looks like fine breadcrumbs. Add the sugar, cream, brandy and egg and process until the dough forms around the knife. Wrap the dough in a floured cloth and chill in a refrigerator for 1 hour. Roll out on a well floured board to ¼ in. (0·75 cm) thickness and cut into ¾ in. (1·5 cm) wide strips 2 in. (5 cm) long.
Heat deep oil until a haze rises from it. Fry the biscuits, not too many at a time, until they are crisp, and light golden in colour. Drain them on kitchen paper and sprinkle with icing sugar when cold.

Crunchies

These are the sort of quickly made buns that are very popular at children's parties.

3 oz (75 g) butter or margarine
6 oz (175 g) soft brown sugar
7 oz (200 g) porridge oats
4 oz (100 g) wholemeal flour
½ teaspoon bicarbonate of soda

Pinch salt
2 oz (50 g) raisins
2 oz (50 g) mixed candied peel
2 small eggs

Double-bladed knife

Melt the butter or margarine in a small saucepan and leave to cool.
Combine the melted butter and eggs and process until smooth. Add the sugar, oats, flour, bicarbonate of soda, salt, raisins and mixed peel and process until the ingredients are well mixed and form a stiff dough.
Shape the dough into small balls the size of a walnut and put them on to a greased baking sheet, leaving about 2 in. (5 cm) between the balls to allow them to spread during the cooking time. Bake in a moderately hot oven (350°F. 175°C. Reg. 4) for about 10 minutes until firm and lightly browned. Cool on the baking sheets and then transfer to a wire rack with a spatula.
Store in an airtight tin.

Fairings

Rich ginger biscuits with a spicy flavouring.

4 oz (100 g) self-raising flour
1 teaspoon ground ginger
Pinch mixed spice, ground nutmeg and
   cloves
1 teaspoon bicarbonate of soda

1½ oz (40 g) granulated sugar
2 oz (50 g) butter or margarine
2 tablespoons golden syrup

Double-bladed knife

Roughly chop the butter or margarine.
Combine the flour, ginger, spices, soda and sugar, add the butter and process until the mixture resembles coarse breadcrumbs. Add the syrup and process until the ingredients are well mixed. Form the mixture, in the hands, into balls the size of small walnuts and place them on an oiled baking sheet with plenty of room in between the balls. Flatten the balls slightly with the palm of the hand and bake them in a hot oven (375°F. 190°C. Reg. 5) for 15–20 minutes until spread and lightly cracked on top. Leave to cook on the tray and remove to a rack with a spatula. Store in an airtight tin.

My Cake

When I am doing cookery demonstrations for charity I like to do the odd dish that won't turn out quite as it was meant to – it happens in everyone else's kitchen so why shouldn't it happen in mine? I start with this cake and, because I open the oven while it is cooking, literally throw it together and even move it from shelf to shelf during the cooking time, I expect it to be a cake failure and plan to make everything all right by pouring over the finished failure adequate sherry to turn it into a masterpiece. Never once has that cake failed me, despite subjecting it to the sort of pressures no cake in its right mind would stand. Each time it appears, risen, moist and aromatic from the oven it improves with keeping and is an unfailing favourite.

7 oz (200 g) self-raising flour	2 tablespoons cider
5 oz (150 g) soft brown sugar	2 tablespoons marmalade
4 oz (100 g) softened butter	5 oz (150 g) mixed dried fruit
2 standard eggs	2 oz (50 g) glacé cherries

Double-bladed knife

Process the flour, sugar and butter with the eggs until a smooth dough is formed. Add the marmalade and cider and process to mix the ingredients. Add the dried fruit and cherries and switch the machine on and off for just long enough to process the ingredients without cutting up the fruit.

Turn into an oiled 2 lb (900 g) loaf tin, lined with non stick paper and bake in a moderately hot oven (350°F. 175°C. Reg. 4) for about 1 hour until a skewer plunged into the centre of the cake will come out clean.

Victoria Sandwich Cake

A classic cake which can be eaten with jam, as given, or made into something special by spreading a layer of whipped cream over the jam. A real party cake can be made by filling it with the rich chocolate filling on page 229.

6 oz (150 g) butter or margarine, softened	1 teaspoon baking powder
6 oz (150 g) caster sugar	3 large eggs
6 oz (150 g) self-raising flour	4 tablespoons strawberry jam
	Icing sugar to dust

Double-bladed knife

Place the butter, sugar, flour, baking powder and eggs in the bowl. Process for 15 – 25 seconds until well mixed and creamy but not runny.

Turn into two bottom-lined and greased 7 in. (18 cm) sandwich tins. Spread evenly and bake in a moderate oven (325°F. 160°C. Reg. 3) for 25–35 minutes or until risen, golden brown and firm to the touch. Cool on a wire rack. Sandwich the cakes together with the jam and sift a little icing sugar over the top.

Rich Chocolate Cake

A deliciously rich and slightly fudgy cake with a combined chocolate and coffee flavouring.

8 oz (225 g) soft butter
8 oz (225 g) caster sugar
4 eggs
5½ oz (160 g) plain chocolate

2 tablespoons strong coffee (liquid)
8 oz (225 g) plain flour
1 teaspoon baking powder

Double-bladed knife

Melt the chocolate with the coffee in a bowl over hot, not boiling water. Process the butter until soft. Add the sugar and process until the mixture is light and fluffy. Add the eggs, one at a time, processing after each addition, until the mixture is light and smooth.

Add the chocolate mixture to the other ingredients and process until smooth. Add the flour and baking powder and switch on and off a few times for just enough time to incorporate the ingredients – do not overprocess. Pour the mixture into an oiled 8 in. (20 cm) cake tin lightly dusted with cocoa powder and bake in a moderately hot oven (325°F. 160°C. Reg. 3) for one and a quarter hours, covering the cake with a sheet of greaseproof paper half-way through the cooking time.

Rich Chocolate Filling for a Sponge Cake

2 oz (50 g) plain chocolate
2 oz (50 g) blanched almonds

2 oz (50 g) unsalted butter
2 oz (50 g) caster sugar

Grating disc
Double-bladed knife

Grate the chocolate through the grating disc. Remove the chocolate. Put the almonds in the bowl and process until the almonds are very finely ground. Add the butter and sugar to the almonds and process until the mixture is smooth, light and creamy. Add the grated chocolate and process for just long enough to mix the ingredients.

Butter Filling

2 oz (50 g) butter

3 oz (75 g) icing sugar

Double-bladed knife

Place the butter in the bowl and process until the butter is light and creamy. Add the icing sugar and process until the mixture is light and pale in colour.

Flavourings
1.   *Chocolate:* dissolve 1 oz (25 g) plain chocolate in a tablespoon water. Add the melted chocolate to the butter icing and process until the ingredients are well mixed. Or add 2 teaspoons cocoa powder and a few drops of vanilla essence into the butter icing and process until the ingredients are well mixed.
2.   *Coffee:* add 2 teaspoons instant coffee to the butter icing and process until the ingredients are well mixed.
3.   *Lemon:* add 2–3 teaspoons lemon juice to the butter icing and process until the ingredients are well mixed.
4.   *Orange:* add 2–3 teaspoons orange juice to the butter icing and process until the ingredients are well mixed.

Swedish Tosca Cake

This is a cake I remember from my childhood (my mother is Swedish) and I only made it myself recently. It is a winner, either to serve as a tea time cake or, with fruit and cream, as a pudding.

2 eggs	**For the topping**
5 oz (50 g) caster sugar	3½ oz (90 g) blanched almonds
1 oz (25 g) soft brown sugar	2 oz (50 g) butter
2 oz (50 g) melted butter	2 oz (50 g) sugar
Grated rind of 1 orange	1 tablespoon double cream
5 oz (150 g) plain flour	2 tablespoons plain flour
1½ teaspoons baking powder	
4 tablespoons double cream	

Double-bladed knife   Process the eggs until fluffy. Add the white and brown sugar and process until light and smooth. Add the melted butter and orange peel and process to mix. Add the cream, flour and baking powder and process for just long enough to mix the ingredients (do not over process).

Pour the cake mixture into a well oiled and floured 10 in. (25 cm) flan case and bake in a moderate oven (350°F. 175°C. Reg. 4) for about 20 minutes until well risen and golden brown. While the cake is cooking make the topping.

Double-bladed knife and a clean dry bowl   Process the almonds until fairly finely chopped. Add the butter, sugar, cream and flour and process well to mix.

Sprinkle the topping over the hot cake and return to a hot oven (400°F. 200°C. Reg. 6) for a further 15 minutes until the topping is golden brown.

Tarte-aux-Fruits (Page 241)

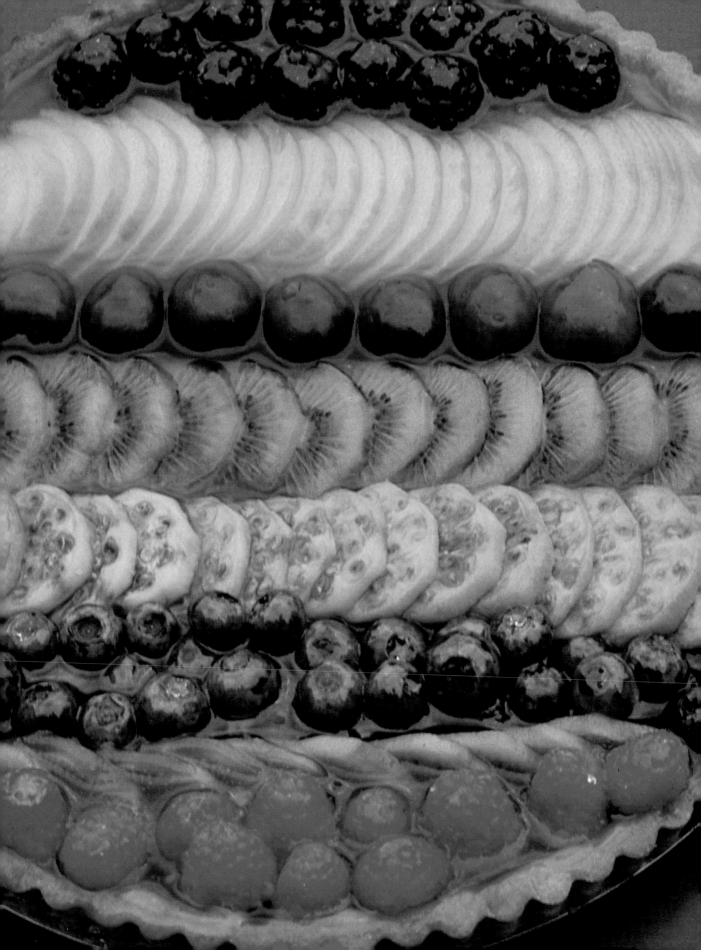

Magimix Banana Cake

8 oz (225 g) self-raising flour
Pinch salt
4 oz (100 g) butter
6 oz (175 g) sugar
1 lb (450 g) bananas

2 eggs
1 oz (25 g) shelled walnuts
4 oz (100 g) glacé cherries
2 oz (50 g) candied peel

Double-bladed knife

Roughly chop the butter. Peel and chop the bananas. Wash and drain the cherries. Combine the flour and salt, add the butter and process until the mixture is reduced to fine breadcrumbs. Add the sugar and process to mix. Add the eggs, bananas, and process until the bananas are mashed and the mixture is smooth. Add the walnuts, cherries and peel and process until the walnuts and cherries are roughly chopped. Well oil a loaf tin, place a strip of oiled greaseproof or non-stick paper over the bottom of the tin and spread in the cake mixture.

Bake in a moderate oven (350°F. 175°C. Reg. 4) for 1½ hours. Cool in the tin.

Note: This cake is best if kept in an airtight tin for a day or two.

Syrup Fruit Cake

6 oz (75 g) butter
4 oz (100 g) caster sugar
4 tablespoons golden syrup
3 eggs

4 tablespoons milk
8 oz (225 g) plain flour
1½ teaspoons baking powder
8 oz (225 g) mixed dried fruit

Double-bladed knife

Process the butter and sugar until light and creamy. Add the syrup and process to mix. With the machine running, add the eggs, one at a time through the feed tube processing after each addition until the eggs are well mixed into the other ingredients. Add the milk and process to mix. Add the flour, baking powder and fruit and process to mix well.

Turn the mixture into a well oiled and lined loaf tin and bake in a moderate oven (325°F. 160°C. Reg. 3) for 1½–2 hours. Cover with foil if browning too much.

Mincemeat (Page 277)

Honey and Spice Cake

2 oz (50 g) butter or margarine
5 fl oz (150 ml) thick honey
5 oz (125 g) soft brown sugar
10 oz (275 g) plain flour
Pinch salt
1 teaspoon bicarbonate of soda
1 teaspoon baking powder

1 teaspoon mixed spice
1 teaspoon cinnamon
1 teaspoon ground ginger
2 oz (50 g) chopped mixed candied peel
1 egg
¼ pint (5 fl oz 150 ml) milk

Melt the butter in a saucepan. Add the sugar and honey and heat gently, stirring every now and then until the sugar and honey have melted. Remove from the heat and leave to cool for 10 minutes.

Double-bladed knife Combine the flour, salt, bicarbonate of soda, baking powder, spices and peel in the Magimix bowl and switch on and off to mix. Add the cooled butter and sugar mixture, egg and milk to the flour mixture and process until smooth. Pour into a well oiled 1 lb (450 g) loaf tin and bake in a moderate oven (325°F. 160°C. Reg. 3) for about 1¼ hours until firm. Remove from the tin and cool on a wire rack. Wrap in a polythene bag and leave in the refrigerator overnight and then cut into slices and spread the slices with softened butter.

Carrot Cakes

Up until about the 18th century carrots were used almost entirely as a sweet rather than a vegetable ingredient and, in fact, were often known as "honey underground" because of their sweetness. These carrot cakes or cookies are inexpensive and, with the Magimix, exceptionally easy to make – few people would ever guess their carrot content.

1 egg
1 fl oz (30 ml) sunflower oil
1½ oz (40 g) cooked carrot
2 oz (50 g) caster sugar
2½ oz (65 g) plain flour

⅔ teaspoon baking powder
¼ teaspoon salt
2 teaspoons grated orange rind
4 tablespoons raisins
½ teaspoon ground ginger

Double-bladed knife Place the carrot in the bowl and process until puréed. Add all the ingredients, except the raisins, to the Magimix bowl and process until the mixture is smooth and well mixed. Add the raisins and switch on and off two or three times to mix the raisins into the other ingredients. Drop from a teaspoon onto an oiled baking sheet and bake in a moderate oven (350°F. 175°C. Reg. 4) for 8–10 minutes until firm and golden brown.

Cheese Straws

2 oz (50 g) Cheddar cheese
4 oz (100 g) plain flour
salt

2 oz (50 g) butter or margarine
1 egg yolk

Grating disc
Double-bladed
knife

Grate the cheddar cheese through the grating disc. Remove the cheese before replacing the grating disc with the double-bladed knife, then combine the flour, a pinch of salt, cheese and the butter or margarine (roughly chopped) in the bowl and process until the mixture is reduced to the consistency of fine breadcrumbs. Add the egg yolk and continue to process for just long enough for the dough to form a ball around the metal blade.

Roll out the pastry to ¼ in. (0·75 cm) thickness on a floured board and cut into strips ¼ in. (0·75 cm) wide and 2 in. (5 cm) long. Place the strips on a greased baking sheet and bake in a hot oven (400°F. 200°C. Reg. 6) for 8–10 minutes until golden brown.

Serve warm.

Wholemeal Oatey Biscuits

Make your own brand of cheese biscuits. Serve these at the end of a meal with Brie and crisp celery and you have something very special indeed.

4 oz (100 g) wholemeal flour
4 oz (100 g) porridge oats
2 tablespoons soft brown sugar

½ teaspoon salt
4 oz (100 g) butter or margarine
1 egg

Double-bladed
knife

Roughly chop the butter or margarine.
Combine the butter and margarine with the flour, oats, sugar and salt and process until the ingredients are well mixed. Add the egg and process into a firm dough. Turn on to a floured board and roll out thinly to ¼ in. (0·75 cm) thickness. Cut into 2 in. (5 cm) circles with a biscuit cutter, arrange on an oiled baking sheet, and bake in a hot oven (375°F. 190°C. Reg. 5) for about 10 minutes and then transfer with a spatula to a wire rack. Store the biscuits in an air tight tin.

Mexican Tortillas

If you are going to serve chilli con carne, chilli beans, gazpacho or any other Mexican dish then you should also take the trouble to make Mexican tortillas. You can buy the tortillas in tins and, unfortunately, it is difficult to buy the corn flour which is used for the tortillas de maiz but it is a simple affair to make the plain 'flour' tortillas and from them to produce delicious crisp triangles of Mexican bread which go so well with cold soups and chilli dishes.

Makes 12 tortillas

1 lb (450 g) plain flour	1 teaspoon salt
2 teaspoons baking powder	About 7 fl oz (210 ml) warm water

Dough blade or Double-bladed knife

Combine the flour, baking powder and salt in the Magimix bowl and process until mixed. With the machine running add enough warm water through the feed tube for the dough to form a ball around the blade. Run the machine for about 30 seconds to knead. Turn the dough on to a floured board and knead lightly until smooth. Wrap in cling film and leave to stand for 15 minutes. Roll out into a thick sausage and cut into 12 pieces. Spread the dough with the ball of your hand until it is about ½ in. (1·25 cm) thick then roll it with a floured rolling pin until the tortilla is paper thin (roll from the centre outwards all the time and if the tortilla becomes an uneven shape, trim it with scissors to a circle).

Cook the tortillas in a well greased large heavy frying pan, until they bubble and become pale golden on the bottom, turn them over and cook until pale gold in spots on the other side. Stack the tortillas as they are made in a folded, dampened, kitchen cloth.

How to serve the tortillas Serve the tortillas at once or they will keep for a short time in a plastic bag (over the kitchen cloth). To re-heat the tortillas. Damp them slightly, wrap them in foil and put them into a moderate oven for 10–15 minutes. Cut each tortilla into four triangles and fry them until crisp and golden in ¼ in. (0·75 cm) hot cooking oil. Hot tortillas can be spread with butter and rolled up like pancakes or they can be used as a wrapping for savoury creamed dishes of seafood, leftover meat or poultry and topped with a cheesey cream sauce.

Christmas Cake

This light Christmas cake will keep well in an airtight tin. It can be eaten as it is or covered with almond paste and Royal icing.

2 oz (50 g) blanched almonds	8 oz (225 g) butter (softened)
8 oz (225 g) sultanas	8 oz (225 g) soft brown sugar
8 oz (225 g) seedless raisins	1 tablespoon black treacle
8 oz (225 g) currants	Grated rind of a lemon
4 oz (100 g) chopped candied peel	4 eggs
4 oz (100 g) glacè cherries	2 tablespoons brandy or rum
10 oz (275 g) plain flour	2 tablespoons rose water

Double-bladed knife Put the almonds in the bowl and process until chopped. Remove them to a large bowl and mix them in with the dried fruit, candied peel, halved and washed glacè cherries and a good tablespoon of the sieved flour to give them a dry coating.

Cut the butter into 1 in. (2·5cm) cubes and place it with the sugar in the bowl. Process until soft and light. Warm the treacle until runny and add it with the lemon rind, then process to mix. Then, with the motor running, add the eggs, one at a time, through the feed tube. Finally add the flour and process in short bursts until it is mixed in.

If using the Grande Famille you can now add the fruit, together with the brandy or rum and the rose water (which gives it a lovely soft flavour) and process again very briefly. You want to mix in the fruit without chopping it too much. If using the standard Magimix (or if you prefer) empty the cake mixture into the bowl of fruit, add the brandy or rum and rose water and mix with a spoon.

Spoon the mixture into a greased and lined 8 in. (20 cm) cake tin. Make a hollow in the centre and tie a piece of grease-proof paper round the tin (so that it projects at least an inch (2·5 cm) above the top of the tin.

Place the cake in the middle of a slow oven (300°F. 150°C. Reg. 2) for two hours and then lower the heat to (275°F. 140°C. Reg. 1) for a further hour and a half. It is cooked if a skewer placed in the centre comes out clean. Leave the cake to cool in the tin.

Almond Paste

8 oz (225 g) ground almonds
4 oz (100 g) caster sugar
4 oz (100 g) icing sugar (sieved)

1 small egg
1 egg yolk
½ teaspoon almond essence

Double-bladed knife Place all the ingredients in the bowl and process until well mixed. Turn out onto a surface dusted with icing sugar and knead lightly. Wrap in cling film or foil and refrigerate until needed.

Royal Icing

4 large egg whites
1 lb 12 oz (800 g) icing sugar (sieved)

1 tablespoon lemon juice
2 teaspoons glycerine

Double-bladed knife Place the egg whites in the bowl and process for five seconds or until lightly frothy. Add the sugar, lemon juice and glycerine and process to mix. If the consistency is wrong add more sugar or lemon juice to correct it. If you do not want to use the icing immediately it will keep for a short time in a bowl covered with a damp cloth.

PASTRY

Special Pastry Dough

Use for savoury flans and pie toppings. Chill the pastry before cooking to stop it from shrinking.

Enough for one
10 in. (25 cm)
flan case or
a pie topping

8 oz (225 g) plain flour
¾ teaspoon salt
5 oz (150 g) butter

1 small egg
White wine

Double bladed
knife

Roughly cut up the butter.
Combine the flour, salt and butter and process until the mixture resembles fine breadcrumbs. Add the egg and process for just long enough to mix the egg into the other ingredients. With the machine running add just enough wine to form the dough into a ball around the knife. (The amount of wine you will need will depend on the size of your egg, and the humidity in your kitchen). The pastry can be rolled out immediately but it must be chilled for at least thirty minutes in a refrigerator before cooking.

Pastry for Sweet Flans

An everyday flan pastry – if you want something richer make the pâté sucrée on page 241.

8 oz (225 g) plain flour
2 teaspoons sugar
Pinch salt

6 oz (175 g) butter
2 small eggs

Roughly cut up the butter.

Double-bladed knife Combine the flour, salt and sugar and process to mix. Add the butter and process until the mixture resembles fine breadcrumbs. Add the eggs and process for just long enough for the dough to form a ball around the knife. Turn on to a well floured board and knead for a few seconds. Leave the dough to rest in a cool place for thirty minutes before rolling out.

Sweet Pastry

Enough for a 10 in. (25 cm) flan case

8 oz (225 g) plain flour
Pinch salt
3 oz (75 g) icing sugar

4 oz (100 g) butter
2 egg yolks

Roughly cut up the butter.

Double-bladed knife Process the flour with the salt and sugar until well mixed. Add the butter and continue to process until the mixture resembles fine breadcrumbs. Add the egg yolks and process for just long enough for the dough to form a ball around the knife. Turn onto a well floured board and knead for a few seconds. Leave to rest in a cool place for thirty minutes before rolling out.

Basic Short Crust Pastry   see photographs page 285

Enough for an 8 in. (20 cm) flan case

6 oz (175 g) plain flour
Pinch salt

3 oz (75 g) butter
1 – 2 tablespoons ice cold water

Double-bladed knife Combine the flour, salt and butter and process until the mixture resembles fine breadcrumbs. With the machine running pour the water in a slow stream through the feed tube adding just enough to enable the dough to form a ball around the knife – the amount of water you use will depend on the temperature of your kitchen and the ingredients – do not over process. Turn the dough onto a floured board and knead lightly for a few seconds only. The dough can be rolled out at once but it benefits from being allowed to 'rest' in a cool place for about thirty minutes.

Pâté Brisée

A classic French pastry for quiches or sweet flans. In France they often add sugar even if the tart is to be a savoury one and it does seem to have a crispening effect on the pastry.

11 oz (300 g) plain flour
1 oz (25 g) caster sugar
4½ oz (125 g) butter

1 egg
Iced water

Double-bladed knife Combine the flour, sugar and the butter, cut into pieces and process until the mixture resembles coarse breadcrumbs. Add the egg and process for just long enough to incorporate the egg into the other ingredients. With the motor switched on add enough iced water for the dough to form a ball around the knife. Do not over process. Turn onto a floured board and knead lightly, wrap in a floured cloth and refrigerate for thirty minutes before rolling out.

Magimix Quiche Pastry

This is the pastry I discovered purely by chance while on a demonstration tour. There I was, on a stage, about to make a quick quiche for my audience, when I found I had neither plain flour nor iced water. I improvised and produced a pastry I have been using ever since for quiches and other pastry cases. Its delight is that you can roll it straight from the Magimix without chilling and that, whatever the filling, the bottom of the case remains crisp.

Making Quiches Roll out the pastry as soon as it is made. Chill the case in the deep freeze while making the filling. Put the hot filling into the chilled case. Sprinkle the top of the quiche with a mixture of fine breadcrumbs and cheese to prevent the top sinking when it is removed from the oven.

To bake 'blind' Line a flan or quiche case with pastry and prick the bottom with a fork. Line the pastry with foil. Chill the case in the refrigerator for thirty minutes and then bake in a hot oven (425°F. 220°C. Reg. 7) for fifteen minutes. Remove the beans and foil and continue to bake for a further ten minutes until the pastry is a crisp and a pale golden colour – leave the case to cool before filling.

Enough to make 2 x 10 in. (25 cm) cases 12 oz (350 g) self raising flour
Pinch Salt
5 oz (150 g) butter or margarine

1 small egg
Dry sherry or dry white wine

Double-bladed knife Roughly chop up the butter.
Combine the flour, salt and butter and process until the mixture resembles coarse breadcrumbs. Add the egg and process until the ingredients are well mixed. With the motor running add just enough sherry or wine for the dough to form a ball around the knife – do not over process.
Roll out the dough on a well floured board, use to line flan cases and chill in the freezing compartment of a refrigerator, while making the filling. Prick the bottom of the pastry lightly with a fork before filling.

Pâte Sucrée (1)

Illustrated page 231

Short sweet pastry for tarts and flans
Enough for 2 x 12 in. (30 cm) flan cases.

10 oz (275 g) plain flour	1 oz (25 g) sugar
7 oz (200 g) butter straight from the refrigerator	1 egg
	Ice cold water

Roughly chop up the butter.

Double-bladed knife Combine the flour, sugar and butter in the Magimix bowl and process until the mixture resembles coarse breadcrumbs. Add the egg and process for long enough to mix the ingredients. With the motor running add just enough ice cold water for the dough to form a ball around the knife. Do not overprocess – stop the machine as soon as that ball has formed. Dust the pastry with flour and put into a plastic bag. Refrigerate the pastry for 30 – 45 minutes before rolling out. Roll out thinly on a well floured board and use to line pastry cases.

For a **tarte aux fruits** (illustrated page 231). Line a 10 or 12 in. (25 or 30 cm) flan case with pate sucrée and bake blind. When the case is cold glaze the bottom with a little melted redcurrant jelly to stop the pastry going soggy. Then arrange a variety of fresh fruit, either whole or sliced, in stripes in the case. Melt 4 oz (100 g) sugar in 3 tablespoons water (or 2 tablespoons water and 1 tablespoon rose water) and rapidly boil for three minutes. Dribble the syrup over the fruit and leave to set before serving.

Pâte Sucrée (2)

Sometimes known as pâte royale this is a delicate, fine pastry, to use when making sweet tarts and flans.

8 oz (225 g) plain flour	2 egg yolks
Pinch salt	A little double cream
6 oz (175 g) butter	1 tablespoon icing sugar

Roughly chop up the butter.

Double-bladed knife Combine the flour, salt, icing sugar, butter and egg yolks and process for just long enough to finely chop the butter and mix the ingredients. With the machine running add just enough cream for the dough to form a ball around the knife. Remove, knead for two seconds on a well floured board and chill in the refrigerator for fifteen minutes before rolling out.

Pastry Shells

Savoury A wonderful crisp and light pastry which can be shaped over scallop shells before baking and which makes a good vehicle for savoury dishes. (See recipe on page 149).

7 oz (200 g) plain flour	1 egg
Pinch salt	1 tablespoon single cream
3 oz (75 g) butter	

Double-bladed knife

Roughly chop the butter.
Combine the flour, salt and butter and process until the mixture looks like fine breadcrumbs. Add the egg and cream and process for just long enough for the dough to form a ball around the blade. Turn onto a floured board, knead lightly for a second or two, wrap in a cloth and chill in the refrigerator for one hour. Roll out the pastry thinly (about ⅛ in. 0·5 cm thick) and shape over oiled scallop shells or flat patty tins. Trim edges of pastry and bake in a hot oven (425°F. 220°C. Reg. 7) for 8 minutes. Remove from the moulds and turn upside down and return to the oven for a further three to four minutes until the pastry is crisp and golden.

Sweet

7 oz (200 g) plain flour	1 teaspoon grated lemon rind
3 oz (75 g) butter	1 egg
1 tablespoon caster sugar	1 tablespoon single cream

Make the pastry as above and fill with fresh sliced strawberries or kiwi fruit topped with sweetened cream.

Almond Pastry

A nice crisp pastry that is good for sweet flans and tarts. This recipe makes enough for 1 x 10 to 12 in. (25–30 cm) flan case.

3 oz (75 g) blanched almonds	1 tablespoon brandy
9 oz (250 g) plain flour	1 egg
1 oz (25 g) sugar	Ice cold water to mix
5 oz (150 g) butter	

Roughly chop up the butter.

Double-bladed knife Process the almonds until they are finely ground. Add the flour, sugar and butter and process until the mixture resembles coarse breadcrumbs. Add the brandy and egg and process to mix.

With the machine running, add a little ice cold water through the feed tube processing for long enough for the dough to form a ball around the blade.

Remove from the bowl, dust the pastry with flour, put it in a polythene bag and refrigerate for thirty minutes before rolling out on a well floured board.

Biscuit Pie Crust

This can be a boon when you feel you don't have time to make a pastry pie crust and it is also ideal for cheesecake recipes. You can make the crust from either digestive biscuits or ginger biscuits – I prefer the latter.

For an 8 x 10 in. (20–25 cm) pie crust:

6 oz (175 g) digestive or ginger biscuits   3½ oz (90 g) unsalted butter, melted

Break up the biscuits.

Double-bladed knife Process the biscuits until they are reduced to coarse crumbs. Add the melted butter and process for long enough for the butter to be absorbed into the crumbs. Press the biscuits into the bottom and sides of a flan tin and bake in a moderate oven (350°F. 175°C. Reg. 4) for 10 minutes. Leave to cool before filling.

Hot Water Crust for Raised Pies

12 oz (350 g) plain flour   3 fl oz (90 ml) water
½ teaspoon salt   1½ oz (40 g) lard
1 large egg   1½ oz (40 g) butter

Dough blade or Double-bladed knife Combine the flour, salt and egg and process to mix. Combine the water, lard and butter in a saucepan, bring to the boil and cook until the fats have melted.

With the machine switched on, pour the boiling liquid through the feed tube and process until the dough forms a ball around the knife.

Put the dough in a lightly floured polythene bag and leave to stand at room temperature for 30 minutes.

Roll the pastry out on a well floured board.

Choux Pastry (Cream Puff Pastry)

Illustrated on page 209

¼ pint (150 ml) water
1 teaspoon sugar
2½ oz (65 g) butter

4 oz (100 g) strong plain flour
4 eggs

Combine the water, sugar and butter in a saucepan and bring to the boil, stirring until the butter has melted. Remove from the heat, add the flour all at once and stir until well mixed. Return to a medium heat and beat the mixture until it forms a ball and is thick and smooth.

Double-bladed knife   Turn the dough into the Magimix bowl and process for ten seconds. With the motor running add the eggs, one at a time, through the feed tube, processing after each egg for long enough for the egg to be completely incorporated into the dough. Process until the dough is smooth and shining – do not put the pusher in the feed tube while processing.

Profiteroles or small puffs Spoon the pastry from a dessertspoon into small mounds on an oiled baking sheet and bake in a hot oven (400°F. 200°C. Reg. 6) for about 15 minutes or until dry, golden and crisp. Lower the heat to cool (275°F. 140°C. Reg. 1) and leave for about 20 minutes until completely dried out. Remove from the oven and prick with a skewer so that the hot air can escape. Leave to cool on a wire rack, split threequarters of the way through, remove any soft dough from the inside before filling.
(*Note:* Extra flavour can be given to the puffs by reducing the water by 2 tablespoons and adding 2 tablespoons orange flower water with the eggs). Fill the profiteroles with whipped sweetened cream before arranging on a dish in a 'pyramid'. Finally melt 4 oz (100 g) plain chocolate with ¼ pint (5 fl oz 150 ml) double cream and pour over the 'pyramid' while hot. Leave for the icing to cool and set before serving.

Savoury Puffs

½ pint (300 ml) water
Pinch salt and cayenne
3 oz (75 g) butter
5 oz (150 g) strong plain flour

1 oz (25 g) Cheddar cheese
3 eggs
1 teaspoon water
1 egg yolk

Combine the water, butter, salt and cayenne in a saucepan and bring to the boil stirring until the butter has melted. Remove from the heat and add the flour all at once stirring well. Return to a medium heat and beat the mixture until it forms a ball and comes cleanly away from the sides of the pan. Remove from the heat and leave to cool for two minutes.

Fine grating disc Grate the cheese.

Double-bladed Transfer the mixture to the Magimix bowl and process with the cheese for ten *knife* seconds. With the motor running, add the whole eggs, one at a time through the feed tube processing until the mixture is smooth before adding another egg.

Force the mixture through a pastry bag fitted with a medium nozzle onto an oiled baking sheet. Brush over with the egg yolk mixed with a teaspoon of water and bake in a hot oven (400°F. 200°C. Reg. 6) for 15 minutes. Lower the heat to 275°F. 140°C. Reg. 1 and leave to dry for 10 minutes.

Savoury Pancakes

These are such a versatile standby to have in your deep freeze. I make a great batch at a time (with practice I find you can have three pancake pans going at one time – a bit of a conjuring feat but very rewarding when you master the act). Fill them with any variety of savoury fillings and use them as a vehicle for utilizing small amounts of leftover fish, poultry or cooked meat.

Makes 20 thin 6 oz (175 g) plain flour   ¼ pint (150 ml) water
crêpes Salt and freshly ground black pepper.   1 oz (25 g) melted butter
3 eggs   1 tablespoon Cinzano
½ pint (300 ml) milk

Double-bladed Combine all the ingredients in the bowl and process until well mixed. Leave to *knife* stand for thirty minutes.

Rub an omelette or pancake pan with a thin smear of oil. Heat until a haze rises from the pan. Pour about two tablespoons of batter into the hot pan, swirling it around until the batter forms a thin film over the bottom of the pan. Cook over a moderate heat until the pancake is set firm. Turn over and cook the remaining side until it is pale golden. Stack the pancakes as you cook them with pieces of greaseproof paper in between each one.

Note: Even the very best cooks will tell you that their first pancakes nearly always stick to the pan and have to be scrapped – don't worry the next one is sure to be fine.

SAUCES & DRESSINGS

FRENCH DRESSINGS (Vinaigrette)

Instead of mixing French dressings and all their variations by hand, perform magic in seconds in your food processor producing well flavoured, emulsified dressings that will grace any salad.

Classic French Dressing

2 tablespoons white wine vinegar
6 tablespoons olive or sunflower oil

Salt and freshly ground black pepper

Double-bladed knife or plastic blade

Process the ingredients until well mixed.
Note: Lemon juice can be substituted for vinegar to make a lighter dressing.

French Dressing with Mustard

Double-bladed knife or Plastic blade

Combine 1 teaspoon Dijon mustard with the vinegar or lemon juice.
Process the vinegar and mustard until well mixed and season with salt and pepper. With the machine switched 'on' add the oil in a slow steady stream through the feed tube.

French Dressing with Garlic

Double-bladed knife

Peel two garlic cloves. Process them until finely chopped. Add ½ teaspoon mustard and the vinegar, season with salt and pepper and process until the ingredients are well mixed. With the machine switched 'on' add the oil in a slow steady stream through the feed tube.

French Dressing with Herbs

Double-bladed knife Process a small bunch of parsley with the stalks removed with some roughly chopped chives, a few tarragon leaves and two sprigs of chervil. Process until the herbs are finely chopped. Add ½ teaspoon Dijon mustard, season with salt and pepper, add the vinegar and process until the ingredients are well mixed. With the machine switched 'on' add the oil in a slow steady stream through the feed tube.

Herb Dressing with Sherry

Double-bladed knife Process a small bunch of parsley with the stalks removed with a few roughly chopped chives until the herbs are finely chopped. Add ½ teaspoon Dijon mustard, 1 tablespoon medium dry sherry, 1 tablespoon white wine vinegar, season with salt and pepper and process until the ingredients are well mixed. With the machine switched 'on' add the oil in a slow steady stream.

Tomato Vinaigrette

Cover two tomatoes with boiling water, leave them to stand for three minutes and then slide off the skins. Halve the tomatoes, remove the core and seeds and roughly chop the flesh.

Double-bladed knife Process the tomatoes until reduced to a purée. Add ½ teaspoon tomato purée, ½ teaspoon Dijon mustard, 2 tablespoons white wine vinegar and season with salt and pepper. Process until well mixed. With the machine switched 'on' add 6 tablespoons of oil in a slow steady stream through the feed tube.

French Dressing with Meat Juices

A popular dressing made by the French when there are some delicious meat juices left in a roasting pan. Try this with a spring salad of young spinach leaves, dandelion leaves and chicory.

Double-bladed knife Process a peeled clove of garlic until finely chopped. Season with salt and pepper, add a few drops of Worcestershire sauce, 2 tablespoons red wine vinegar; ½ teaspoon Dijon mustard and 2 tablespoons meat juices with the fat removed. Process until well mixed. With the machine switched 'on' add the oil in a slow steady stream through the feed tube.

Stilton Dressing

Double-bladed knife Combine 2 tablespoons white wine vinegar and 6 tablespoons oil and season with salt and pepper. Process until well mixed and add 2 tablespoons double cream and 2 oz (50 g) Stilton cheese. Process for just long enough to mix the ingredients – do not over-process, the dressing should still retain some texture rather than being absolutely smooth. (See recipe for avocado pears with stilton dressing on page 188).

Other alternatives Add some toasted sesame seeds to a classic French dressing. Add some dried tarragon leaves soaked in a little lemon juice to a classic French dressing.
Add 1 teaspoon curry powder to a classic French dressing.

Ruby Dressing

Especially good with a chicory and watercress salad.

¼ pint (5 fl oz 150 ml) French dressing (see page 246)	2 anchovies
	1 small, cooked, beetroot

Double-bladed knife
Medium grating disc

Roughly chop the anchovies.
Combine the anchovies and vinaigrette in the Magimix bowl and process until the anchovy is finely chopped. Remove the double-bladed knife.
Grate the beetroot into the dressing.
Pour the dressing over the salad and toss lightly to mix.

Ravigote Dressing

French dressing with the addition of capers and herbs which goes well with cold beef, tongue or ham as well as a salad dressing.

½ pint (10 fl oz 300 ml) French dressing (see page 246)	1 small bunch mixed fresh parsley tarragon and chervil
1 small onion	2 teaspoons capers

Double-bladed knife

Peel and roughly chop the onion. Remove any coarse stalks from the herbs. Combine the herbs in a clean dry bowl and process until finely chopped. Add the onion and continue to process until the onion is finely chopped. Add the capers and dressing and process for long enough to chop the capers and mix all the ingredients.

Tomato and Cream Vinaigrette Dressing

4 drained tinned tomatoes
1 teaspoon red wine vinegar
3 fl oz (90 ml) strong chicken stock

4 tablespoons double cream
¼ teaspoon dried tarragon
Salt and freshly ground black pepper

Double-bladed knife Combine all the ingredients in the Magimix bowl, season with salt and freshly ground black pepper and process until well mixed. Serve with tomato salads, cucumber salads and light summer patés.

Cream Cheese Dressing

A rich dressing for summer salads and for coleslaw.

Small bunch parsley
3 oz (75 g) cream cheese
1 small shallot
½ teaspoon dry mustard

1½ tablespoons white wine vinegar
3 tablespoons olive or sunflower oil
Salt and freshly ground black pepper

Double-bladed knife Remove any tough stalks from the parsley. Peel and roughly chop the shallot. Process the parsley until finely chopped in a clean, dry bowl. Add the shallot and process until the shallot is finely chopped. Add the cream cheese and process until well mixed. Add the mustard, vinegar and oil, season with salt and pepper and process until the dressing is smooth.

Avocado Dressing

Delicious with a cucumber or tomato salad.

½ ripe avocado
Little lemon juice
¼ pint (5 fl oz 150 ml) vinaigrette
  dressing (see page 246)

1 tablespoon finely chopped chives or
  spring onion tops

Double-bladed knife Peel the avocado, remove the stone and brush the flesh with lemon juice. Combine the avocado with the dressing and process until the mixture is smooth. Add the chives or spring onion tops and switch on and off to mix.

Mayonnaise

see photographs page 291

This is the sauce, above all sauces, that cookery writers have most problems with. So much depends on the temperature of the ingredients and the temperature of the room in which they are to be mixed. Much depends also on the speed at which the oil is added and, although you can do this more quickly in the food processor, than by any other process, it still has to be a controlled addition. Most of all it depends on the ability of the cook to know when the mayonnaise is on the point of curdling and what to do to adjust it. At home, when I know exactly what the temperature of my ingredients are (they should all be the same whether that be refrigerator temperature or room temperature) I have no trouble at all in producing mayonnaise in a matter of about five minutes at the outside. At cookery demonstrations, however, where there are strong lights on, when my machine has been in constant use for about one hour or more and the spool itself may be quite warm, I have had mayonnaise curdle again and again. Fortunately I don't mind because at least the audience sees that it happens to everyone and frequently, how it is possible to adjust the curdling before it gets too bad or (if this fails) how to make mayonnaise even more quickly the second time using the curdled ingredients.

The process of making mayonnaise is, I believe, one of the magic processes of cooking. What happens, basically, is that oil added to beaten egg yolks with salt, and perhaps a little mustard, forms a liason that makes a thick, globular mixture – why? No one quite knows but, whatever the reason, the result is a very good one indeed.

Once you have your mayonnaise perfected it can be stored in the coolest part of the refrigerator (the bottom) for up to three weeks. It can also be flavoured with a wide variety of ingredients.

2 egg yolks
Pinch salt
¼ teaspoon made English mustard

½ pint (10 fl oz 300 ml) olive oil
2 teaspoons vinegar
White pepper

Double-bladed knife   Combine the egg yolks, and mustard and process for 30 seconds. With the machine switched on, add the oil, a teaspoon at a time, through the feed tube, processing until the ingredients are well mixed after each addition of oil. The egg yolks and oil should form an emulsion after about the third of the oil is used – if the mixture looks at all like curdling (separating) add a few drops of vinegar at that point as this should help to stabilise and thicken the sauce.

As soon as the oil and egg yolks have formed a thick emulsion (it should be thick enough to stand a spoon up in) and all the oil has been absorbed, season the mayonnaise with salt and pepper and with the machine still switched on, add the remaining vinegar.

AT THIS POINT the mayonnaise may be too thick for your purpose – it can be thinned by the addition of warm water, cream or other liquid ingredients such as tomato purée etc.

If, at any point, the mayonnaise curdles beyond control, start the whole process again with a third egg yolk, beating it until smooth with the plastic blade or double-bladed knife and adding the curdled mixture a few drops at a time (with the machine switched on).

Variations Use lemon juice instead of vinegar to give a more sensitive but marked flavouring.
Add ¼ pint (5 fl oz 150 ml) whipped cream to the finished mayonnaise to make a lighter slightly moussey sauce.

Garlic Mayonnaise or Sauce Aioli

A strongly flavoured garlic mayonnaise for serving with crudités (raw vegetables served as a first course i.e. carrot and celery sticks, strips of green and red pepper, firm button mushrooms, cauliflower florettes, spring onions etc.) or with some fish dishes.
Please read the notes for making mayonnaise since this sauce is made exactly the same way and has the same problems.

8 cloves garlic
2 egg yolks
Pinch salt
White pepper

½ pint (10 fl oz 300 ml) olive oil or
    sunflower oil
Juice ½ lemon

Double-bladed knife

Peel and roughly chop the garlic cloves.
Process the garlic until very finely chopped. Add the egg yolks, and pepper and a few drops of lemon juice and process until the yolks are smooth and light in colour. With machine still running add the oil, a little at a time, processing until each addition of oil forms an emulsion with the egg yolks. Continue to add the oil in a steady slow stream until it is absorbed into the yolks. Add the salt and remaining lemon juice (with the machine still switched on) and then check the seasoning. If the sauce is too thick for your purpose thin it with a little warm water added through the feed tube with the motor still running.

Fennel Mayonnaise for Salmon and Trout

A marvellously subtle sauce to serve with cold or grilled fish.

Half a fennel bulb
Salt
1 teaspoon lemon juice
1 teaspoon Dijou mustard

8 fl oz (240 ml) mayonnaise
(see page 250)
Pinch cayenne pepper

Double-bladed knife

Remove the top stalks of the fennel and reserve the feathery leaves. Roughly chop the fennel, cover it with water, season with salt, add the lemon juice and boil for 20 minutes until tender. Leave to cool.
Process the fennel leaves until finely chopped. Add the fennel and process to a purée. Add the mayonnaise, mustard and cayenne and process until the ingredients are well mixed.

Watercress Mayonnaise

Delicious with fish, egg dishes or cold chicken dishes.

For four people

8 fl oz (240 ml) mayonnaise
(see page 250)

1 bunch watercress
1 teaspoon lemon juice

Double-bladed knife

Remove any tough stalks from the watercress.
Process the watercress until finely chopped. Add the mayonnaise and lemon juice and process until the ingredients are well blended.

Tomato Mayonnaise

For four to six people

¼ pint (5 fl oz 150 ml) tomato sauce
(see page 259)

¼ pint (5 fl oz 150 ml) mayonnaise
(see page 250)

Double-bladed knife

Cook the tomato purée over a high heat, stirring every now and then to prevent sticking, until it is thick and reduced by about a third in volume. Leave to cool.
Process the tomato sauce until smooth. Add the mayonnaise and process until the ingredients are well mixed.

Variation Add one teaspoon curry paste to the mixture to give an Oriental flavouring.

Green Mayonnaise

An attractive sauce for serving with cold fish, chicken or egg dishes.

Small bunch parsley
1 sprig tarragon and chervil

3 spinach leaves
½ pint (10 fl oz 300 ml) mayonnaise
(see page 250)

Remove the stalks from the parsley, tarragon, chervil and spinach. Cook the herbs and spinach in a little boiling salted water for three minutes. Plunge into cold water to stop the cooking process and drain really well in a sieve pressing out excess water gently with your hands.

Double-bladed knife   Process the herbs and spinach until reduced to a smooth purée. Add the mayonnaise and process until the ingredients are well mixed.

Mayonnaise Colée

This mayonnaise is used for coating cold foods such as chicken joints, salmon steaks or halved hard boiled eggs.

½ pint (10 fl oz 300 ml) mayonnaise
(see page 250)

½ a packet ¼ oz (0·6 g) gelatine
2 tablespoons boiling water

Double-bladed knife   Dissolve the gelatine in the boiling water. Place the mayonnaise and the dissolved gelatine in the bowl and process until shiny and smooth.
Place the food to be covered on a wire rack, and carefully pour over the mayonnaise. Leave to set before moving to a serving dish.

Whole Egg Mayonnaise

This makes a lighter mayonnaise than one made with egg yolks and since it uses all the egg instead of having some white left over it can sometimes be preferable in terms of economy.

1 small egg
Salt and freshly ground black pepper
1 teaspoon Dijon mustard

7 fl oz (210 ml) olive or sunflower oil
2 teaspoons – 1 tablespoon white wine
vinegar (or use lemon juice)

Double-bladed knife   Combine the egg with a little salt, some freshly ground black pepper and the mustard and process for 30 seconds. With the machine switched 'on' add the oil in a slow, steady, stream until the sauce has emulsified and most of the oil has been used. With the machine still switched 'on' add the vinegar or lemon juice through the feed tube and then add any remaining oil. Taste for seasoning and add some more salt if necessary.

Note: Use ingredients that are at the same temperature. If the ingredients seem like curdling during the addition of the oil, add a few drops of vinegar to stabilize the sauce.

Gribiche Sauce

A cold, mayonnaise, type sauce made with hard boiled eggs which goes well with salads, fish or cold chicken.

3 hard boiled eggs	8 fl oz (240 ml) olive or sunflower oil
Small bunch parsley, chives and chervil	1 teaspoon white wine vinegar
1 tablespoon Dijon mustard	Salt and white pepper

Double-bladed knife   Remove the stalks from the herbs. Separate the white and yolks of the eggs. Process the herbs until finely chopped and remove. Process the egg whites until finely chopped and remove. Combine the egg yolks with the mustard in the Magimix bowl and process until smooth. With the motor running gradually add the oil, in a thin stream through the feed tube until all the oil has been used up and the sauce is thick and satiny. Season with salt and pepper, add the vinegar and process to mix well. Add the egg whites and herbs and switch on and off to mix.

Additions I have had this sauce with the addition of capers and pickled gherkins making it more like a sauce tartare. Add the capers and gherkins before mixing in the egg whites and herbs, and process until the capers and gherkins are finely chopped.

Sharp Egg and Cream Sauce

A good sauce to serve with hard boiled eggs dishes as an alternative to an egg mayonnaise or to accompany fish.

2 hard boiled egg yolks	Salt and a pinch of paprika
2 raw egg yolks	2 tablespoons vinegar
2 teaspoons Dijon mustard	½ pint (10 fl oz 300 ml) whipping cream

Double-bladed knife Process the hard boiled egg yolks until smooth. Add the raw egg yolks and process until the ingredients are really well mixed and smooth. Add the mustard, season with salt and a pinch of paprika, add the vinegar and process until smooth. Add the cream and process for just long enough to thicken the ingredients.

Cooked Egg Dressing

This was a popular dressing during the war since it used only one egg and is also more easily digested than a rich mayonnaise. You end up with a thick dressing but one of a pouring consistency rather than the thickness of a mayonnaise.

2 tablespoons plain flour
1 teaspoon dry English mustard powder
Salt and freshly ground black pepper
Pinch cayenne pepper
2 teaspoons sugar

1 egg
½ pint (10 fl oz 300 ml) boiling water
4 tablespoons white wine vinegar
3 tablespoons olive or sunflower oil

Double-bladed knife Break the egg into the bowl, add the flour, mustard, seasoning and sugar and process to mix well. With the motor switched on pour in the boiling water through the tube. Add the vinegar, process to mix and transfer the mixture to a small heavy saucepan. Cook over a low heat, stirring continually, until the sauce thickens and is satiny smooth. Cool, transfer back to the Magimix bowl and, with the machine switched on, gradually add the oil. Check the seasoning before serving.
Note: The sauce can be covered with cling film and kept in the refrigerator (if it separates return the sauce to the Magimix bowl and process till smooth. If necessary add a few teaspoonfuls of boiling water to adjust the curdling).

Hollandaise

I used to get bored with making Hollandaise over a stove (all that stirring in double boilers and wondering if *anything* at all was going to happen). Now I follow this recipe with my Magimix and it works perfectly and will keep well providing the vinegar mixture and the butter are really hot when they are added to the egg yolk mixture. Hollandaise can be served with egg, fish and some poultry dishes. I do not personally think the sauce needs to be warm when served and feel it is safer to serve it at room temperature – the sauce is so delicious that I doubt if any of your guests will comment on its temperature.

1 tablespoon white wine vinegar
3 tablespoons water
3 egg yolks

Freshly ground black or, if necessary,
   white pepper
5 oz (150 g) unsalted butter

Double-bladed knife   Process the egg yolks until really smooth and well mixed. Combine the vinegar and water in a small saucepan, season with pepper, bring to the boil and boil until the mixture is reduced to about a teaspoon. Melt the butter until boiling (but without browning) in a small saucepan. With the machine switched on add the vinegar and then the butter, in a slow, steady stream, through the feed tube. The mixture should emulsify and thicken as the vinegar and butter are added producing a consistency that is the same as a thick mayonnaise.

Variations

Sauce Mousseline Cool the Hollandaise sauce. Whip ¼ pint (5 fl oz 150 ml) double cream with the plastic disc, add the Hollandaise sauce and process for just long enough to mix the ingredients.
Add 1 teaspoon of green peppercorns but no salt to the vinegar mixture to produce a sharp but delicious Hollandaise sauce.
Add 1 teaspoon mixed herbs to the vinegar and water mixture to produce a well flavoured Hollandaise sauce.

Sauce Charon Add 1 tablespoon homemade, concentrated tomato purée to the finished sauce.

Hermes Sauce

This is one of the many sauces that my Magimix and I have invented together. Its a kind of Hollandaise but lighter with an almost mousse-like texture. It goes well with fish, chicken or vegetables and I called it 'Hermes' because it looks expensive and tastes expensive. *Fromage frâiche* can be bought from good supermarkets and delicatessen stores but if you cannot find it use cream cheese thinned with some single cream.

4 egg yolks	1 teaspoon Dijon mustard
Juice of ½ small lemon	Salt and freshly ground black pepper
3 tablespoons tinned consommé	2 oz (50 g) butter
4 tablespoons fromage frâiche	

Double-bladed knife   Process the egg yolks until smooth. Add the lemon juice, consommé, fromage frâiche and mustard and season with salt and pepper. Process until smooth. Turn into a small heavy bottomed saucepan, and stir over a low heat until the sauce thickens to the texture of custard and will coat the back of a wooden spoon. Add the butter, cut into small pieces and stir over a low heat until the butter has become amalgamated into the sauce.
Note: I have found this sauce just does not seem to curdle but if, by some chance yours does, put it back into the bowl and process it with the double-bladed knife until it is smooth again.

Spring Onion and Wine Sauce

A nice delicate sauce to serve with light poultry and fish dishes.

1 bunch spring onions	3 tablespoons dry white wine
2 oz (50 g) butter	½ teaspoon Dijon mustard
2 tablespoons flour	Salt and freshly ground black pepper
¼ pint (5 fl oz 150 ml) milk	¼ pint (5 fl oz 150 ml) single cream

Double-bladed knife

Trim the spring onions and cut into lengths of about 1 in. (2·5 cm). Process the onions until chopped.

Melt the butter in a small saucepan. Add the spring onions and cook over a low heat until the onions are soft. Add the flour and mix well. Stir in the mustard and gradually add the milk and wine stirring continually over a medium high heat until the sauce is thick and smooth. Season with salt and pepper and simmer for three minutes. Stir in the cream and heat through without boiling. If you want a completely smooth sauce turn it all back in the bowl and process.

Note: If a sharper sauce is required you can add a little lemon juice.

Pesto

A Mediterranean sauce or amalgamation which is used for flavouring soups and stews and also as a sauce for pasta. Made by hand this deliciously aromatic sauce takes a long time to prepare but with your Magimix it can be done in seconds.

4 cloves garlic	4 tablespoons olive oil
Small bunch basil (about 12 sprigs)	Salt and freshly ground black pepper

Double-bladed knife

Peel and roughly chop the garlic.

Process the basil until finely chopped. Add the garlic and continue to process until the garlic and basil are reduced to a purée (you may have to scrape down the sides of the bowl during the processing time). With the machine running, add the oil in a slow steady stream in the same way as you would for a mayonnaise. Season the finished sauce with salt and pepper and process to mix well.

Add the sauce to vegetable soups or to stews just before serving.

Salsa Verde

A strongly flavoured Italian and Spanish style vinaigrette which goes well with meats, fish, vegetables, etc.

1 small bunch parsley with the stalks
   removed
2 anchovy fillets, drained
1 tablespoon capers

1 tablespoon lemon juice
¼ pint (5 fl oz 150 ml) olive or
   sunflower oil
Freshly ground black pepper

Double-bladed knife   Process the parsley until finely chopped. Add the anchovy fillets and process until the mixture is reduced to a paste. Add the capers and lemon juice and process until well mixed. Season with pepper (salt will not be necessary because of the saltiness of the anchovies) and, with the machine switched 'on' add the oil in a slow, steady, stream through the feed tube. The sauce should be quite thick and emulsified and should be used as soon as possible before it has time to separate.

Sauce Verte

A handful of young spinach with the
   stalks removed
Small bunch parsley
Few sprigs chervil with the stalks
   removed

Small bunch of chives
Few tarragon leaves
½ pint (10 fl oz 300 ml) mayonnaise
   (see page 250)
2 teaspoons capers

Wash the spinach and cook it with a little salt over a medium heat until the spinach is soft. Leave to cool.

Double-bladed knife   Process the parsley, chervil, chives and tarragon leaves until finely chopped. Add the spinach and process until the spinach is reduced to a purée. Add the mayonnaise and capers and process until the ingredients are well mixed.
This is very good if served with cold salmon or trout.

Barbecue Sauce

A good all round sauce for basting spare ribs of pork, chops, sausages, chicken joints, etc. You can also use the sauce to serve on the side with barbecued ingredients.

1 onion	2 tablespoons white wine vinegar
2 cloves garlic	2 teaspoons soft brown sugar
1 oz (25 g) butter	1 teaspoon Dijon mustard
1 tablespoon oil	Salt and freshly ground black pepper
1 small (8 oz) (225 g) tin tomatoes	Pinch paprika pepper
2 teaspoons tomato purée	

Double-bladed knife

Peel and roughly chop the onion and garlic.
Process the onion and garlic until finely chopped and remove. Heat the oil and butter in a frying pan. Add the onion and garlic and cook over a low heat until the onion is soft and transparent.
Process the tomatoes with the remaining ingredients, seasoning with salt and freshly ground black pepper, until they are reduced to a purée. Add to the onion and garlic and stir over a medium heat for five minutes. Use for basting barbecue ingredients.

Quick Tomato Sauce

A useful and versatile sauce which can be stored in the refrigerator for some days without loss of flavour.

1 medium onion	¼ pint (5 fl oz 150 ml) red wine
2 cloves garlic	½ teaspoon dried mixed basil and
2 tablespoons sunflower oil	oregano
1 tin (15 oz 400 g) tomatoes	Salt and freshly ground black pepper

Double-bladed knife

Peel and roughly chop the onion. Peel the garlic cloves.
Process the onion and garlic until the onion is very finely chopped.
Heat the oil in a medium sized saucepan, add the onion and garlic and cook over a medium high heat until the onion is soft and transparent. Add the tomatoes, wine, herbs and seasoning and cook over a high heat, without a lid, for 20 minutes, stirring every now and then to break up the tomatoes, until the sauce has thickened and is rich and ruby red. Serve the sauce hot or cold.
Note: This recipe is for a coarse sauce, if you prefer a smoother sauce return it to the Magimix and process with the double-bladed knife until it is almost smooth. Rub the sauce through a fine sieve to remove any pips.

Tomato Coulis

A light raw tomato sauce which goes well with light pâtés, terrines, fish mousses etc.

4 firm, ripe tomatoes

1 clove garlic

Salt and freshly ground black pepper

2 tablespoons dry white wine

Cover the tomatoes with boiling water for three minutes, drain, slide off the skins and halve the tomatoes. Scoop out the seeds and any tough cores and leave the tomatoes upside down to drain for 30 minutes. Roughly chop the tomato flesh. Peel and roughly chop the garlic.

Double-bladed knife Process the garlic until finely chopped. Add the tomato flesh and process until the tomatoes are reduced to a purée. Season with salt and pepper, add the wine and process to mix well.

Variations To give a more strongly flavoured sauce add a tablespoon of tomato purée to the tomato pulp. Add a tablespoon of finely chopped fresh basil and chives to the tomato sauce.

For a lighter sauce add half a packet of gelatine powder softened in tomato juice and ¼ pint (5 fl oz 150 ml) whipped cream to the tomato pulp.

Portuguese Tomato Sauce

1 large onion

3 cloves garlic

3 tablespoons oil

1½ lb (675 g) firm ripe tomatoes

4 tablespoons dry white wine

Salt and freshly ground black pepper

¼ teaspoon oregano

¼ teaspoon sugar

2 bay leaves

2 teaspoons tomato purée

2 oz (50 g) unsalted butter

Peel and roughly chop the onion and garlic cloves. Cover the tomatoes with boiling water, leave them to stand for 3 minutes and then drain and slide off the tomato skins. Halve the tomatoes and scoop out the seeds and any hard cores. Stand the tomatoes upside down to drain for 15 minutes.

Double-bladed knife Process the onion and the garlic until finely chopped and remove.

Process the tomatoes until finely chopped.

Heat the oil in a saucepan, add the onions and garlic and cook over a low heat until the onion is soft and transparent. Add the tomatoes, season with salt and pepper, add the sugar, wine, tomato purée, oregano and bay leaves stir well, bring to the boil and simmer uncovered for 30 minutes.

Add the butter, cut into small pieces, and stir over a medium heat until the butter has been absorbed into the sauce just before serving.

Sweet and Sour Sauce

A sauce that can be served with mixed salads, with grilled prawns or with a summer salad of prawns, lettuce, radishes and some crisply cooked young vegetables.

2 tablespoons clear honey
½ teaspoon lemon juice
1 teaspoon white wine vinegar
½ teaspoon soy sauce

½ teaspoon made English mustard
Salt and freshly ground black pepper
1 tablespoon tomato ketchup

Double-bladed knife   Combine all the ingredients in the Magimix bowl and process until well mixed and smooth.

Curried Cream Sauce

1 oz (25 g) butter
1 small onion
1½ tablespoons flour
¼ pint (5 fl oz 150 ml) chicken stock
1 teaspoon hot curry paste or powder

¼ pint (5 fl oz 150 ml) double cream
2 teaspoons honey
1 teaspoon lemon juice
Salt and white pepper

Peel and coarsely chop the onion.

Double-bladed knife   Process the onion until finely chopped.
Melt the butter, add the onion and cook over a low heat, stirring, until the onion is soft and transparent. Add the flour and hot curry paste or powder and mix well. Gradually blend in the stock, stirring continually, over a medium high heat until the sauce is thick and smooth. Lower the heat, add the cream, honey and lemon juice and (if necessary) enough stock to make a thick sauce, season with salt and pepper and simmer without boiling for three minutes.
Transfer to the Magimix bowl and process until the sauce is smooth.
Serve hot with fish, chicken mousseline, shellfish etc.

Onion and Cider Sauce

A delicious sauce to go with boiled bacon or gammon. It goes well too with roast pork or pork chops.

2 medium onions	1 chicken stock cube
1 oz (25 g) butter	Freshly ground black pepper
1 tablespoon flour	Pinch nutmeg
¼ pint (5 fl oz 150 ml) dry cider	Pinch dried sage
¼ pint (5 fl oz 150 ml) milk	1 teaspoon made English mustard

Peel and halve the onions.

Thin slicing disc   Slice the onions through the thin slicing disc. Heat the butter in a small saucepan. Add the onions and cook over a low heat, stirring until the onions are soft. Add the flour and mix well. Gradually blend in the cider and milk, stirring continually over a medium high heat until the sauce comes to the boil and is thick and smooth. Add the stock cube and stir until the cube has melted. Season with pepper and nutmeg, stir in the sage and mustard and simmer, stirring every now and then to prevent sticking, for 20 minutes.

Note: The sauce should be the consistency of thick custard, if necessary add a little more milk.

Sauce Smitane

A lovely onion and cream sauce to serve with plainly cooked fish or chicken.

1 large onion	1 pint (20 fl oz 600 ml) double cream
1½ oz (40 g) butter	Salt
3 fl oz (90 ml) dry white wine	¼ teaspoon lemon juice

Peel and roughly chop the onion.

Double-bladed knife   Process the onion until finely chopped.

Heat 1 oz (25 g) butter in a saucepan, add the onion and cook over a low heat, without browning, until the onion is soft and transparent.

Add the wine, bring to the boil and boil until the wine has evaporated. Add the cream, season with salt and bring to the boil and cook over a high heat until the sauce has reduced by about one third. Strain the sauce.

Double-bladed knife   Process the onion until smooth adding a little of the cream liquid through the feed tube during the processing. Return the onion purée and cream liquid to a clean pan, heat through without boiling. Stir in the lemon juice and the remaining batter. Check seasoning before serving.

Sauce Espagnole

This basic sauce is added to other sauce bases to give them flavour and colouring. It is a rich sauce and can be used by itself with roast lamb or it can be thinned with stock to serve with other meat and poultry dishes. If you make a quantity of the sauce it can be stored in a screw top jar in the refrigerator and can be added to soups, stews and casseroles to give extra flavour.

2 oz (50 g) streaky bacon rashers with the rinds removed	4 tablespoons dry white wine
1 medium carrot	2 bay leaves
1 onion	2 pints (1·1 litres) beef stock (or use tinned consommé).
Small stalk celery	2 oz (50 g) butter
1 sprig of thyme or a pinch of dried oregano	4 tablespoons flour
2 tablespoons sunflower oil	3 tablespoons tomato purée
	Salt and freshly ground black pepper

Roughly chop the bacon. Peel and roughly chop the carrot. Peel and roughly chop the onion. Roughly chop the celery.

Double-bladed knife Process the bacon until finely chopped and remove. Process the carrot, onion and celery until finely chopped. Heat the oil. Add the vegetables and cook over a medium high heat, stirring now and then until the vegetables are lightly browned. Add the wine, bring to the boil and stir for 2 minutes to reduce the wine. In a heavy saucepan, melt the butter, add the bacon and cook, stirring, over a high heat until the bacon and butter are lightly browned. Stir in the flour over a high heat, continuing to stir until the flour is the colour of a hazelnut. Gradually add the stock, stirring continually over a medium high heat until the sauce comes to the boil and is thick and smooth. Add the vegetables and wine, season with salt and pepper add the thyme (or oregano) and bay leaves. Bring to the boil and cook, uncovered, for 1½ hours, skimming off any scum that rises to the surface as it cooks. Add the tomato purée and continue to cook for a further 30 minutes. Remove the bay leaves.

Double-bladed knife Process the sauce until almost smooth.

Note: Thin the sauce if necessary with stock; add it to sauces, soup, casseroles and stews for flavouring.

Variations Add ½ pint (10 fl oz 300 ml) good brown stock and 1 tablespoon sherry to the Espagnole sauce, simmer until the sauce is reduced by a third and strain through a sieve to make a *demi-glace* sauce.

Piquant Sauce

I find this is an admirable sauce (as is the Sauce Robert which follows) for reheating leftover meat or chicken if you want to serve leftovers as a hot rather than a cold dish. Instead of the flour, stock and tomato purée you can substitute ½ pint (10 fl oz 300 ml) Espagnole sauce (see page 263) and thinned, if necessary.

1 medium onion	½ pint (10 fl oz 300 ml) stock
2 spring onions	Salt and freshly ground black pepper
3 oz (75 g) butter	1 tablespoon tomato purée
2 tablespoons flour	2 gherkins
3 tablespoons red wine vinegar	

Double-bladed knife

Peel and roughly chop the onion and spring onions. Finely chop the spring onions. Add the onion and process until the onion is finely chopped. Heat half the butter in a saucepan, add the spring onions and onion and cook over a low heat until softened and golden brown. Add the flour and mix well over a medium heat until the flour is the colour of a hazelnut.

In a small saucepan, boil the vinegar until reduced by half. Add the vinegar to the onion and flour mixture and then gradually blend in the stock and tomato purée stirring continually over a medium heat until the sauce comes to the boil and is thick and smooth. Season with salt and pepper and simmer gently for 15 minutes.

Double-bladed knife

Process the gherkins until finely chopped and add them to the sauce with the remaining butter cut into small pieces. Heat through before serving.

Note: If you add some Dijon mustard and a pinch of sugar to the sauce with the gherkins it then becomes a Sauce Robert.

Sauce Chasseur

Another robust and versatile sauce which can be used for meat, chicken or fish.

½ pint (10 fl oz 300 ml) demi glace sauce (see page 263)	4 oz (100 g) firm button mushrooms
Small bunch parsley and a few leaves of fresh or dried tarragon	¼ pint (5 fl oz 150 ml) dry white wine
1 small shallot	2 tomatoes
	1 oz (25 g) butter
	Salt and freshly ground black pepper

Remove any tough stalks from the parsley. Peel and roughly chop the shallot. Cover the tomatoes with boiling water, leave to stand for three minutes and then drain and slide off the skins. Halve the tomatoes, scoop out the seeds and any hard core and leave the tomatoes upside down to drain for 10 minutes. Roughly chop the tomatoes.

Double-bladed knife

Process the parsley and tarragon until finely chopped and remove.

Process the shallot until finely chopped and remove.

Medium slicing disc

Process the mushrooms through the slicing disc and remove.

Double-bladed Process the tomatoes until reduced to a purée. Melt half the butter in a saucepan and
knife add the shallot. Cook gently over a low heat until the shallot is soft and transparent.
Add the mushrooms and wine and cook until the wine is reduced by half. Add the
demi-glace sauce and tomato purée and boil for five minutes. Add the parsley and
tarragon and stir in the remaining butter cut into small pieces. Season with salt and
pepper if necessary.

Madeira Sauce

A delicious sauce to serve with meat or game.

4 oz (100 g) firm button mushrooms	½ pint (10 fl oz 300 ml) Espagnole
1 oz (25 g) butter	sauce (see page 263)
4 tablespoons Madeira	Extra stock as needed

Thin or medium Slice the mushrooms.
slicing disc Melt half the butter in a saucepan. Add the mushrooms and cook over a high heat
for two minutes. Add the Espagnole sauce and enough stock to make a fairly liquid
sauce and stir gently until hot through. Boil the Madeira in a small saucepan until
reduced by a third. Add the Madeira to the sauce bring to the boil, lower the heat,
beat in the remaining butter and check the seasoning before serving.

Sauce Brune

Use this to serve instead of a gravy with meat or poultry or incorporate the sauce as
the basis of a stew, casserole or soup.
When you have time make the sauce in a quantity and freeze it, you will find it a
great freezer standby. The secret is to allow the flour to get nicely browned before
adding the stock – this takes longer than you may think so be patient.

3 oz (75 g) butter	2 oz (50 g) plain flour
1 large onion	1½ pints (30 fl oz 900 ml) strong beef
2 medium carrots	stock (or use tinned beef consommé)
2 large sticks celery	Bouquet garni
2 rashers bacon	Salt and freshly ground black pepper

Melt the butter in a saucepan until foaming and then strain through a very fine sieve
to clarify. Peel and roughly chop the onion and the carrots. Roughly chop the

Double-bladed knife

celery. Remove the rinds from the bacon and roughly chop the rashers.
Process the onion, carrots, celery, and bacon together until finely chopped.
Heat the clarified butter in a saucepan, add the onion, carrot, celery and bacon and cook over a medium heat, stirring, for about ten minutes until all the vegetables are really soft. Add the flour and continue to stir over a medium high heat until the flour is the colour of a hazelnut. Gradually add the stock, stirring continually over a medium high heat until the sauce comes to the boil.
Add the bouquet garni, season with salt and pepper and cook over a medium heat (just above simmering heat) for 1 hour.
Remove the bouquet garni and strain the sauce through a coarse sieve.

Double-bladed knife

Process the vegetable residue from straining the sauce until it is reduced to a smooth purée. Add this to the sauce and use as required – check seasoning before using.

Curry Sauce

Serve with chicken or eggs.

1 clove garlic	1 tablespoon curry powder
1 small onion	Salt and freshly ground black pepper
2 medium, firm eating apples	1 pint (20 fl oz 600 ml) chicken stock
1 oz (25 g) butter	1 tablespoon tomato purée
2 tablespoons flour	1 tablespoon grated coconut (optional)

Double-bladed knife

Peel and roughly chop the onion and garlic. Peel, core and roughly chop the apples. Process the onion and the garlic until finely chopped and remove.

Medium or coarse grating disc

Process the apple through the grating disc. Heat the butter in a saucepan. Add the onion and garlic and cook over a low heat, stirring to prevent sticking, until the onion is soft and transparent. Add the flour and mix well. Add the curry powder and stir over a medium heat for three minutes. Mix in the apple and gradually blend in the stock stirring continually over a medium high heat until the sauce comes to the boil and is thick and smooth. Add the tomato purée, coconut (if used) and season with salt and pepper, simmer for 30 minutes.

Sauce Mornay

One of the most useful of sauces – serve it with eggs, chicken or fish or use it as a base for ingredients that are to be used as a filling for savoury pancakes, savoury puffs, vol-au-vents etc.

2 oz (50 g) butter
2 oz (50 g) flour
1 pint (600 ml) milk
1 onion
1 bay leaf

1 clove
3 oz (75 g) Gruyère cheese
Salt and freshly ground black pepper
2 egg yolks

Thin or medium grating disc
Double-bladed knife

Make a Bechamel sauce by combining the milk with the peeled onion, bay leaf and clove. Bring to the boil and simmer gently for 6 minutes. Strain off the milk. Melt the butter in a saucepan, add the flour and mix well. Gradually add the hot milk, stirring continually over a medium high heat until the sauce comes to the boil and is thick and smooth. Season with salt and pepper and cook gently for 10 minutes. Grate the cheese.

Combine the egg yolks with the cheese and process until the yolks are well beaten and smooth. With the machine switched on, add the Bechamel sauce through the feed tube and process until the ingredients are well mixed and satiny. Transfer the sauce to a clean pan and heat through without boiling and stirring all the time, if necessary. (If the sauce is to be combined with other ingredients to use as a filling which will be re-heated anyway it is not necessary to heat the sauce at this point).

Mint Sauce

The traditional British accompaniment to roast lamb, lamb chops or cutlets. It is a sauce which tastes far better fresh than it does out of a bottle and is best of all made in a Magimix where the full potency of the mint flavour is extracted into the sauce.

For four servings

1 bunch fresh mint leaves
1 tablespoon sugar

150 ml (5 fl oz ¼ pint) white or red wine vinegar

Double-bladed knife

Strip all the leaves from the mint stalks and discard the stalks.
Place the mint leaves in the Magimix bowl and process until the leaves are finely chopped, scraping down the sides of the bowl if necessary.
Add the sugar and process until the sugar is absorbed by the mint juice. Add the vinegar and process until the ingredients are well mixed. Leave to infuse in a refrigerator for at least an hour before using.
Note: The sauce can be made in larger quantities and stored in airtight screw top jars or in the deep freeze.

Sauce Suprême

A rich white sauce to serve the fish, chicken, vegetables, eggs etc.

2 oz (50 g) butter
1 oz (25 g) flour
¾ pint (15 fl oz 450 ml) chicken stock

Salt and white pepper
¼ pint (5 fl oz 150 ml) cream
2 small egg yolks

Melt the butter in a saucepan. Add the flour and mix well. Gradually blend in the stock stirring continually over a medium high heat until the sauce comes to the boil and is thick and smooth.
Season with salt and pepper and simmer for 10 minutes.

Double-bladed knife   Process the cream with the egg yolks until smooth. With the machine on add the white sauce through the feed tube in a slow, steady stream, processing until the ingredients are well mixed.
Transfer to a clean saucepan and heat through, stirring all the time, without boiling.

Cranberry Sauce

Serve with roast turkey, roast chicken or roast game.

8 oz (225 g) cranberries
8 oz (225 g) granulated sugar
¼ pint (5 fl oz 150 ml) water

2 tablespoons port
pinch thyme

Combine the cranberries, sugar and water in a saucepan, bring to the boil, cover and simmer for 10 minutes.

Double-bladed knife   Transfer the cranberry mixture to the Magimix bowl, add the port and thyme and process until smooth.

Cumberland Sauce

A traditional sauce for cold ham, but one that is also good with cold game or venison.

4 tablespoons redcurrant jelly
grated rind and juice of 1 orange
2 teaspoons cornflour

½ teaspoon French mustard
Salt and freshly ground black pepper
(10 fl oz 300 ml) port or red wine

Double-bladed knife
Put the redcurrant jelly, orange rind and juice and cornflour in the bowl and process until mixed. Season sparingly and add the port. Process to mix well.
Pour the sauce into a saucepan and bring to the boil stirring continuously. Cook for a few minutes and leave to get cold before serving.

Sauce Soubise

A rich onion flavoured sauce which goes well with boiled bacon, roast chicken, beef or lamb.

4 onions	1 oz (25 g) flour
4 tablespoons dry Vermouth	½ pint (10 fl oz 300 ml) milk
¼ pint (5 fl oz 150 ml) beef consommé	Salt and pepper and a pinch of ground
2 oz (50 g) butter	nutmeg and mace

Peel the onions.

Medium slicing disc
Slice the onions. Plunge the onions into boiling salted water, and cook for 10 minutes. Drain well.
Boil the consommé until reduced by half. Melt 1 oz (25 g) butter in a saucepan, add the onions, dry Vermouth and consommé, season with salt, pepper and nutmeg and mace and simmer for 10 minutes. Melt the remaining butter in a clean pan. Add the flour and mix well. Gradually add the milk stirring continually over a medium high heat until the sauce comes to the boil and is thick and smooth.

Double-bladed knife
Process the onion mixture until almost smooth (I like to retain some texture), add the purée to the white sauce, mix well and check seasoning. Simmer for three minutes before serving.

Horseradish Cream

1 x 4 in. (10 cm) piece horseradish root, peeled	½ teaspoon made English mustard
1 teaspoon white wine vinegar	¼ pint (5 fl oz 150 ml) double cream
	salt

Fine grating disc
Double-bladed knife
Grate the horseradish.
Add the vinegar, mustard and cream to the horseradish, season with salt and process until thick and well mixed.

Pink Horseradish Cream Add 1 tablespoon grated raw beetroot to the cream.

Horseradish and Cucumber Cream An unusual and very good sauce to serve with fish: Add 4 tablespoons grated peeled cucumber to the horseradish cream.

Apple Sauce with Horseradish

An excellent sauce to serve with roast and grilled pork dishes.

¾ lb (375 g) cooking apples
2 oz (50 g) fresh horseradish root
1 teaspoon lemon juice

½ oz (13 g) butter
Salt and white pepper

Fine grating disc
Double-bladed
knife

Peel, core and roughly chop the apples. Cook the apples in a couple of tablespoons of water until soft. Peel the horseradish.
Grate the horseradish.
Combine the apples with the horseradish and butter and process until smooth. Add the lemon juice, season with a little salt and pepper and if the apples are very tart, add a pinch of sugar. Serve hot or cold.
Note: If you cannot get fresh horseradish root use dried, horseradish from a jar.

Duxelles

Duxelles is a classic French preparation which is used as a flavouring ingredient for sauces, stuffings, soups and sauces. A quantity can be made in advance and frozen or kept in a refrigerator for a few days and I find it a most convenient flavour source to have handy. You will find a recipe utilizing duxelles on page 74 but it is also a winner when you find your gravy for a roast dish is a little uninteresting, a soup needs more body or a sauce is disappointing – add a little well flavoured duxelles and you will be delighted with the results.

4 oz (100 g) firm button mushrooms
½ oz (13 g) butter
1 small onion

2 tablespoons tomato purée
Salt and freshly ground black pepper

Double-bladed
knife

Peel and roughly chop the onion.
Process the onion until finely chopped and remove. Process the mushrooms until finely chopped.
Melt the butter in a small saucepan. Add the onion and cook over a low heat until the onion is soft and transparent. Raise the heat, add the mushrooms and cook over a medium high heat, stirring until the onions and mushrooms are lightly browned. Stir in the tomato purée and season with salt and freshly ground black pepper.

To store the duxelles: Cool the mixture, put it into a bowl and cover it with cling film and store it in a refrigerator. Or divide the mixture into small quantities and freeze them.

Variations: Add 2 tablespoons of white wine to the browned ingredients and simmer for three minutes.
Add 2 oz (50 g) finely chopped ham to make a richer mixture.

SAVOURY BUTTERS

Savoury butters add an attractive but easily made last minute garnish to chicken dishes, steaks, hamburgers, chops, cutlets and grilled, poached or fried fish. Keep a range of savoury butters in your freezer or refrigerator so that you have some always on hand. Make the butters in seconds in your Magimix. Shape savoury butter into a neat sausage on a piece of foil, roll up tightly and refrigerate until set solid. Unwrap and cut into thin slices to serve.

Garlic Butter

Serve with steaks or hamburgers.

2 cloves garlic   2 oz (50 g) butter
¼ teaspoon salt

Double-bladed knife
Peel and roughly chop the garlic. Combine the garlic and salt and process until the garlic is finely chopped. Add the butter and process until the butter and garlic are well mixed. Shape and chill as above. This butter can also be used to make garlic bread. Cut a French loaf in diagonal slices ¾ of the way through the loaf. Spread the cut slices with the garlic butter. Wrap lightly in foil. Bake in a hot oven (400°F. 200°C. Reg. 6) for 20 minutes until the bread is crisp and the butter has melted.

Stilton Butter

Serve with poultry, fish or steaks.

2 oz (50 g) stilton cheese   2 oz (50 g) butter

Double-bladed knife
Combine the Stilton and butter and process until well mixed. Shape and chill as above.

Herb Butter

Serve with poultry, meat or fish.

Small bunch parsley
2 sprigs tarragon
2 sprigs watercress

½ small onion or 1 shallot
2 oz (50 g) butter
Salt and white pepper

Double-bladed knife

Peel and roughly chop the onion or shallot. Remove any tough stalks from the herbs.
Combine the parsley, tarragon and watercress in the Magimix bowl and process until the herbs are finely chopped. Add the onion or shallot and process until that is finely chopped. Add the butter, season with salt and pepper and process until the ingredients are well mixed. Shape and chill as above.

Maître d'hôtel Butter

Serve with poultry, meat or fish.

2 oz (50 g) butter
1 teaspoon lemon juice

Small bunch parsley
Salt and white pepper

Double-bladed knife

Remove the tough stalks from the parsley.
Process the parsley until finely chopped. Add the butter and lemon juice, season with salt and pepper and process until well mixed. Shape and chill as above.

Minty Butter

Serve with roast lamb, lamb steaks, cutlets or chops.

3 oz (75 g) butter
Small bunch of mint

1 teaspoon French Dijon mustard
Salt and white pepper

Double-bladed knife

Remove any tough stalks from the mint.
Process the mint until finely chopped.
Add the butter and mustard, season with salt and pepper and process until the ingredients are well mixed. Shape and chill as above.

Anchovy Butter

Serve with fish.

2 anchovy fillets

1 clove garlic

3 oz (75 g) butter

Freshly ground black pepper

Double-bladed knife   Peel and roughly chop the garlic.
Process the garlic until finely chopped. Add the anchovy fillets and butter, season with pepper and process until very well mixed. Shape and chill as above.

CURRY ACCOMPANIMENTS

Onion and Peach Chutney Condiment

1 small onion

1 clove garlic

4 tablespoons peach or mango chutney

1 teaspoon lemon juice

Peel and roughly chop the onion and garlic.

Double-bladed knife   Process the onion and garlic until coarsely chopped. Add the chutney and lemon juice and process until the onion and chutney are finely chopped.

Tomato and Onion Condiment

1 small onion

1 clove garlic

2 ripe tomatoes

1 tablespoon tomato ketchup

Few drops Worcestershire and Tabasco sauce

Salt and freshly ground black pepper

Peel and roughly chop the onion and the garlic. Cover the tomatoes with boiling water, leave to stand for three minutes then slide off the skins and roughly chop the tomatoes.

Double-bladed knife   Process the onion and garlic until coarsely chopped.
Add the tomatoes and process until the tomatoes are fairly finely chopped. Add the tomato ketchup season with a few drops of Worcestershire and Tabasco sauce and salt and pepper and process until the ingredients are finely chopped and mixed well.

Cucumber Mint and Yoghurt Relish

1 small bunch mint   1 carton 5 oz (150 ml) yoghurt
½ cucumber   Salt and white pepper

	Remove any coarse stems from the mint. Peel the cucumber.
Double-bladed knife	Process the mint until finely chopped and remove.
Coarse grating disc	Grate the cucumber and remove.
Plastic blade	Combine the mint, cucumber and yoghurt, season with salt and pepper and process to mix well.

Tomatoes with Onion and Yoghurt

A traditional curry accompaniment which goes well with hot or cold fish dishes.

3 small ripe firm tomatoes   Salt and freshly ground black pepper
2 spring onions   ½ teaspoon lemon juice
1 carton (5 fl oz 150 ml) yoghurt

	Trim and roughly chop the spring onions.
Double-bladed knife	Process the onions until finely chopped. Add the yoghurt, season with salt and pepper and add the lemon juice and process until well mixed.
Chipper disc	Leave the yoghurt mixture in the bowl and process the tomatoes through the chipper disc. Turn the mixture into a bowl and chill before serving.

PICKLES & PRESERVES

Pickled Red Cabbage

I find it a good idea not to pack this pickle in too large a jar since it seems to have a tendency to loose its colouring once it is opened. I pack it in ½ lb (225 g) jars and find it a good contrast to serve with cold cooked turkey, beef or pork; my family also insist on the pickle being served with toad in the hole (see page 131) and any other sausage or sausage meat dish.

1 red cabbage (about 4 lb (1·8 kg) in weight)
5 oz (150 g) cooking salt
¾ pint (15 fl oz 450 ml) malt vinegar
4 cloves
6 all spice

2 blades mace
½ in. (1·25 cm) stick cinnamon
1 piece dry root ginger
6 peppercorns

Coleslaw disc

Cut the cabbage into quarters and remove any tough outside leaves and the core. Shred the cabbage through the coleslaw disc (having washed and drained it if necessary) and put it into a basin sprinkling the salt between the layers of cabbage. Cover and leave to stand for 2 days.
Combine the vinegar with all the spices in a basin, cover the basin with a plate and place it in a saucepan with enough water to come half way up the basin. Bring slowly to the boil and when the water boils remove from the heat and leave to stand until the vinegar is cold. Strain the vinegar.
Rinse the cabbage in cold water, drain well and pack loosely in jars with the spiced vinegar poured over. Cover with cling film and then with cellophane and leave to mature for at least 1 month before using.

Potted Cheese

Unless you have tasted potted cheese you don't know what you have missed. It's got a sort of tangy, memorable flavour which is delicious.

4 oz (100 g) cottage cheese
4 oz (100 g) Cheddar cheese
1 pickled cucumber

4 fl oz (120 ml) light ale
1 tablespoon brandy
½ teaspoon of dry mustard

Double-bladed knife

Roughly chop up the Cheddar cheese. Roughly chop the cucumber. Process the Cheddar cheese until very finely chopped. Add the cucumber and process until the cucumber is very finely chopped. Add the cottage cheese and process until the ingredients are reduced to a paste. Add the mustard and process until smooth. With machine running, add the ale and brandy through the feed tube processing until the ingredients are smooth and creamy. Pack into a pot, cover with cling film and leave to mature in a refrigerator before serving as a cheese spread or in place of a cheese.

Orange and Ginger Marmalade

2 lb (900 g) oranges
2 lb (900 g) cooking apples
2 lemons
½ lb (225 g) preserved ginger

2 teaspoon ground ginger
5 lb (2·2 kg) sugar
5 pints (3 litres) water

Citrus fruit juice extractor
Double-bladed knife
Medium slicing disc

Wash the fruit and remove the top third of the oranges and lemons. Peel and core the apples.
Squeeze the oranges and lemons. Reserve the pips.

Process the orange and lemon peel until fairly coarsely chopped and remove. Process the ginger until finely chopped and remove.
Process the apples.
Combine the orange and lemon peel in a pan with 4¾ pints (3·9 l) water, add the fruit juice and the pips in a muslin bag, bring to the boil and simmer for 1½ hours or until the peel is soft and the liquid has reduced by about half. Cook the apples in the remaining ¼ pint (5 fl oz) water until soft.
Add the apples to the citrus fruit with the ginger, ground ginger and sugar and bring to the boil, stirring until the sugar is dissolved. Boil rapidly for 30 minutes, check for setting and then leave to stand for 15 minutes before potting in the usual way.
Note: I like to cut two or three thin slices of orange off the top of the fruit before squeezing them and add these with the fruit. Extract the slices when the marmalade is cooked and use to decorate the sides of your jars.

Chunky Orange and Lemon Marmalade

2 lb (900 g) oranges
1 lb (450 g) lemons

4 lb (1·8 kg) sugar
3½ pints (2·4 litres) water

Citrus juice extractor
Double-bladed knife

Wipe the fruit and cut a third off the tops of the oranges and lemons.
Squeeze the juice from the oranges and lemons.
Reserve the pips.
Process the fruit peel in three batches until fairly coarsely chopped. (If using the Grande Famille you will be able to do it in one or two batches).
Tie the pips in a piece of muslin.
Combine the fruit peel, fruit juice, water and pips in a preserving pan. Bring to the boil and simmer gently for 2 hours. Remove the bag of pips squeezing it well, add the sugar and boil rapidly for 30 minutes. Test for setting, leave to stand for 15 minutes then pot in the usual way.

Mincemeat

Illustrated page 232

Makes approx-imately 6 lb

1¼ lb (575 g) cooking apples
14 oz (400 g) seedless raisins
14 oz (400 g) sultanas
8 oz (225 g) candied peel
14 oz (400 g) soft brown sugar

14 oz (400 g) shredded suet
2 oz (50 g) blanched almonds
Good pinch ground cinnamon, cloves, allspice and nutmeg
6 tablespoons brandy

Double-bladed knife

Peel and core the cooking apples.
Process the almonds until chopped and remove.
Process the apples until fairly finely chopped and add to the nuts. Pour 3 tablespoons brandy over the apples and nuts.
Combine the raisins and candied peel and process until the ingredients are fairly finely chopped. Add the sugar, suet and sultanas and process until the ingredients are well mixed. Unless you are using the Grande Famille you may have to do this in two batches. Add these ingredients to the apples and almonds, mix in the spices and mix the whole lot well together. Cover with a cloth and mix three times a day for three days. Add the remaining brandy, mix well and pot in jars, cover with wax circles and then with tight cling or cellophane. Keep for up to 1 year before using (I make mine at Christmas time for next Christmas).

Chestnut Stuffing for Turkey

1 lb (450 g) chestnuts
1 lb (450 g) fat pork, with the skin
   removed
1 onion

Salt and freshly ground black pepper
Pinch dried thyme and sage
1 tablespoon brandy
2 oz (50 g) butter

Score the chestnuts with a sharp pointed knife in a cross across the top. Cover the chestnuts in a saucepan with cold water, bring to the boil and then remove from the heat, leave to cool and remove the chestnut shells and inner skins. Cut the pork into cubes. Peel and roughly chop the onion.

Double-bladed knife   Process the onion until finely chopped.
Add the pork and process until the pork is very finely chopped. Season with salt and pepper, add the thyme, sage, brandy and the butter and process to mix. Remove the mixture.

Coarse grating disc   Process the chestnuts through the coarse grating disc add them to the pork and onion and mix well.

Special Rice Stuffing for Turkey

This stuffing is also delicious with a large chicken or capon.

1 onion
1 clove garlic
1 carrot
1 courgette
1 stick celery
4 dried apricots

3 tablespoons sunflower oil
6 oz (75 g) cooked rice
Salt and freshly ground black pepper
Pinch ground cumin and coriander
6 fl oz (180 ml) chicken stock

Peel and roughly chop the onion and garlic.

Double-bladed knife   Process the onion and garlic until finely chopped and remove.
Process the apricots until finely chopped and remove.

Coarse grating disc   Grate the carrot and remove.
Grate the courgette and remove.

Thin slicing disc   Slice the celery stalk.

Heat the oil in a frying pan. Add the onion, garlic, celery and carrot and cook until the vegetables are soft. Add the courgette, apricots and rice, season with salt, pepper, cumin and coriander, stir in the stock and simmer for 15 minutes. Cool the ingredients before stuffing the bird.

Simple Herb Stuffing

Use for roast chicken.

1 bunch parsley with the stalks removed
4 oz (100 g) white bread with the crusts
  removed
2 oz (50 g) suet
½ teaspoon mixed herbs

Grated rind 1 lemon
Salt and freshly ground black pepper
Pinch ground nutmeg
1 egg

Double-bladed knife   Process the parsley until finely chopped. Add the bread and process until the bread is reduced to fine crumbs. Add the suet, herbs and the lemon rind, season with salt, pepper and nutmeg, and process until the ingredients are well mixed. Finally add the beaten egg and process to bind the stuffing.

Simple Sage and Onion Stuffing

Use for stuffing poultry or boned pork joints.

4 oz (100 g) white bread with the crusts
  removed
2 onions
½ teaspoon dried sage

2 oz (50 g) butter
1 egg
Salt and freshly ground black pepper
Pinch nutmeg

Peel and roughly chop the onions.
Double-bladed knife   Process the bread until reduced to coarse crumbs and remove.
Process the onions until finely chopped.
Melt the butter, add the onions and cook over a low heat, stirring to prevent browning, until the onion is soft and transparent. Leave to cool.
Double-bladed knife   Combine the onions, the juices from the pan and the breadcrumbs, season with salt, pepper and nutmeg, add the egg and sage and process until the ingredients are well mixed.

Capacities

Follow the table of capacities. Your Magimix will perform miracles for you twenty or more times a day in the normal course of household and entertaining cookery but, like any other machine, it will balk if you expect it to perform the impossible. The table below gives capacities for the Standard Magimix (RC 1), the Grande Cuisine 2800 (RC 8) and the Grande Famille 3500 (RC 7).

Standard Magimix 1800 (RC 1)
1¼ lb (575 g) pastry (made with 12 oz (350 g) flour)
1 lb (450 g) meat (cut into cubes)
2 lb (900 g) bread dough (made with 1 lb 2 oz (500 g) white flour)

2 lb (900 g) cake mixture (a 4 egg victoria sandwich)
Up to 1 pint (20 fl oz: 600 ml) soup or liquid

Grande Cuisine 2800 (RC 8)
2 lb (900 g) pastry (made with 1¼ lb (575 g) flour)
2 lb (900 g) meat (cut into cubes)
2 lb (900 g) bread dough (made with 1 lb 2 oz (500 g) white flour)

3 lb (1.3 kilo) cake mixture (a 6 egg victoria sandwich)
Up to 3 pints (60 fl oz: 1.8 L) soup or liquid

Grande Famille 3500 (RC 7)
2½ lb (1.2 kilo) pastry (made with 1½ lb (675 g) flour)
3 lb (1.3 kilo) meat (cut into cubes)
4 lb (1.8 kilo) bread dough (made with 2 lb 4 oz (1 kilo) white flour

4 lb (1.8 kilo) cake mixture (an 8 egg victoria sandwich)
Up to 2 pints (40 fl oz: 1.2 L) soup or liquid

Step by step instructions for using your Magimix and its accessories

The Machine

The Base
Your Magimix runs off a strong direct drive motor contained in a sealed base onto which the all purpose bowl fits. The base should never be immersed in water.

The Bowl
The all purpose bowl is made of strong, durable and unbreakable plastic. To position the bowl place it over the central spindle and slide it round to the right so that it slots firmly into place with the handle facing towards you – use the handle to click the bowl into a locked position.

The Lid and Feed Tube
The lid and feed tube are made of the same durable, strong, unbreakable plastic as the bowl (both are able to take boiling liquids). To position the lid hold it by the feed tube, place the lid over the bowl with the feed tube a little to the left of the handle and slide the lid to the right so that it clicks into a rigid position – in the case of the standard Magimix this positioning will start the machine – with the other machines the lid should be positioned in the same way but the machine is started or 'pulsed' by two buttons situated on the base of the machine.

The Pusher
The white plastic pusher fits snugly into the feed tube and is used as a stopper for the machine as well as a pusher to press ingredients through the feed tube for slicing, grating and shredding etc.

The Double-bladed Knife
Once the bowl is in place the double-bladed knife or other attachments can be placed in position. Slot the double-bladed knife over the central spindle and then spin it around until it clicks into place and push the top firmly to make sure the double-bladed knife is on the bottom of the machine. The double-bladed knife is used for chopping (mincing) ingredients, puréeing, pulping, grinding and mixing. To remove the blade, remove the lid and twist the bowl to the left and lift the bowl off with the blade still in place. Put the bowl down on surface and lift the blade out.

The standard Magimix RC1 and its accessories.

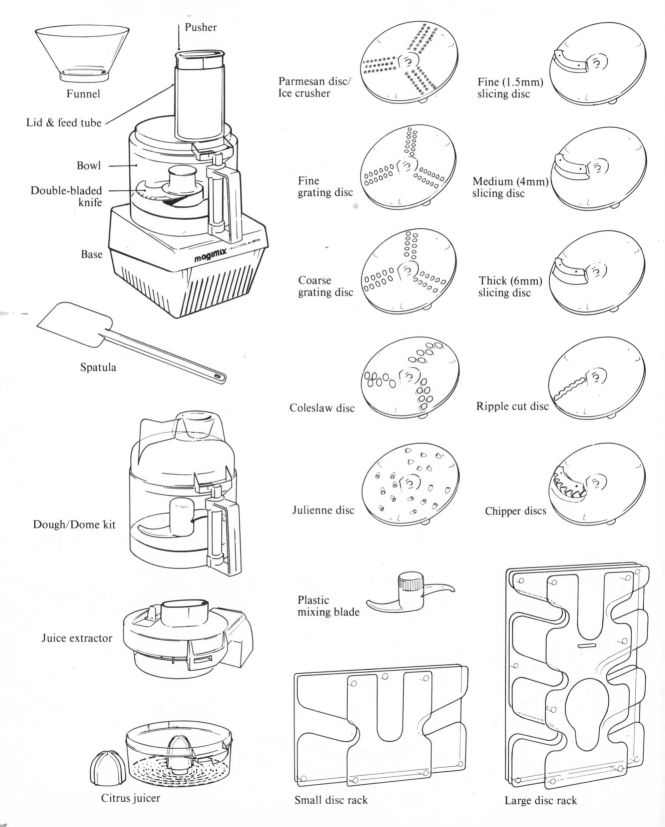

Funnel

Pusher

Lid & feed tube

Bowl

Double-bladed knife

Base

Spatula

Dough/Dome kit

Juice extractor

Citrus juicer

Parmesan disc/ Ice crusher

Fine grating disc

Coarse grating disc

Coleslaw disc

Julienne disc

Plastic mixing blade

Small disc rack

Fine (1.5mm) slicing disc

Medium (4mm) slicing disc

Thick (6mm) slicing disc

Ripple cut disc

Chipper discs

Large disc rack

Machine cover and 'Magimix' apron are also available.

The Dough Blade

The white plastic dough blade can be used for all doughs and breads and will process a slightly larger quantity than the double-bladed knife.

The Grating Discs

Your machine comes supplied with a fine grating disc. Follow the instructions to fit this and you will find that it is ideal for grating cheese, chocolate, dry bread crumbs, etc. There are other grating discs available for all the machines, the selection includes very coarse ones to an extra fine Parmesan disc. Your local stockist should know exactly what is available for your particular model.

The Slicing Discs

Your machine comes with a fine slicing disc, which is perfect for slicing cucumber and potato crisps. There are other discs for thicker slices available for all machines and your local stockist should be able to supply you with details.

New accessories for all models are continually being introduced. Your local stockist will have an up-to-date list of what is available.

Using the Machine

photographs pages 285–296

Switching on and off

Having placed the bowl and blade or disc in position, slide the lid onto the bowl with the feed tube just to the left of the handle. To start the machine slide the lid to the right so that it clicks in place over the handle and starts the motor. To stop the machine slide the lid to the left, holding the feed tube, so that the machine switches off. To pulse ingredients that should not be over processed or to mix ingredients lightly hold the feed tube while ingredients are processing and slide the lid onto the on and then the off position (in Grande Cuisine and the Grande Famille machines the lid is put firmly into place and processing is done by pressing the on or pulse buttons).

Using the Double-bladed Knife

Chopping (mincing) Prepare ingredients by peeling them if necessary. Cut meat into even sized cubes; roughly chop vegetables. Place ingredients in the bowl with the double-bladed knife in position (make sure it is pressed firmly down onto the bottom of the central spindle), switch on the machine and process until ingredients are chopped to the desired consistency – if ingredients are not to be too finely chopped pulse them by switching the machine on and off until the desired consistency is reached. (The Grande Cuisine and Grande-Famille have a pulse switch).

Mixing Place the double-bladed knife in position, add ingredients that are to be mixed and process until the desired consistency is obtained. While ingredients are being processed liquid, eggs etc. can be added through the feed tube.

If ingredients are to be both chopped and mixed you can obtain different textures by chopping one ingredient and then adding others so that both a fine and coarse texture is obtained in the same mixture – this is particularly useful for pâtés etc.

Puréeing Be careful not to incorporate too much liquid into ingredients that are to be puréed – strain off excess stock from soup ingredients for instance before processing them into a purée.

Using the Grating and Slicing Discs

If necessary peel ingredients which are to be grated or sliced. For longer slices (i.e. carrots or courgettes) cut the ingredients to fit the food tube sideways rather than upright.

If slicing only one carrot or courgette etc. position it at the right hand side of the feed tube.

With the ingredients in the feed tube position the pusher on top of them and, with the motor switched on, exert an even pressure on the pusher; use a firm pressure for hard foods such as cheese, root vegetables, lemon etc. Exert a light pressure for soft foods such as sliced strawberries etc.

When using the julienne disc (this is only available for the standard Magimix) cut the vegetables to fit the feed tube sideways rather than upright to produce long julienne strips. When slicing ingredients like mushrooms into even slices arrange the mushrooms neatly sideways in the feed tube before processing. Cut a slice from onions, carrots etc that require to be evenly sliced before positioning them in the feed tube.

Pastry: (For recipes see pastry chapter pages 238 – 245).
For shortcrust pastry (page 239) place 6 oz (175 g) plain flour in the bowl together with 3 oz (75 g) butter (or half-in-half butter and lard) cut into cubes and a pinch of salt.

Process until the mixture resembles fine bread-crumbs. (If the butter or fat were from the freezer these will be suitably cold for lighter pastry).

With the machine running add 1 – 2 tablespoons of very cold water in a slow stream.

Stop the machine the moment a ball of pastry forms. Do NOT over-process. If you have used frozen butter or fat the pastry will be cold and ready for rolling out, otherwise rest in the refrigerator for 30 minutes.

Cakes: (See recipes pages 218 – 237).
A Victoria Sandwich (recipe page 228) is a good example of a quick and simple All-In-One Magimix cake.
Place all the ingredients in the bowl: 6 oz (150 g) softened butter or soft margarine, 6 oz (150 g) caster sugar, 6 oz (150 g) self-raising flour, 1 teaspoon baking powder, 3 large eggs and any flavourings – vanilla essence, chocolate powder etc. Process for 10 seconds, then after stopping to scrape down the sides of the bowl, process for a further 5 seconds or until well mixed.

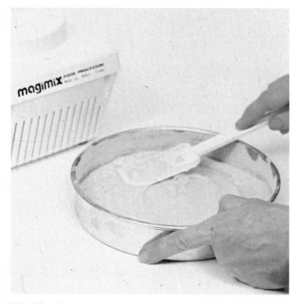

Divide the mixture between two 8 inch (20 cm) prepared tins and spread level. Bake for 30 minutes at 350°F, 180° C, Reg 4.

Bread: For detailed instructions see recipe on page 218. Process the flour, lard and salt together, then, with the machine running add the prepared yeast mixture.

When a ball of dough has formed continue to process for a further 20 seconds to knead it. Remove the dough, shape it on a floured board, and place it in a greased polythene bag and leave it in a warm place to rise.

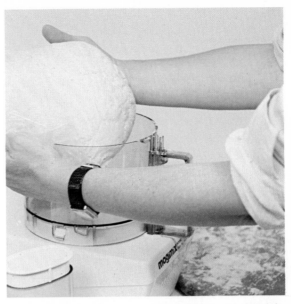

After about an hour, or when it has doubled in bulk, return it to the machine and process to 'knock-back' for a further 10 seconds.

Form the dough into a rectangle, fold into three and place in a well greased loaf tin. Return to the oiled polythene bag and leave in the warm for a further 40 minutes or until doubled in bulk.

Bake in a hot oven 450°F, 230°C, Reg 8 for 30 minutes, or until golden. Turn the loaf onto a wire rack to cool.

Raw Meat: This is quickly and easily chopped with the double-bladed knife – See the recipes in the chapter on Meat pages 98 – 131.

Meat can be chopped to the degree of fineness required for mince, hamburgers, pâtes, meat loaves etc.

If you are using onions or herbs, process them first, then add the meat and process together.

Cooked Meat: Place chunks of cooked meat in the bowl and it is chopped in a few seconds. Use the left-overs from Sunday's leg of lamb with your favourite recipe for Monday's shepherd's pie, or there are several recipes in the chapter on Meat pages 98 – 131.

It is just as easy to chop cold chicken for which there are many uses. See the Poultry and Game chapter pages 132 – 150 for recipes including a Pancake Filling (page 142), Curried Chicken and Ham (page 141), Chicken Pie (page 139) and Maidenwell Rissoles (page 142).

Pâte's and Terrines: (See pages 52 – 56) For Chicken Liver Terrine (complete recipe page 52) chop the parsley, add the chicken livers, process and then add the sausage meat. Process again before adding the brandy, herbs and seasonings. When mixed add the roughly chopped belly of pork and process to coarsely chop.

Marinate overnight before turning into a terrine lined with bacon. Cover with more bacon and bay leaves.

Cook in a medium oven 350°F, 175°C, Reg. 4 in a bain marie for about 1½ hours or until the contents are coming away from the sides of the terrine.

Cool and cover with a piece of board wrapped in foil. Weigh down and refrigerate. Serve in slices with hot toast.

Chopping Onions: Process quartered onions with the double-bladed knife until the desired fineness is reached. Because the bowl is covered, tears in the kitchen are a thing of the past.

Chopping Parsley: Remove tough stalks from parsley or other herbs. Place in a clean bowl, process for a few seconds, until coarsely or finely chopped as desired.

Soup: To make soup strain off the stock and place the vegetables in the bowl. Process until they are puréed (coarse or fine according to recipe) then return the vegetables to a saucepan and stir in the stock. For Soups see pages 16 – 30.

Baby Food: For a young baby meat and vegetables can be puréed, or, chopped to a suitable fineness.

Mayonnaise: (See pages 250 – 253)
Place two egg yolks in the bowl with pepper and ¼ teaspoon mustard. Process for half a minute.

With the motor running very slowly start adding ½ pint olive or sunflower oil. When the mayonnaise starts to thicken and stabilise you can increase the pouring rate to a thin stream.

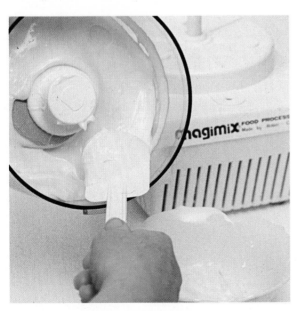

Continue processing while adding two teaspoons vinegar or lemon juice and salt. Turn the mayonnaise into a dish and use as required.

Chopping Nuts: All nuts, the picture shows hazelnuts, can be quickly chopped for use in puddings, cakes etc.

Potatoes: Shown being sliced with the thick (6 mm) slicing disc. Thinner slices can be obtained by using either the 1·5 mm or 4 mm slicing discs.

Slicing Vegetables: When slicing use the appropriate disc to obtain the thickness of slice you require. This shows peppers being sliced with the medium (4 mm) disc.

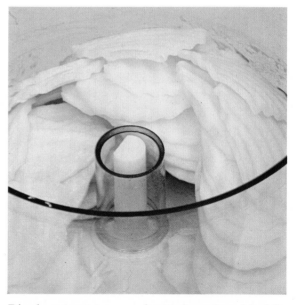

Chipped Potatoes: The photograph shows potatoes that have been through the chipper disc for French fried chips. Try chipping, rather than slicing carrots or courgettes before cooking them.

Ripple cut potatoes are fun to do and are ideal for game chips.

Really thin slices of cucumber can easily be achieved with the thin (1.5 mm) slicing disc, and all the slices will be equally thin.

Grating Vegetables: Cabbage being processed with the special coleslaw disc. This is ideal for winter salads.

You can use the julienne disc for carrots, celeriac, turnips, etc., or either of the grating discs. Choose the one that suits your recipe or salad best.

Grating Cheese: This is very easy through the coarse grating disc. Soft and hard cheeses can be quickly and easily grated.

Freshly grated Parmesan really adds something to a pasta dish. The Parmesan disc is also a very effective ice crusher.

Grating Chocolate: The fine grating disc is ideal for chocolate. A difficult process to do by hand as the chocolate tends to melt or smear. See recipe for cake filling on page 229.

Extracting Vegetable and Fruit Juices: Use the juice extractor for grapes, apples, pears, pineapple, tomatoes, carrots, spinach. Juice can be extracted from citrus fruits with the pith removed. But for clear citrus juice use the special citrus juicer.

Citrus Juicer: Cut the end off the fruit and press down on the cone while the machine is running. Continue holding the fruit until the inside is smooth. The shells can be used filled with sorbets or desserts. (See pages 193 and 194). Or for attractive prawn and melon cocktails etc.

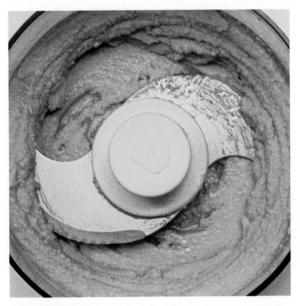

Peanut Butter can be simply and economically made by processing 8 oz (250 g) peanuts with two teaspoons groundnut or vegetable oil until smooth.

Ices and Sorbets: (See recipe page 201). Drain the juice from a can of apricots and process the fruit until puréed. Add the syrup and the juice of a lemon and process to mix. Turn into a freezing tray and freeze for about an hour.

Return the semi-frozen sorbet to the bowl.

Process until completely smooth (this will 'knock out' any crystals that may have formed), then return to the freezing tray and complete the freezing.

Taramasalata: Home made Taramasalata is a delicious starter to any meal. Place 4 oz (100 g) skinned smoked cod's roe in the bowl together with a clove of garlic and two slices of bread that have been soaked in milk. Process until smooth,

then with the motor running slowly add ½ pint (300 ml) oil, two teaspoons lemon juice and two tablespoons yoghurt. Process until all the ingredients are well amalgamated.

Thickening Cream: Use the plastic blade or double-bladed knife to thicken cream which can

then be used for many types of savoury and sweet dishes.

When slicing lemons cut the lemon in half and cut a slice off the bottom and top of the lemon to enable it to stand squarely in the feed tube. Exert an even, firm pressure on the pusher.

Using the Chipper Disc

Cut peeled potatoes and other root vegetables to fit the feed tube sideways and cut a slice off the bottom of vegetables so that they are flush to the bottom of the feed tube. Exert a firm pressure on the pusher to ensure even chips.

Save time and washing up by processing your ingredients in the right order

Ingredients like herbs and breadcrumbs should be processed in a dry bowl so always process these first in a recipe that calls for a combination of many ingredients.

After having processed these 'dry' ingredients then chop items like garlic, onion, etc. Sliced and grated ingredients do not need a clean dry bowl and neither do chopped vegetables, meat, etc.

If you are using your Magimix to make sweet puddings or pies, etc. after processing savoury ingredients always wash and dry your bowl, cover, pusher, knives, blades, etc. before use to avoid any tainting by savoury ingredients.

Adapting recipes for use in a Magimix

Once you are thoroughly at home with your Magimix you will easily see how to adapt other recipes for use with your machine. Read the recipe through first, tick those steps which can utilize your processor and then work out the best order in which the ingredients can be processed to avoid having to wash the bowl in between.

Cut down your preparation time for your favourite dishes by chopping, slicing and grating ingredients in your food processor. Use the plastic or double-bladed knife to mix sauces, blend and purée ingredients for recipes. Never waste time and effort by doing any process by hand that can be done more quickly and more efficiently in your Magimix.

Taking care of your Magimix

Your Magimix is a strong durable machine and the plastic bowl, cover and pusher are virtually indestructable and will not break if dropped.

Wipe the motor with a soft, damp cloth, using a little detergent – do not immerse the motor in water.

Wash the bowl, blades, discs, etc. in hot water with detergent, rinse in clean, warm water and dry well. The plastic bowl, blades, discs etc. can be washed in a washing up machine. Your Magimix has an automatic cut out mechanism which acts if the machine is overloaded and the motor becomes overheated. The machines will stop automatically and will start again as soon as the motor has cooled sufficiently to be within the safety level once more.

Note: The only occasion on which the motor will overheat is if it is overloaded. Do not try to process too much at one time or to process ingredients that are too thick (i.e. dough to which not enough liquid has been added).

The Magimix food processors have a sharp Sabatier blade which, providing you take care of it, should remain razor sharp for years.

Problems

The main problem I have found with those who write to me about their Magimix machines is that of *over* processing. At first it is difficult to realise quite how swiftly and strongly your food processor performs, or quite how amazingly efficient it is. Overprocessing results in ingredients losing their texture and in too much air being driven out of ingredients such as cakes, batter, dough, etc.

Over-filling the bowl A table of capacities is given on page 280. Do not over-fill or the result will be liquid seeping through the cover and bowl or through the central spindle.

Note: The Magimix has such a fast performance that it is unnecessary to overfill the machines – it will only take a matter of minutes to process ingredients in two batches.

Puréeing Ingredients that are to be puréed should be drained of most excess liquid if a smooth purée is to be obtained – in the case of cream of vegetable soups, for instance, strain off stock before puréeing vegetables adding a little of the stock through the feed tube, if necessary, halfway through the processing.

Cakes and Doughs It is important that the pusher should not remain in the feed tube while cake and dough mixtures are being processed. This is to allow as much air as possible to be incorporated into the mixture.

It is easy to *over* process cake mixtures resulting in heavy, flat cakes. *Remember* that your food processor works at a revolutionary fast rate and always process ingredients, other than those that are to be 'creamed', for the minimum time needed to mix ingredients together.

Uneven slices Make sure you exert an *even* pressure on the pusher when slicing ingredients.

Foods that will not process successfully

While a food processor is one of the most efficient, fast and versatile of machines available to the 1980s housewife and gourmet cook there are some things it will not do.

A food processor will not mash potatoes successfully – the starch and liquid in cooked potatoes results in their becoming a 'gluey' purée.

Do not attempt to process Exceptionally hard cheese except through the Parmesan disc; Bones or hard gristle; Roast coffee beans; Hard spices such as cloves.

How to use your Magimix for basic preparations

Whether you want to chop, slice, grate, mix or blend ingredients your Magimix will do the job faster and more efficiently than any other machine. Here are some ideas of the capacity of your machine for use with basic cookery preparations.

Baby Food

The best food for a growing baby is the food you eat yourself providing it is not too highly spiced or too rich. Save money by processing meat, vegetables, gravy, fruit etc. with the double-bladed knife until it is the right consistency for your baby.

Baking

Cakes that do not involve the mixing in of whipped egg whites, scones, rock cakes, biscuits etc. all can be mixed in seconds with your food processor. Use the double-bladed knife to process butter and sugar together and to reduce flour and fats to coarse breadcrumbs. Remember not to put the pusher in the feed tube while processing cakes, scones etc.

If your butter is hard, cream it with the double-bladed knife before adding the sugar. Roughly chop hard butter before processing.

Add dried fruit for the final processing and switch the machine on and off to incorporate dried fruit without chopping it.

You will probably find that you need to use slightly *less* liquid in baking than may be specified in standard recipes.

Most problems with baking come from *over* processing; your Magimix is an astonishingly strong machine and when you first use it you may find it hard to believe how quickly ingredients will be processed. If in doubt switch the machine on and off while processing rather than keeping it switched on all the time.

We have found that the best and easiest cakes and other baking products to produce from your food processor are those which involve creaming the butter and sugar and then adding all the other ingredients at the same time or all-in-one cakes in which all the ingredients are added together.

Batters

Process the ingredients for batters for pancakes, coating ingredients, Yorkshire pudding etc. in seconds with the plastic blade or double-bladed knife to provide light, smooth batters. Do not have the pusher in the feed tube when processing batters so that air will be able to be incorporated with the other ingredients.

Barbecueing

Make marinades for your barbecue ingredients with your food processor and the double-bladed knife. Process garlic, onion and root ginger until finely chopped, add tomato ketchup, mustard, brown sugar, lemon juice, chilli sauce, a little Worcester sauce and oil and blend into a basic marinade for barbecue ingredients.

Produce delicious sauces and accompaniments with your Magimix and the slicing or grating discs and the double-bladed knife to give finesse to your barbecued ingredients.

Beating
When a recipe calls for 'beating' ingredients perform this preparation in your Magimix using either the double-bladed knife or plastic blade. When beating butter with sugar, process the butter first with the double-bladed knife until it is smooth, light and creamy. Add caster sugar through the feed tube, in a slow steady stream, with the machine switched 'on' to obtain a light mixture.

In the same way, when beating eggs with sugar for sweet dishes, process the eggs or egg yolks until light and foaming before adding the sugar in a slow steady stream through the feed tube. Do not have the pusher in the feed tube when 'beating' ingredients of this kind.

Binding
Sauces and other ingredients which require to be bound with eggs or other ingredients should be processed with the plastic blade or double-bladed knife.

Biscuits
A wide range of biscuits and cookies can be made with your Magimix. Follow your favourite recipes but remember to add any fruit at the last minute and avoid over-processing so that the fruit becomes finely chopped.

Bread Making
Your Magimix will make excellent bread and cuts out most of the hassel of long kneading. You will probably find you need to use a little less liquid than normally required and you should take care not to overprocess so that too much air is driven from the dough. Having processed the main ingredients, add the liquid through the feed tube with the motor switched on. As soon as enough liquid has been added to enable the ingredients to form a ball around the double-bladed knife or the dough blade cease to add any more liquid, allow the dough to make about ten turns around the bowl and then switch off. Do not have the pusher in the feed tube while making bread.

After processing turn the dough onto a well floured board and knead lightly to shape.

Cakes
Excellent all-in-one cakes, fruit cakes, tea cakes etc. can all be made with great success and astonishing speed in your Magimix. You may find you will need less liquid than is normally required in recipes.

Fruit for fruit cakes should be added at the end of the processing and the machine switched on and off to mix the ingredients without chopping the fruit.

Casseroles
Chop or slice vegetables for casseroles with your food processor.

Cereals
Chop fruit and nuts etc. with the double-bladed knife for adding to home made *muesli*.

Chinese Dishes
Slice ingredients for Chinese 'stir fry' dishes through the thin, medium or thick slicing discs. Pork, chicken breast or steak can be cut to the size of the feed tube, chilled in the freezer until firm but not solid and cut into wafer thin slices through the medium slicing disc.
For varying texture in mixed vegetable and meat 'stir fry' dishes try processing some vegetables through the julienne disc or the chipper disc.
Sweet and sour sauce can be blended in your food processor with the double-bladed knife.

Creaming Ingredients
Creaming butter can be done in seconds with the double-bladed knife. Roughly chop the butter before processing and scrape down the sides of the bowl with the spatula during the creaming process if necessary.

Curries
Many curry recipes call for the onions (and garlic etc) being reduced to a paste for a curry sauce. This process can be done in seconds with the double-bladed knife. You can also use the double-bladed knife to grind many spices, and finely chop garlic, ginger root and chillis. Do not attempt to grind oily, hard, spices such as peppercorns, coriander or cloves as these may scar the bowl and always use a clean, *dry* bowl when grinding suitable spices.

Custards
Mix and blend eggs and cream or milk for custards, ice creams and quiches etc with the plastic blade or double-bladed knife until the ingredients are smooth. Custards will not need to be strained when they are processed in your Magimix.

Dals
Make rich and inexpensive dals from cooked pulses with your double-bladed knife – most dals are more delicious if they retain some texture so take care not to over process.

Dips
Make a wide variety of avocado, cheese, smoked fish and other dips by processing ingredients with the double-bladed knife. Add ingredients grated with the fine or coarse grating discs to provide a texture contrast.

Dog Food
Chop leftover meat to mix with dog biscuits with your double-bladed knife.

Doughs
Make delicious bread with your food processor in minutes. Use the dough blade or double-bladed knife.
You will probably find that you need to use less liquid than you would for a standard recipe – add just enough liquid, through the feed tube with the motor running, when

the other ingredients for a dough have been incorporated and processed, to make the dough form a ball around the central spindle.

Your Magimix will do most of the work of kneading the dough for you (I like to count ten turns for the dough around the spindle for a normal kneading). Once the dough is ready knead it briefly on a floured board to shape it.

DO NOT OVERLOAD THE MACHINE.

Maximum quantities for the standard Magimix: 2 lbs finished bread dough.

Maximum quantities for the Grande Cuisine: 2 lbs bread dough.

Maximum quantities for the Grande Famille: 4 lbs bread dough.

There is a dough/dome kit available for the standard Magimix which enables you to make 40% more dough at a time.

Drinks

Citrus fruit juice for drinks is speedily produced with your citrus juicer.

The bases for many drinks and cocktails can be made by processing the ingredients with the double-bladed knife or plastic blade.

Many different fruit and vegetable juices can easily be obtained by using the juice extractor.

Fruit Dishes

Purée raw or cooked fruit with the double-bladed knife for a wide variety of fruit dishes. Slice firm fruit through the medium or thick slicing discs for fresh fruit dishes and fruit salads etc.

Garnishes

Prepare attractive chopped, sliced and grated garnishes with your Magimix. Finely chop parsley and other herbs to scatter over dishes at the last minute. Slice cucumber etc. through the thin slicing disc to decorate cold food. Finely chop hard boiled eggs to sprinkle over hot and cold dishes. Grate raw carrots or raw beetroot through the fine or coarse grating disc or process them through the julienne disc to add a final touch of colour to salads.

Goulashes

Process vegetables through the slicing disc, or chipper disc to add to well flavoured goulashes.

Gratinés

Grate cheese for gratinés through the fine or coarse grating disc. Gratiné sauces can be enriched with cream and eggs and the cheese for the sauce can be blended into it by processing the ingredients with the double-bladed knife ensuring a smooth, rich and satiny sauce.

Ice Creams

Process custards and purée fruit for ice creams with the double-bladed knife. When ice cream requires to be beaten once ice crystals have formed in the mixture this process can be efficiently, quickly and easily done with the double-bladed knife.

Hashes

Excellent hashes made from corned beef or leftover roast meat etc. can be made by processing the ingredients with the double-bladed knife.

Iced Drinks

While your food processor will not actually crush or shave ice cubes you can get an excellent effect with ice drinks by adding ice cubes to the drink and processing the ingredients with the double-bladed knife.

Leftovers

Make the best possible use of leftovers to provide delicious and inexpensive dishes. Chop meat, poultry and leftover fish etc. with the double-bladed knife. Chop or slice cooked vegetables with the double-bladed knife or through the thin, medium or thick slicing discs.

Finely chop leftover ingredients to add to soups. Process stale bread with the double-bladed knife to make fresh or dried breadcrumbs. Process stale cheese through the thin or medium grating discs for savoury sauces and toppings.

Note: If the cheese is exceptionally hard it should be processed through the Parmesan grating disc.

Marinades

Slice or chop onions and herbs etc. for marinades using the double-bladed knife. Process ingredients for a marinade using the plastic or double-bladed knife.

Marmalades

Extract the juice for marmalades from citrus fruit using the citrus juicer. Chop citrus fruit peel with the double-bladed knife, slice it with the thin slicing disc or even put it through the chipper disc.

Mayonnaise

Make all types of mayonnaise quickly and with ease using the double-bladed knife.

Meat Dishes

Chop meat to the desired fineness with the double-bladed knife.

Firm, cooked meat can be cut to fit the feed tube and sliced with the medium or thick slicing discs.

Raw meat and chicken breast can be cut to fit the feed tube, chilled until firm but not solid in a freezer and then sliced through the medium or thick slicing discs.

Milk Shakes

If you have trouble trying to get your children to drink milk try whisking up a delicious fruit milk shake in your Magimix. Purée fresh or cooked fruit with the double-bladed knife, add milk, sugar and a few ice cubes and process until the ingredients are frothy and well mixed.

Minced Meat and Poultry Dishes

Finely chop meat, poultry or fish with the double-bladed knife and ensure you retain all the blood and juices in the ingredients resulting in minced dishes having far more flavour and goodness than if they were put through a mincing machine which has a disadvantage of 'wringing' the ingredients. Your Magimix will reduce ingredients evenly to a 'minced' consistency in seconds. Do not try to process too large a quantity of ingredients at one time (the food processor performs so quickly this is not necessary) and take care not to over process so that the ingredients are too finely chopped.

Mixing

Almost all 'mixing' can be performed in your Magimix with the double-bladed knife or plastic blade. When mixing light ingredients do not have the pusher in the feed tube so that the maximum amount of air is able to be incorporated into the mixed ingredients.

Mousses

Purée poultry, fish etc. for savoury mousse bases with the double-bladed knife. Beat eggs and sugar together with the double-bladed knife or plastic blade for sweet mousse bases.

Pancakes

Make pancake batters by processing ingredients with the double-bladed knife or plastic blade (see batters).
Make delicious potato pancakes by grating raw potatoes through the medium grating disc and adding them to basic pancake batters.
Add interest to pancake batters by adding some bacon, finely chopped with the double-bladed knife, finely chopped herbs or some finely chopped or grated onion.
Make sweet pancakes by processing ingredients with the double-bladed knife or plastic blade.

Pastry

Make the best and lightest pastry in the world with your Magimix. Combine the flour and fat and process with the double-bladed knife. Add an egg if this is required and process to mix. Add just enough liquid through the feed tube to bind the pastry into a ball around the double-bladed knife. You will probably find that less liquid is required than if you make pastry by hand.
Take care not to over-process pastry as this will result in it becoming tough – process for just long enough for the pastry to form a ball around the blade.

Pâtés

Process ingredients for delicious pâtés and terrines using the double-bladed knife. If the pâté is to be coarse grained take care not to over process the ingredients. Do not attempt to process too great a quantity of ingredients for pâtés and terrines at one time – your Magimix will process ingredients so quickly that it takes no time at all to process them in two or more batches.
Finely chop herbs to be incorporated into pâtés in a clean, dry bowl using the double-bladed knife.
Finely chop garlic and onions to be incorporated into pâtés or terrines before adding other ingredients.

Pies

Make the pastry for pies, the fillings and a wide variety of sauces in your Magimix.

Poultry

Process poultry that is to be minced or reduced to a paste with the double-bladed knife. Raw chicken breast can be cut to fit the feed tube, chilled in the freezer until firm but not solid and sliced through the medium or thick slicing blade. Pressed cooked chicken or turkey can also be sliced for salads.

Purées

Purée ingredients for soups, sauces and vegetable dishes with the double-bladed knife. When puréeing ingredients for soups drain off the stock before processing the ingredients with the double-bladed knife. Purée raw or cooked fruit with the double-bladed knife for puddings and sweet dishes.

Salads

Most salad ingredients require to be sliced, chopped, grated or shredded. Perform all these chores with your Magimix. Slice or shred ingredients through the fine, medium or thick slicing discs. Grate ingredients through the coarse grating discs or, if using the standard Magimix, through the julienne disc or the coleslaw disc for coleslaw and other salads. Finely chop salad ingredients with the double-bladed knife.

Salad Dressings

Process herbs and other chopped ingredients for salad dressings with the double-bladed knife. Process dressing ingredients into an emulsion using the double-bladed knife or plastic mixing blade.

Sauces

Finely chop ingredients for sauce bases with the double-bladed knife. Grate cheese, horseradish root etc. for sauces through the fine or medium grating discs. Give your sauces a marvellously smooth and satiny consistency by adding an egg and some cream to the sauce and processing with the plastic mixing blade or double-bladed knife. Unsnarl curdled or lumpy sauces by processing them for a few seconds with the double-bladed knife.

Purée ingredients (cooked onions, spinach etc.) for sauce flavourings with the double-bladed knife.

Sausages and Sausage Meat

Make home made sausages and sausage meat by processing ingredients with the double-bladed knife. Cut pork and pork fat into fairly small cubes before processing. Sausage skins can be bought from family butchers. Some butchers will also fill sausage skins with your own mixture providing there is enough of it (usually a minimum of 5 lb of sausage meat). Skins can also be filled by attaching them to the nozzle of a piping bag – use the largest piping nozzle.

Scones

Make scone doughs with the double-bladed knife. Process the flour with any fat and then add enough liquid, to enable the dough to form a firm ball around the double-bladed knife, through the feed tube with the machine switched 'on'. You may find you need to use less liquid than if you were making scone dough by hand.

Take care not to over process when making scone dough and do not put the pusher in the feed tube so that air is able to be incorporated into the ingredients.

Add fruit to scone mixtures at the last stage of their processing and switch the machine on and off for just long enough to incorporate the ingredients without chopping the fruit.

Sorbets

Purée raw or cooked fruit for sorbets using the double-bladed knife.

Soups

Many soups call for a purée or chopped vegetable base. Both these processes can be done in your Magimix with the double-bladed knife in seconds. A small quantity of finely chopped, mixed, fresh vegetables can provide an almost instant, delicious and nourishing soup base; cooked vegetables can be puréed to provide cream of vegetable soups in no time at all.

When cooking vegetables in stock which are to be puréed, drain off excess liquid and purée the softened vegetables without liquid to produce a thick, smooth purée – make sure the vegetables are tender before puréeing.

Use the grating discs to provide varying textures for vegetable soups. Beat egg yolks and cream together with the plastic mixing blade or double-bladed knife to add to soups to give a creamy, satiny, texture – do not boil the soup after the egg mixture has been added.

Make small meat, poultry or fish forcemeat balls by processing raw ingredients with the double-bladed knife to add to soups to produce nourishment. Chop herbs and other ingredients to add to soups at the last minute with the double-bladed knife to provide a garnish.

Stews

Chop or slice vegetables for stews using the thin, medium or thick slicing discs. Process root vegetables for stews using the ripple cut or chipper disc.

Stuffings

Make delicious stuffings for meat, poultry and fish dishes using the double-bladed knife. Chop herbs in a clean dry bowl with the double-bladed knife before adding other ingredients. Process breadcrumbs with the double-bladed knife in a clean dry bowl before adding other ingredients.

Tarts

Make the pastry and fillings for tarts using the double-bladed knife. Process custard for sweet tarts with the double-bladed knife or plastic blade. Chop ingredients for tart fillings with the double-bladed knife. Process purées for tart fillings with the double-bladed knife.

Terrines (See Pâtés)

Index

Figures in italic refer to photographs